Elliott Anthony

**The Constitutional History of Illinois**

Elliott Anthony

**The Constitutional History of Illinois**

ISBN/EAN: 9783337326180

Printed in Europe, USA, Canada, Australia, Japan

Cover: Foto ©ninafisch / pixelio.de

More available books at **www.hansebooks.com**

# THE

# CONSTITUTIONAL HISTORY

OF

# ILLINOIS.

BY

HON. ELLIOTT ANTHONY,

Judge of the Superior Court of Chicago.

CHICAGO:
CHICAGO LEGAL NEWS PRINT.

1891.

# CONTENTS.

|  | PAGE. |
|---|---|
| CHAPTER I.—This is an Age of Written Constitutions | 5 |
| CHAPTER II.—The Advantages of Written Constitutions | 8 |
| CHAPTER III.—The American Constitutional Form of Government the Strongest in the World | 11 |
| CHAPTER IV.—The Ordinance of 1787—The Great Organic Law of the Northwest | 14 |
| CHAPTER V.—The Efforts to Perpetuate Slavery Notwithstanding the Ordinance | 16 |
| CHAPTER VI.—The First Court Ever Held in the Northwest Territory | 18 |
| CHAPTER VII.—The Organization and Admission of New States | 20 |
| CHAPTER VIII.—The Admission of Ohio and Indiana into the Union | 23 |
| CHAPTER IX.—The Admission of Michigan and Wisconsin into the Union | 27 |
| CHAPTER X.—Illinois and Virginia—George Rogers Clark and the Backwoodsmen | 29 |
| CHAPTER XI.—Illinois County | 33 |
| CHAPTER XII.—Constitutional Conventions in Illinois | 38 |
| CHAPTER XIII.—The Founders of the Commonwealth | 46 |
| CHAPTER XIV.—Governor Coles, and his Immediate Friends and Contemporaries | 50 |
| CHAPTER XV.—The Great Convention Struggle of 1823-4 to make Illinois a Slave State | 66 |
| CHAPTER XVI.—The Development of Infant Industries, or how Banking can be Carried on by Politicians | 73 |
| CHAPTER XVII.—Repeal of the Black Laws of Illinois | 77 |
| CHAPTER XVIII.—Mason and Dixon's Line in Illinois | 87 |
| CHAPTER XIX.—The Period Preceding the Calling of the Constitutional Convention of 1847 | 91 |
| CHAPTER XX.—The Partisan War on the Supreme Court and the Reorganization of the Same | 93 |
| CHAPTER XXI.—The Constitutional Convention of 1847 | 103 |
| CHAPTER XXII.—Constitutional Convention of 1862 | 109 |
| CHAPTER XXIII.—Constitutional Convention of 1869-70 | 116 |
| CHAPTER XXIV.—Is a Constitutional Convention Needed | 124 |
| CHAPTER XXV.—Radicalism and Conservatism | 128 |
| CHAPTER XXVI.—Limitations and Restraints are Necessary in all Free Governments | 136 |
| CHAPTER XXVII.—The Power and Scope of a Constitutional Convention | 139 |
| CHAPTER XXVIII.—Legislative Provisions in Modern Constitutions | 143 |
| CHAPTER XXIX.—An Examination of Some of the Objections Which Are Urged against the Present Constitution | 145 |

## CONTENTS.

PAGE.

CHAPTER XXX.—The Administration of the Criminal Law in the State of Illinois.................................................................. 148
CHAPTER XXXI.—State and Federal Judges.............................153
CHAPTER XXXII.—Constitutional Convention Necessary to Induce the Supreme Court to Recognize and Enforce the Statutes Relating to the Common Law...................................................... 156
CHAPTER XXXIII.—The Address of the Delegates to the People, Showing the Changes made in the Old Constitution and the Reforms Proposed.. 161
CHAPTER XXXIV.—How State Taxes have been Diverted, School Lands Stolen, and other Abuses under the old Regime, with some Remarks on the Value of the "Pay as You Go" Policy.................................. 171
CHAPTER XXXV.—The Organization and Government of Great Cities...... 176
CHAPTER XXXVI.—Frequent Changes in the Organic Law of a State not Desirable.................................................................. 185
CHAPTER XXXVII.—Illinois ought to be a Model Republic, with a Constitution and Laws to Correspond..................................... 189
CHAPTER XXXVIII.—Public Virtue........................................ 191
CHAPTER XXXIX.—No State will ever be Prosperous under any Constitution unless the People are Educated..................................... 195
CHAPTER XL.—The Right of American Citizens to be Protected in Exercising the Elective Franchise................................................ 197
CHAPTER XLI.—Conclusion................................................ 202

# INTRODUCTION.

WITHIN the period of seventy-three years the people of Illinois have held four constitutional conventions and have become somewhat conversant with constitution-making and political science.

The genius of our people for statecraft was early developed, and the number of state-artificers which was then produced, shows no signs of abatement.

Of the four conventions referred to it has fallen to our lot to be a member of two of them, one in 1862 and the other in 1870, which framed our present Constitution.

Many of the members of these conventions were men of great experience, and whose knowledge of events reach back to the very beginnings of our history as a State.

It had long been in contemplation by us to write a sketch of these various conventions, together with an account of events that preceded and called them into existence, and of some of the public men that took part in them, when we received an invitation from the State Bar Association to read a paper before that body upon the needs of a constitutional convention to revise and amend our present Constitution. Upon considering the matter we resolved to at once make use of the materials already on hand, not only by way of review of some of the most interesting events in our State history, but to discuss in the light of experience at considerable length the whole subject of written constitutions and what, if anything, was required by way of amendments to our own organic law as it at present exists. Such a work we have ventured to characterize as a "Constitutional History of Illinois," and which may be regarded as a special study of one phase of our history not hitherto treated of by any of our historians.

We submit it with great deference to our fellow-citizens, hoping that we may be able to contribute in some slight degree to a better understanding of some of the most stirring events in the formative period of this great commonwealth, and of the men who took part in them.

ELLIOTT ANTHONY.

CHICAGO, January 23, 1891.

# CHAPTER I.

## This is an Age of Written Constitutions.

THE present is an age when the powers of the government are sought to be defined and limited so that the people may know their rights, and those who govern may not invade them.

It is an age of written constitutions, and it is a curious fact that to-day there is not a government in Europe, except those of Russia and Turkey, but what are constitutional governments; while upon the American continent, since Brazil became a republic, not a single monarchy exists. Most European constitutions are usually found written in some law which has been passed and promulgated by representatives of the people, which the king or ruler has been graciously pleased to approve, conferring upon the people the right of representation and taking part in making the laws; while in the United States, where it is held that "all power is inherent in the people and all free governments are on their authority and instituted for their peace, safety and happiness," a much more elaborate form is made use of, and the most exact details are required to define and regulate the sovereign powers and the measure of authority of all the departments of the government—legislative, executive, judicial, civil and military—general and local, and each and every function of the government.

The problem is to confer authority and so reserve liberty that each shall serve as a check or balance upon the other, and that each, without being dangerous in itself, may help and not encroach upon the other.

The days of charters and special privileges have passed away, and absolute equality before the law is the only condition which the people of this country will accept or tolerate.

The publicists of Europe hold that all power of government is derived from God through the instrumentality of kings, while the political creed of America is that the impartial governor of the universe has not communicated his attributes of power, wisdom, justice and mercy to kings only, and denied the least portion of them to every other class of mankind, but that the only divine right that any king or ruler has is derived from the people themselves.

Indeed, as Winterbottom says in his "View of the United States," in 1796:

"The creed of an American colonist was short, but substantial. He believed that God made all mankind originally equal; that he endowed them with the rights of life, property, and as much liberty as was consistent with the rights of others; that he had bestowed on his vast family of the human race the earth for their support; and that all government was a political institution between men naturally equal, not for the aggrandizement of one or a few, but for the general happiness of the whole community."

And one, long after this time, in reviewing the tracks of the early American pioneers, says:

"Without the infection of wild or social theories, they were animated by a love of liberty and a spirit of personal independence unknown to the great body of the people of Europe, while at the same time recognizing the law which united the individual to the family and to the society in which he is appointed to live; to the municipality and the commonwealth which gave him protection, and to a great nation which met and satisfied the natural sentiment of country."

In this country sovereignty is in the people. In them are those inherent powers of society, which no climate, no time, no constitution, no contract, can ever destroy or diminish. In them, as the supreme power, resides the right of command or the right to institute organic law, to establish public authority and to compel obedience to it. On this foundation rose the American superstructure of government.

James Otis once said that there could be no prescription old enough to supersede the law of nature and the grant of Almighty God, who had given all men a right to be free; that nothing but life and liberty were hereditable; that in solving practically the grand, political problem the first and simple principle must be equality and the power of the whole.

In its practical sense sovereignty means nothing more nor less than the *power to originate and secure* the performance of all governmental acts.

The powers of sovereignty in the people of the United States are parceled out between the Nation and the State, by the creators of sovereignty itself, that is by the people.

The sixteenth and seventeenth centuries were engaged very much in discussing the prerogatives of kings, and the contest never died out till the last heir of the royal house of the Stuarts had passed away.

In Blackstone's time (1753) prerogative had assumed such definite shape as to be capable of being defined, and he defines it as follows: "By the word prerogative we usually understand that special pre-eminence, which the king had over and above all other persons, and out of the ordinary course of the common law, in right of his real dignity. It signifies in its etymology (from *præ* and *rogo*) something that is required and demanded before or in preference to others. And hence it follows that it must be in its nature singular and eccentrical; that it can only be applied to those rights and capacities which the king enjoys alone in contradistinction to others, and not to those which he enjoys in common with any of his subjects; for if once any prerogative of the crown could be held in common with the subject it would cease to be prerogative any longer, and, therefore, Finch lays it down as a maxim, that the prerogative is, that law on the case of the king, which is law in no case of the subject."

St. George Tucker in commenting upon this in his edition of Blackstone in (1803) says, that "This definition of prerogative is enough to make a citizen of the United States shudder at the recollection that he was born under a government in which such doctrines are received as Catholic."

It was one of the wise utterances of Locke, that "The freedom of a people under Government is dependent upon *standing rules* to live by, so that the Government may become a government of laws and not of men."

## CHAPTER II.

### The Advantages of Written Constitutions.

THERE has always been, since the Government of the United States was established, and long before, a controversy between publicists and jurists as to the advantages and disadvantages of written and unwritten constitutions, and good and plausible reasons may be assigned why unwritten constitutions should be preferred to written constitutions, and *vice versa*. This opens a wide field and we shall not enter it. It is sufficient for us to express our decided preference for a written constitution, rather than an inference from disconnected facts or customs, which may become the playthings of judicial tribunals. It gives a strong feeling of right and a powerful impulse of action to have the written law clearly on one's side, and though power, if it comes to the last, may succeed, yet unless wielded by frenzy will pause before it dares to pass the Rubicon, and to declare revolution.

A written constitution has the peculiar advantage of serving as a beacon to apprise the people when their rights and liberties are invaded or in danger—and Thomas Jefferson says: "Though written constitutions may be violated in moments of passion or delusion, yet they furnish a text to which those who are watchful may again rally and recall the people; they fix, too, for the people principles of their political creed."

If every man in the community had studied political economy and the science of government, and had been trained to understand his political rights and duties, and the rights and duties of his fellow-man, had mastered checks and balances, and would constitute himself a watchman to see that there were no violations of these functions and prerogatives, and that no public functionary usurped any of the rights of the people, then perhaps an unwritten constitution would be sufficient for all purposes, and possibly be regarded the best. It could, by common consent, be made to yield to all the exigencies, wants and necessities of the people, as they arose and were required, and constitutional conventions would be unknown and unnecessary. But for a community whose training has been

## ADVANTAGES OF WRITTEN CONSTITUTIONS.

imperfect, whose opportunities for observation have been limited, and which has not reached a high degree of development, then a written constitution becomes indispensable, and is far preferable.

To render a written constitution safe, however, we admit that it must provide efficient machinery for its own amendment, and not be too unyielding—but it never should be degraded to that of an ordinary statute, which may be passed to-day and repealed to-morrow.

Thomas Jefferson once expressed an opinion, that no constitution ought to go longer than twenty years, without an opportunity being given to the citizens to amend it. This opinion he based upon the consideration that by the European tables of mortality it appeared that a generation of men lasted on the average about that number of years, and that every succeeding generation, like its predecessor, had "a right to choose for itself the form of government it believed most productive of its own happiness; and to accommodate to the circumstances in which it finds itself, and that which it received from its predecessors."

But in expressing this opinion he did not hold it to be necessary that a constitutional convention should be called together every twenty years. And we judge from other opinions that he expressed that it would meet every contingency, if amendments could from time to time be proposed, and voted upon by the people.

It does not follow that because defects have been discovered here and there in the structure of an organic law, or that some of its provisions have fallen short of the requirements or expectations of the people, that a great convention should be called together to consider the same and rectify it, when the same result can be brought about by other and simpler means.

Is our constitution so unyielding in its provisions as to prevent amendments as speedily as they are required?

And what, allow me to ask, is the grievance that can not now be remedied by appropriate legislation on the part of the General Assembly?

A constitution is nothing more nor less than a limitation of power on the part of the Legislature and in the absence of a prohibitory clause, actually prohibiting the General Assembly of the State of Illinois from legislating upon any given subject, it is as omnipotent as that of the British Parliament.

If the people of this country were more homogeneous than they are—if they were influenced by the same traditions, the same general customs and systems of law and structure of government, but few laws would probably be required, and we would not perhaps be always striving for something new and employing our highest courts to settle doubtful questions. But the fact is the tendency of all of our legislators is in the direction of innovation and not of conservatism. Here men pass from private to public employment, with but little knowledge of governmental principles, and with no knowledge whatever of formulating them, and the result is that we need constitutional limitations to restrain the rashness and rawness of those whom we select to act as Solons and law givers, however fiercely they may beat against the barriers that hem them in.

Indeed it is the leading principle of our American system of government to rest its permanency upon laws rather than upon men, and as a general rule, if the laws are wise and right, it would make but a very little difference to the people by whom they are administered, so long as they are actually, honestly and efficiently enforced.

Thus the Constitution and the laws are our real rulers; the men who for the time being are our real rulers, the men who for the time being are at the head of the government, are the servants of the laws, and are simply called upon to see that they are properly respected and administered. And so it may be well that it is even better to have as rulers honest men of moderate ability, who will strive diligently to know their duty and to do it, than to have men of higher capacity, whose consciousness of their great abilities might tempt them, in the interest of their ambition, to leave the old and safe ways and experiment in new and dangerous ones.

There are but very few men in this country but what discourse long and learnedly upon the Constitution and constitutional government. There are but very few laws ever passed either by our National or State Legislatures but what sooner or later are attacked as being unconstitutional, and it is nothing uncommon for justices of the peace and those of a little higher grade, to boldly announce that this or that law need not be obeyed, and if anybody does undertake to obey the same they shall be indicted and punished for so doing.

## CHAPTER III.

### The American Constitutional Form of Government the Strongest in the World.

THE English theory of government is that its constitution is pliable, is always yielding, and can be made to fit any emergency. Its constitutional convention they say is always in session unless adjourned for short intervals, or prorogued by the supreme ruler of the empire, whose power to do so dates back to the remote past. An act of Parliament when passed and approved becomes a part of the Constitution, while in the United States every law must be subject to a still higher law, to wit, an organic law, which no power can change or destroy except by certain methods prescribed by the people themselves. It is true that English jurists and English statesmen constantly refer to their constitution, and when they refer to an act as being unconstitutional they mean that it conflicts with their system of government and with the principles embodied in Magna Charta, the Bill of Rights, the Petition of Rights, the Habeas Corpus Act or Act of Settlement, but they can refer to no great body of organic law or established system of government, outlined on parchment or paper, which has ever been formally adopted and promulgated by a vote of the people, as the rule and guidance of rulers and ruled, and they glory in this as something remarkable and as evidence of the highest wisdom. Indeed the tories of England have never ceased to laugh at and ridicule our constitution, but we think that the time will come when it will be taken as a model for every government in Christendom, and every government of the world will become a representative government.

Mr. Gladstone, the great English liberal, deserves to be excepted from most of the English statesmen of past and present ages, for he says: "I think the Constitution of the United States represents the most admirable creation that has ever been produced by one effort of human intelligence." If these are his sentiments it is no wonder that he is in favor of Home Rule in Ireland, and every other country where intelligent human beings have their abode.

When the constitution of this country was drafted, but few

such documents had ever seen the light. "It consisted of a few sheets of paper, which, when held in the hands of the secretary of the convention that formed it, appeared so weak, so frail and imperfect that it seemed as if it would have but very little force and effect in binding together the various States of the Union or commanding the respect of the people." It was in fact a mere skeleton, and the powers conferred upon the new government were merely enumerated but not defined. Their definition would ultimately depend upon the extent to which it would be prudent or practicable to assert and employ them. Skill, courage and energy would make good a broad definition. Timidity, cowardice or disloyalty would shrivel them into insignificance. To-day our government is, in my judgment, the strongest government on earth.

We began our national life by adopting a form and system of government by vote of the people, and so did most of the States constituting the American Union.

It is true that a number of the States were granted charter governments, some of which existed until long after the Revolution—notably Connecticut, which existed under the charter of Charles, in 1662, down to 1818, and Rhode Island, from 1665 down to 1842—but the people established their own governments without any authority from the Crown, and afterward procured the charters, which conferred the same authority they had already exercised.

The people elected their governors and assemblies, and the king reserved no power to veto their laws.

The traveler to Europe as he visits country after country, and sees in many of them the sad results of poverty, misery and misgovernment, is moved with pity.

France, Spain, Italy, Austria, Bohemia, Poland and Turkey are not advancing with rapidity, and there is much in them that may be regarded as benighted. It is true that France, Spain and Italy have grappled with many of the social problems of the age, and have taken advantage of steam and electricity and many of the modern appliances with which we are so familiar, but these you meet with in the cities and along their crowded thoroughfares; but back in the country is "the stillness of the ages." The people stand aghast or remain stolid and indifferent. They are a hundred years behind the age. The absence of the school house is noticeable everywhere, while the night of the middle ages seems to have settled down upon the rural population of Bohemia, Poland and Austria, and that of Italy and France is destitute of all enterprise. The Turkish Empire is in a worse condition than in the age of Theodosius, and seems to be incapable of regeneration.

There are yet large portions of Europe which seem to have come to a standstill, and to have arrived at

> "That last dread mood
> Of sated lust and dull decrepitude.
> No law, no art, no faith, no hope, no God.
> When round the freezing founts of life in peevish ring,
> Crouched on the bare-worn sod,
> Babbling about the unreturning spring,
> And whining for dead creeds that can not save,
> The toothless nations shiver to their grave."

In this country we are happy to say things are different, and efforts at reform are observable everywhere. Reforms in the laws and in the methods of domestic government are matters of State concern, and under our form of government the powers reserved to the people in these respects embrace nearly every governmental power essential to a wise and liberal government.

The Constitution of the United States, in fact, enjoins and promotes, instead of restricting, the best possible domestic government, republican in form, which the people can devise for their respective States.

The National Legislature has its limited range of legislative powers; the State Legislatures have the rest.

Forty-two State Legislatures keep watch and ward against National encroachment, and the Supreme Court of the United States towers above them all, directing, restraining and nullifying the action of either National or State Legislature which infringes the other.

The States of this Union are unfettered in their powers to regulate their domestic affairs, except in a very few particulars. The form of government which we adopt must be republican in type, the rights of the citizens must be respected, and in the language of our Bill of Rights "elections must be free and equal," even if it requires force to make them so.

Our interests center in domestic and local affairs.

"We are interested in the concerns of our neighborhood, town, county and State. Aside from the post-office officials, we rarely come in contact with a Federal officer, except now and then a military or naval officer on leave of absence. If we take an interest in moral, social, educational or humanitarian reforms the Nation can not lawfully help us; our field is the State or under its favor."

## CHAPTER IV.

### The Ordinance of 1787—The Great Organic Law of the Northwest.

IN the history of every country there are supreme events to which may be traced the influence that shaped the destiny of the people for good or evil; in that of the United States it is customary to refer to the Declaration of Independence and the adoption of the Constitution in encomiastic phrase, as exhibiting wisdom and genius of the highest order. But whatever may be said of these may be applied to the ordinance of 1787, with equal justice.

Aye, more; the spirit of the ordinance has conferred blessings in addition to those derived from the Constitution upon the citizens of the States erected under its provisions. "Upon the surpassing excellence of the ordinance," said Judge Timothy Walker, " no language of panegyric would be extravagant. The Romans would have imagined some divine Egeria for its author. It approaches as nearly to absolute perfection as anything to be found in the legislation of mankind; for, after the experience of fifty years, it would perhaps be impossible to alter without marring it."

In short it is one of those matchless specimens of sagacious forecast, which even the reckless spirit of innovation would not venture to assail. As long as human government shall endure, the influence for good of this remarkable charter shall be witnessed. It was the one really great act of legislation by Congress under the old Confederation, and it was the happy fortune of Arthur St. Clair to be the president of the body at that time and have the opportunity to give the measure his hearty support. 1 St. Clair papers, 118.

It was of this ordinance that the great Daniel Webster, in his first speech upon Foot's Resolution in the Senate of the United States, on the 20th of January, 1829, said:

## THE ORDINANCE OF 1787.

"At the foundation of the Constitution of these new Northwestern States, lies the celebrated ordinance of 1787.

"We are accustomed, sir, to praise the law givers of antiquity; we help to perpetuate the fame of Solon and Lycurgus, but I doubt whether one single law of any lawyer, ancient or modern, has produced effects of more distinct, marked and lasting character than the ordinance of 1787. That instrument was drawn by Nathan Dane, then and now a citizen of Massachusetts.

"It was adopted, as I think I have understood, without the slightest alteration; and certainly it has happened to few men to be the authors of a political measure of more large and enduring consequence. It fixed forever the character of the population in the vast regions of the Ohio, by excluding from them involuntary servitude. It impressed on the soil itself, while it was yet a wilderness, an incapacity to sustain any other than freemen. It laid the interdict against personal servitude in original compact, not only deeper than all local law, but deeper also than all local constitutions. Under the circumstances then existing, I look upon the original and seasonable provision as a real good attained. We see its consequences at this moment, and we shall never cease to see them, perhaps, while the Ohio shall flow. It was a great and salutary measure of prevention."

In these late years many publications have been put forth to show that Nathan Dane was not the author of the ordinance of 1787, and the claim of Dr. Manasseh Cutler, of Massachusetts, has been most strenuously urged. We do not deem it necessary to engage in the discussion of this subject at this time, and are content to leave it to contemporary history.

But there is one thing that may be affirmed of the ordinance of 1787, and that is it was the first great Constitution which was prepared in advance to govern and control a vast territory that was soon to develop into a great commonwealth.

"Save New England alone, there is no section of the United States embracing several States, that is so distinct an historical unit, and that so readily yields to historical treatment, as the old Northwest.

"It is the part of the great West first discovered and colonized by the French. It was the occasion of the final struggle for dominion between France and England in North America. It was the theatre of one of the most brilliant and far reaching military exploits of the Revolution. The disposition to be made of it at the close of the Revolution, is the most important territorial question treated in the history of American diplomacy. After the war the Northwest began to assume a constantly increasing importance in the national history. It is the original public domain and part of the West first colonized under the authority of the national government. It was the first and the most important territory ever organized by Congress. It is the only part of the United States ever under a secondary constitution like the ordinance of 1787."

Out of this territory five great States have been carved, and each one has framed a constitution for itself, and there is probably no region of the world where constitution making has been indulged in to such an extent, and in no region where the science of government is better understood.

## CHAPTER V.

### The Efforts to Perpetuate Slavery Notwithstanding the Ordinance.

THE whole country was, from the earliest period, devoted to freedom, but it is quite astonishing at this day, to know how early and what persistent efforts were made to establish and perpetuate slavery in this territory, notwithstanding it was expressly prohibited by the ordinance of 1787.

The French residents of St. Vincents and at Kaskaskia and Cahokia had been permitted to hold slaves by the king of France, and this permission was continued under the government of Great Britain, and was not interfered with during the territorial period. Some slaves were removed to the Louisiana Territory, but others were retained as indentured servants. Memorials soon began to pour into Congress asking a suspension of the sixth article.

The first of these, signed by John Edgar, and the others, were reported on May 12, 1796, by Joshua Coit, of Connecticut, to whom they had been referred, adversely.

In December, 1802, a meeting of citizens of the Indiana Territory, held at Vincennes and presided over by William Henry Harrison, resolved to make an effort to secure a suspension of the sixth article of the ordinance.

A memorial was drawn up, and in February following, it and a letter from Mr. Harrison were referred to a special committee of which John Randolph, of Virginia, was chairman. March 2, 1802, Mr. Randolph reported the following resolution:

*Resolved*, That it is inexpedient to suspend, for a limited time, the operation of the sixth article of compact between the original States and the people and States west of the river Ohio.

This resolution was accompanied by these most pertinent and sensible remarks: " The rapid population of the State of Ohio sufficiently evince, in the opinion of your committee, that the labor of slaves is not necessary to promote the growth and settlement of colonies in that region ; that this labor, demonstrably the dearest of any, can only be employed to advantage in the cultivation of products more valuable than any known to that quarter of the United States; that the committee deem it highly dangerous and inexpedient to impair a provision wisely calculated to promote the happiness and prosperity of the Northwestern country, and to give strength and security to that extensive frontier. In the salutary operation of this sagacious and benevolent restraint it is believed that the inhabitants of Indiana will, at no distant day, find ample remuneration for a temporary privation of labor and of emigration."

In March, 1804, Cæsar Rodney, of Delaware—afterward Attorney General of the United States—reported the resolution of a special committee in favor of the suspension of the inhibition for ten years.

A similar report was made in 1806 by James Garnet, of Virginia; and in 1807 Mr. Parker, delegate from Indiana, reported favorably on a memorial of William Henry Harrison and the Territorial Legislature praying for a suspension of the sixth article of the ordinance. But subsequently no action was ever taken by the House on these favorable reports. Subsequently General Harrison and his Legislature went before the Senate, and a special committee, consisting of Mr. Franklin, of North Carolina, Mr. Kitchell, of New Jersey, and Mr. Tiffin, of Ohio, was appointed.

They brought in an adverse report, and that put an end to the efforts to destroy the anti-slavery clause of the ordinance.

What if Ohio had formed a slave State constitution in 1802. What if Illinois had actually made the proposed change in 1824? What would Congress and the Supreme Court possibly have done with the hard questions that would have arisen in such a contingency? And if one or both of those States had become slave States, what then? What would have happened if slave State men had been in a majority in Ohio, Indiana and Illinois, no one can do more than conjecture.

Fortunately, at the decisive tests, the free State men were in the majority. Moreover, the ordinance helped to create the majority as well as to protect it against assault. Governor Reynolds, who had lived in Illinois since 1800 and who was a slave State man in 1824, although he afterwards rejoiced at his own defeat, said in 1855: "This act of Congress was the great sheet anchor that secured the States of Ohio, Indiana and Illinois from slavery. I never had any doubt but slavery would now exist in Illinois if it had not been prevented by this famous ordinance."

## CHAPTER VI.

### The First Court Ever Held in the Northwest Territory.

THE county of Washington, having within its limits about half of the present State of Ohio, was erected on the 26th of July, 1788. Officers for the militia were appointed. The governor appointed three distinguished gentlemen justices of the peace, viz.: Rufus Putnam, Benjamin Tupper and Winthrop Sargent, and on the 30th of August, established a Court of Quarter Sessions, of which he appointed another distinguished citizen and soldier, Return Jonathan Meigs, clerk. Gen. Putnam was also made judge of probate, with Colonel Meigs as clerk.

Laws having now been framed, civil officers appointed thereunder, a county erected, and the population having increased on the Ohio to one hundred and thirty-two souls, there remained to complete the Government only the formal inauguration of the judiciary; with just laws, bench and forum, the liberties of the people would be made secure. Tuesday the 2d day of September, 1788, was the day set apart for the ceremony.

## FIRST COURT IN NORTHWEST TERRITORY.

The account of an eye witness enables us to enter into the spirit of the occasion and to feel, after an interval of more than a hundred years, something like a just appreciation of the greatness of the work of those Revolutionary heroes.

It is the duty, as it should be the pleasure, of all who enjoy the blessings conferred by the most liberal Government, and equal and beneficent laws, to study the sources of these and the character of the men who framed and established them.

They builded for posterity. The scene is laid at Marietta at the mouth of the Muskingum, September 2, 1788. On that memorable first Tuesday of September, 1788, the citizens, Governor St. Clair and other territorial officers and military from Fort Harmar, being assembled at the point, a procession was formed, and as became the occasion, with Colonel Ebenezer Sproat, sheriff, with drawn sword and wand of office, at the head, marched up a path that had been cut through the forest, to the hall in the northwest block-house of Campus Martius, where the whole counter-marched, and the judges, Putnam and Tupper took their seats on the high bench. Prayer was fittingly offered by our friend, Reverend Manasseh Cutler, who was on a visit to the new colony, after which the commissions of the judges, clerk and sheriff were read and the opening proclaimed in deep tones by Colonel Sproat in these words: "O, yes! a court is opened for the administration of even-handed justice, to the poor and the rich, to the guilty and the innocent without respect of persons; none to be punished without trial by their peers, and then in pursuance of laws and evidence in the case."

Paul Fearing, Esq., was admitted as an attorney and was the first lawyer in the territory. This was the opening of the Common Pleas.

The Indian chiefs who had been invited by Governor St. Clair to attend a convention were curious witnesses of this impressive scene.

On the Tuesday following September 9th, the first Court of Quarter Sessions was held in the southeast block-house, occupied by Colonel E. Battelle. Hildreth describes this event as follows:

"Colonel Meigs, clerk, read the general commission issued by the governor, after which Colonel Sproat's deep bass voice commanded the solemn attention of all.

"General Rufus Putnam and General Benjamin Tupper were all the justices of the quorum, and Isaac Pierce, Thomas Lord and

Colonel Return Jonathan Meigs assistant justices; Colonel Meigs was also clerk. Paul Fearing was admitted an attorney of this court, and appointed court counselor for the United States in the county of Washington.

"The grand jury was constituted as follows: William Stacy, foreman; Nathaniel Cushing, Nathaniel Goodale, Charles Knowles, Anselm Tupper, Jonathan Stone, Oliver Rice, Ezra Lunt, John Matthews, George Ingersol, Jonathan Devol, Samuel Stebbins, Jethro Putnam and Jabez True. The charge was given with much dignity and propriety by Judge Putnam. At one o'clock the grand jury retired, and the court adjourned for thirty minutes. At half past one the court again opened, when the jurors entered and presented a written address to the court, which, after being read, was ordered to be filed. Judge Putnam replied to the address. There being no suits before court, it was adjourned without day."
—*St. Clair Papers.*

## CHAPTER VII.

### The Organization and Admission of New States.

ON Friday, the 5th of October, 1787, Congress elected General Arthur St. Clair governor of the Northwestern Territory; James M. Varnum, Samuel Holden Parsons and John Armstrong, judges, and Winthrop Sargent, secretary. John Armstrong having declined the office of judge, John C. Cleves Symmes was appointed to fill the vacancy. Judge Varnum died January 10, 1789, and Parsons, 1790. These vacancies were filled by the appointment of George Turner and Gen. Rufus Putnam, an old revolutionary soldier who had taken up his abode at Marietta, at the mouth of the Muskingum. Judge Putnam served until 1796 when he resigned to accept the office of surveyor-general. Joseph Gillman, of Point Harnar, was appointed to the vacancy. Judge Turner removed from the Territory and resigned in 1796. In his place Return Jonathan Meigs was appointed in February, 1798. There were no further changes until Ohio was erected as a State.

At this time no congressional legislation had taken place to carry into effect the ordinance, and General St. Clair improved the earliest opportunity after the assembling of the First Congress under the Federal Constitution to secure the necessary action. In July, 1789, Mr. Fitzsimmons, of Pennsylvania, reported in the House of Representatives a bill which had been drafted by St. Clair for the government of the Northwestern Territory, which passed the House and Senate without opposition. This act gave the sanction of the National Legislature to all of the important provisions of the ordinance, including the compact for the inhibition of slavery, which was a formal assertion of the right of the National Legislature to regulate that institution in the Territories.

By the ordinance of 1787, the governor and judges which were to be selected were empowered to adopt and publish such "laws of the original States" as they deemed fit and necessary, reporting them to Congress from time to time, which laws were to continue in force until the organization of the General Assembly, unless disapproved by Congress. This method of legislation was followed in constituting all the Territories carved out of the old Northwest, except Wisconsin in 1836, and also in the act of 1790, for the territory south of the Ohio.

This Legislature thus constituted, soon found that their authority was altogether too limited, and without any regard to the provisions of the ordinance of 1787, commenced to legislate *de novo*.

The Legislature met at various times and places—at Marietta, Cincinnati and Vincennes, and promulgated laws; but among the very first ones in June, 1795, which was copied from an old Virginia statute of the colonial period, was one which provided that "the common law of England and all general statutes in aid of the common law prior to the fourth year of James I, should be in force in the territory." The other laws passed in 1795, were principally derived from the statute book of Pennsylvania.

The next thing in order was to constitute counties in order to provide for local governments, and while these counties were not as large as those that Virginia had bounded on the west by the South Sea or even by the Mississippi river, they were still of truly imperial proportions. Washington county, for example, reached from the Ohio to Lake Erie and from the Pennsylvania line to the Cuyahoga-Tuscarawas line and the Scioto; St. Clair county embraced all Southern Illinois. But Wayne county, organized in 1796, was the most extensive of all, including all the territory within the following limits: North by the International boundary line, east by the Cuyahoga, the portage path and the Tuscarawas; south by a line reaching from the forks above Fort Laurens; west and northwest to the head of the Miami in the Ohio; thence northwest to the portage between the Miami of the lake and the Wabash, where Fort Wayne now is, and thence northwest to the head of Lake Michigan; and west by a line running north to the International boundary, including all the lands in Wisconsin draining eastward to the same lake.

It is needless to say, that as time passed, the original counties had to be divided into smaller ones, and that the General Assembly, after 1799, claimed the power to make the subdivision, but the governor denied the Assembly's claim, and vetoed its bills erecting new counties, the result being a controversy that was finally carried to Congress and decided against him. Much of the bitterness which was engendered by this controversy, is said to have been due to land speculators, who were anxious to organize new counties in order to provide for office holders, and also for the profits that might be derived from the location of county seats.

### THE PAN HANDLE.

In the beginning Virginia had been organized by a charter of James I, in 1609, with movable boundaries on the west, extending "up into the land throughout from sea to sea, west and northwest, so that as settlers took possession of the country jurisdiction was extended over them. The authorities of that old commonwealth claimed the earth. In 1738 the General Assembly created Augusta county, bounding it on the east by the Blue Ridge, and on the west and northwest by "the utmost limits of Virginia, whether these limits were the Pacific Ocean or the Mississippi river. They included all western Pennsylvania. It took years to settle the disputes which this claim of Virginia gave rise to, and it was not until 1779 that commissioners appointed by the respective States met at Baltimore and agreed upon common boundaries, which was "To extend Mason and Dixon's line due west five degrees of longitude, to be computed from the river Delaware, for the southern boundary of Pennsylvania, and that a meridian line drawn from the western extremity thereof to the northern limit of the said State, be the western boundary of Pennsylvania forever." This contract was duly ratified by the Legislatures of the two States. In

1785 Mason and Dixon's line was extended and the southwestern corner of Pennsylvania established.

The "Pan Handle" is what was left of Virginia east of the Ohio river and north of Mason and Dixon's line after the boundary was run from this point to Lake Erie, in 1786.

When the State of Ohio was formed, in 1802, the "Pan Handle" first showed its beautiful proportions on the map of the United States. It received its name in legislative debate from Hon. John McMillan, delegate from Brooke county, to match the Accomac projection, which he dubbed the Spoon Handle.*

## CHAPTER VIII.

### The Admission of Ohio and Indiana into the Union.

IN May, 1800, an act was passed by the Congress of the United States, dividing the Northwest Territory by what is known as the Greenville line, from the Ohio up to Fort Recovery, and thence directly north through Michigan. All eastward of this boundary continued to be the Northwest Territory.

The country westward was established as the Indiana Territory, but in all other respects was governed by the ordinance.

Chillicothe and Vincennes were made the seats of government of the respective districts or territories until otherwise ordered by their Legislatures.

On April 30, 1802, an act was passed authorizing a convention of delegates to be elected in September, and a convention to be held November 1st, at Chillicothe, to determine whether to establish a State government, and, if so, to proceed at once to form and adopt a constitution, provided the same should be republican in form 'and conform to the compact of the ordinance of 1787. On the 29th of November a constitution was adopted without being submitted to a vote of the people, the enabling act not requiring it.

The action of the people thus taken was reported to Congress, together with the constitution which had been adopted by the convention, and asking for its approval.

---

*Creg. Hist. of Wash. Co., Pa.; Old Northwest, p. 109, note.

But before this was done a question was raised whether Mr. Fearing, who, it will be recollected, was the first lawyer ever admitted to the bar of the State of Ohio, and who was then a delegate in Congress, was entitled to his seat as a delegate—which was not settled until January 31st. Then a further delay took place in regard to certain " additional donations" which the convention had proposed, which were finally consented to by a bill which was not passed until March 3, 1803.

The Senate also had taken up the subject by a bill introduced January 5th, to " provide for giving effect to the laws of the United States, within the State of Ohio." A communication was presented from Worthington on the 7th, as agent, inclosing a copy of the State Constitution. A committee was directed to report what legislative measures, if any, were necessary for admitting the State of Ohio into the Union, and extending the laws of the United States over the State. The bill reported by this committee, after reciting that a constitution and State government had been formed by the people pursuant to the enabling act, passed by Congress, and that they had given it the name of the State of Ohio, ordained that it be established as a judicial district of the United States; that a district court be organized, and hold its term on the first Monday in June, at Chillicothe; and that the laws of the United States should be of the same force and effect in the said State as elsewhere in the United States. This bill was passed by Congress February 19th.

Rufus King, in his work on Ohio, in discussing this matter, among other things says:

" Here, then, were two acts of Congress recognizing the State of Ohio, but no State yet established which could accept or act upon them; and the Constitution expressly recognizing the Territorial government as in force until the State government should be established. The elections were held January 11th.

The first General Assembly met at Chillicothe on the 1st of March. Upon organizing and canvassing the votes for governor, Edward Tiffin was declared to be elected. In the course of the session Return Jonathan Meigs, Jr., Samuel Huntington and William Sprigg were appointed judges of the Supreme Court. Thomas Worthington and John Smith were chosen as Senators to Congress, and an act passed for holding an election of a representative to Congress, on June 11th. Jeremiah Morrow was elected. But

Congress had adjourned on the 3d of March, and the Senators and Representatives of Ohio were not actually admitted until the next session.

As there was no formal act of admission by Congress, much dispute has arisen as to the time when Ohio was admitted as one of the United States, the various hypotheses ranging all along from the date of the enabling act, April 30, 1802, to the actual seating of her Senators and Representatives in Congress, October 17, 1803. It is quite clear that the enabling act did not form the State. It is also certain that the inchoate State, which was framed by the convention, was postponed, by its express submission, to the Territorial government until the State government could be formed and set in operation. The earliest day at which this can be said to have occurred was at the meeting of the Legislature on the first day of March.

The law-making power being the repository and paramount representative of the power and sovereignty of the State, the Territorial government on that day ceased, and Ohio became a State in the Union."

This was the view of the question subsequently adopted by Congress. In March, 1804, Judge Meigs, for himself and his associates of the Territorial court, presented a petition stating that they had continued to exercise the duties until April 15, 1803, and had applied at the treasury for payment of their salaries accordingly.

The accounting officers, on the advice of the attorney-general, had refused to allow it beyond November 29, 1802, the day on which the State Constitution and form of government had been adopted. The judges had thereupon applied to the Legislature of Ohio, and they likewise refused, holding it to be an obligation of the United States.

After reports by two committees, and a warm debate and close division in committee of the whole, an act was passed February 21, 1806, directing the salaries of the Territorial officers to be allowed and paid at the treasury until March 1, 1803.

This, therefore, may be deemed an authoritative decision on the subject.

The instrument so adopted, it would be respectful to pass in silence. It was framed by men of little experience in matters of State, and under circumstances unfavorable to much forecast.

With such a model of simplicity and strength before them as

the National Constitution, which had just been formed, the wonder is that some of its ideas were not borrowed. It seems to have been studiously disregarded; and Ohio, as well as some States further westward, which her emigrant sons with filial regard induced to adopt her example, has suffered ever since from a weak form of government made up in haste, and apparently in mortal dread of Governor St. Clair. He declined to be a candidate for the office of governor, but unluckily not until the convention had adjourned.

In after years Ohio's greatest and wittiest governor was wont to say, that, after passing the first week of his administration with nothing to do, he had taken an inquest of the office, and found that reprieving criminals and appointing notaries were the sole "flowers of the prerogative."

Briefly stated, it was a government which had no executive, a half-starved, short-lived judiciary, and a lop-sided Legislature.

This department, overloaded with the appointing power which had been taken away from the executive, became so much depraved in the traffic of offices, that, in an assembly where there was a tie both between the Democrats and the Whigs, two "Free Soilers" held the balance of power, and were permitted to choose a United States Senator, in consideration of giving their votes, for every other appointment, to the party which aided them in this supreme exploit of jobbery. A new constitution put an end to this, but the shadow of St. Clair still predominates.

One occurrence in the convention deserves notice. In terms for the qualification of voters, as at first adopted, the right of suffrage had been conferred upon negroes and mulattoes. But on a revision, a motion to strike this out was carried only by the casting vote of the President — a strange prelude to the rigorous "Black Laws" soon afterward adopted by the Legislature.

The admission of Indiana was effected without opposition and without causing a single ripple on the surface of public affairs.

In response to a petition from the Territorial Legislature, Congress passed an enabling act April 19, 1816, defining the boundaries and providing for the election of delegates and the calling of a convention to frame a constitution.

The convention convened at Corydon June 10-29, 1816, and framed a constitution, and the State was admitted into the Union December 11, 1816.

# CHAPTER IX.

## The Admission of Michigan and Wisconsin into the Union.

THE history of the admission of Michigan into the Union, forms, perhaps, quite as interesting a chapter as any in our annals. No other part of the United States has seen so many changes of national and local jurisdiction. It has belonged to France, to England and to the United States.

From 1796 to 1803 it was part of the Northwest Territory, from 1803 to 1805 a part of Indiana, and then an independent territory until its admission into the Union, in 1837. In 1832 the people, at a popular election, cast a large majority vote in favor of entering into a State government. Proceeding upon the theory of the Federalists in 1802, that no enabling act was necessary, the Territorial Legislature, January 26, 1835, passed an act calling a convention to frame a constitution, and designating April 4th the day for the election of delegates. The election was held; the convention assembled at Detroit, May 11th to June 29th, and a constitution was drawn up and ratified November 2d. President Jackson laid it before Congress in a special message. A boundary contest immediately sprang up between Ohio and Indiana, which led to "war," and the marshaling of political and military forces, but no blood was shed.

A great presidential contest was imminent, and Andrew Jackson was interested in the candidacy of Martin Van Buren. The State of Arkansas also stood at the door knocking for admittance, and the administration party was anxious that both should be admitted in time to vote, for it was expected that both would be democratic; but Michigan was a free State and Arkansas was a slave State, and although it was understood that in this scale, one would balance the other, there was yet an anxiety on either side lest the other should get the advantage.

Acts for the admission of the two States were finally approved June 15, 1836; the one admitting Arkansas unconditionally, the other Michigan with certain conditions relating to its boundaries, which were required to be assented to by a delegated convention called to sit at Ann Arbor September 4th. The convention rejected

(27)

the propositions and conditions. This caused a great disappointment among the politicians, and the governor was importuned to call another convention to consider the matter, but he replied that there was no time to call another, and he had no authority to do so. The enterprising citizens of that commonwealth were, however, equal to the emergency and accordingly five citizens, "in the name of the people in their primary capacity," called a convention to meet at Ann Arbor December 14th, which it was afterward ascertained to be in accordance with a democratic scheme formed at Washington. The convention was dubbed the "frost-bitten convention," assumed "sovereign powers," assented to all the terms and conditions provided in the act of Congress, and adjourned. They reported their action to the House, and, to the astonishment of the people of Michigan and the civilized world, Congress accepted the action of this convention as amply sufficient and as meeting the requirements of the act of admission, and then and there admitted Michigan into the Union, but *the electoral vote was not counted.*

The admission of Wisconsin into the Union was not accompanied by such "signs and portents" as that of Michigan, and was not effected until two constitutional conventions had been held and two constitutions framed, one of which, on being submitted to the people, was rejected, and the other was not adopted until after the lapse of several years after the first one was rejected; and it was not until May 29, 1848, that the State became a member of the Union.

A controversy first arose between Michigan and Wisconsin as to what was to be her future boundaries, and finally led to a division of the great peninsula which commences in the region of Green Bay and extends to the shores of Lake Superior. Then the people demanded a restoration of that portion of Illinois which includes many of the northern counties of the State, and, strange to say, were aided and assisted in this claim by large numbers of the inhabitants of those counties, who sympathized with the people of Wisconsin. Public meetings were held in various Illinois towns, and adopted resolutions in favor of the Wisconsin claim, and on the 6th of July, 1840, a convention was held at Rockford, which declared that the fourteen northern counties belonged to Wisconsin, and recommended the people to elect delegates to a convention, to be held at Madison in November, for the purpose of adopting such lawful and constitutional measures as may seem to be necessary and proper for the early adjustment of the southern boundary.

In 1842 the territorial governor sent an official communication to the governor of Illinois, informing him that the Illinois jurisdiction over the frontier counties was accidental and temporary.

Great excitement ensued, and the people were kept in a continual agitation over the boundary question, State banking and various other matters, and, as before stated, it was not until May 29, 1848, that Wisconsin was admitted into the Union.

## CHAPTER X.

### Illinois and Virginia—George Rogers Clark and the Backwoodsmen.

THE individual enterprise of Col. George Rogers Clark to lead an expedition into the Illinois country and drive out the English, French and Indians that had their headquarters at Kaskaskia and neighboring villages, or make them acknowledge allegiance to the Americans, was one worthy of the daring and genius of that intrepid and experienced frontiersman.

The story has been too often told to bear repetition. Its great importance arises from the fact that, starting as he did from Virginia, and under the auspices of Virginia, his conquest has been claimed as belonging exclusively "to the Nation of Virginia," as Thomas Jefferson characterized that great commonwealth.

Roosevelt, in his "Winning of the West," says: "It is idle to talk of that conquest as being purely a Virginia affair. It was conquered by Clark, a Virginian, with some scant help from Virginia, but it was retained only owing to the power of the United States, and the patriotism of such northern statesmen as Jay, Adams and Franklin, the negotiators of the final treaty. Had Virginia alone been in interest, Great Britain would not have even paid her claims the compliment of listening to them. Virginia's share in the history of the Nation, has ever been gallant and leading; but the Revolutionary war was emphatically fought by Americans for America; no part could have been won without the help of the whole, and every victory was thus a victory for all, in which all alike can take pride."

The fate of Clark was melancholy, and like that of General Arthur St. Clair, closed in poverty and gloom. He was ultimately made a brigadier-general in the Virginia militia, and to the harassed settlers in Kentucky, his mere name was a tower of strength.

Alone and with the very slenderest means, he had conquered and held a vast and beautiful region, which, but for him, would have formed part of a foreign and hostile empire; he had clothed and paid his soldiers with the spoils of his enemies; he had spent his own fortune as carelessly as he had risked his life, and the only reward that he was destined for many years to receive, was the sword voted him by the Legislature.

Clark felt that he was entitled to some substantial reward rather than an empty bauble for his services, and the tradition is that when the Virginia commissioners offered Clark the sword, the grim old fighter, smarting under the sense of his wrongs, threw it indignantly from him, telling the envoys that he demanded from Virginia his just rights and promised reward of his services, not an empty compliment. The inhabitants of Illinois paid to his shade the posthumous honor of naming a county after him, and the city of Chicago an important street, over which uncounted thousands daily and hourly pass and repass, who never knew of his existence, and never heard of his exploits.

"The country beyond the Alleghanies was first won and settled by the backwoodsmen themselves, acting under their own leaders, obeying their own desires and following their own methods. They were a marked and peculiar people. The good and evil traits in their character were such as naturally belonged to a strong, harsh and homely race, which, with all its shortcomings, was nevertheless bringing a tremenduous work to a triumphant conclusion. The backwoodsmen were, above all things, characteristically American; and it is fitting that the two greatest and most typical of all Americans, should have been respectively a sharer and an outcome of their work. Washington himself passed the most important years of his youth heading the westward movement of his people; clad in the traditional dress of the backwoodsman, in tasseled hunting shirt and fringed leggings, he led them to battle against the French and Indians, and helped to clear the way for the American advance.

The only other man who, in the American roll of honor, stands by the side of Washington, was born when the distinctive work of the pioneers had ended; and yet he was bone of their bone and flesh of their flesh; for from the loins of this gaunt frontier folk sprang mighty Abraham Lincoln." The claims of Virginia to the Northwestern Territory have, first and last, been the subject of very great discussion, and were, at the time when she made her deed of cession to the United States. She claimed in the first place, all of the sovereign powers of a Nation, and laid great stress upon her conquest of the territory by Clark, which was followed by many public acts of the Colonial Government, asserting and exercising dominion over the same.

### THE NATION OF VIRGINIA.

Thomas Jefferson entertained a most exalted opinion of the power of the State of Virginia, and sometimes spoke of that great Commonwealth as the *Nation* of Virginia. As an example, in 1799, the question was extensively discussed whether the Supreme Court of the United States possessed a general common law jurisdiction, and in a letter addressed to Edmund Randolph on the 18th of August, of that year, among other things said: "Before the Revolution, the Nation of Virginia had, by the organs they then thought proper to constitute, established a system of laws, which they divided into three denominations, of:

I. Common Law.

II. Chancery; or if you please into two only: 1. Common law. 2. Chancery.

When by the Declaration of Independence they chose to abolish their former organs of declaring their will, the acts of will already formally and constitutionally declared, remained untouched. For the Nation was not dissolved, was not annihilated; its will, therefore, remained in full vigor; and on establishing the new organs, first of a convention and afterward a more complicated Legislature, the old acts of National will continued in force, until the Nation should, by its new organs, declare its will changed.

The common law, therefore, which was not in force when we landed here, nor till we had formed ourselves into a Nation and had manifested by the organs we constituted that the common law was to be our law, because the Nation continued in being, and because, though it changed the organs for the future declarations of its will, yet it did *not* change its former declarations that the common law was *its* law. Apply these principles to the present case. Before the Revolution there existed no such Nation as the United States; they then first associated as a Nation, but for special purposes only. They had all their laws to make as Virginia had on her first establishment as a Nation. But they did not, as Virginia had done, proceed to *adopt* a whole system of laws ready made to their hand.

That Virginia did, as the settlers passed beyond the Alleghanies, exercise acts of sovereignty over the regions which were, from time to time, reported to the authorities as existing, is not denied, for we find that the county of Orange was created in 1734, Augusta in 1738, and Botetourt in 1769, in which act it is naively stated that it is "bounded west by the utmost limits of Virginia."

Other counties erected before the Revolution, extended to the Ohio, and embraced Kentucky.

Chief Justice Chase, in reviewing the controversy which arose in regard to Virginia's claim to the whole Northwestern Territory and of the various other claims to western lands by eastern States among other things says : "Of these various claims, that of the United States seems to have been the most natural and just. The charter of Virginia had been vacated by a judicial proceeding; the company to whom it was granted had been dissolved, the grant itself had been resumed by the Crown, and large tracts of the country included in its original limits, had been patented to various individuals and associations without remonstrance on the part of the colony of Virginia."

The expenses incurred and the efforts made by Virginia in the reduction of the British posts and in the defense and protection of the frontier, created a just claim upon the treasury of the Union, but could not, of themselves, confer a valid title to the western lands. The western boundary of Connecticut had been so clearly defined in her agreement with New York that her claims to territory beyond that line could not be entitled to much consideration; the pretensions of New York were liable to easy refutation upon an appeal to western geography and an investigation into the real extent of the territory of the six nations, and the claim of Massachusetts rested upon a charter granted at a period when the territory now claimed under it was actually possessed and occupied by France. In opposition to these various pretensions, the Congress, as the common head of the United States, maintained its title to the western lands upon the solid ground that a vacant territory wrested from the common enemy by the united arms and at the joint expense of all the States, ought of right to belong to Congress in trust for the common use and benefit of the whole Union.

In 1776 the Virginia Legislature erected the county of Kentucky, which included about everything southwest of the Ohio.

On the 4th of July, 1778, George Rogers Clark captured Kaskaskia, which had been for nearly a hundred years the capital of what was called the Illinois country, and in October, 1778, the Legislature of Virginia declared, "All citizens of the Commonwealth of Virginia, who are actually settlers there, or who shall hereafter be settled on the west side of the Ohio, shall be included in the District of Kentucky, which shall be called Illinois County." A lieutenant commandant was appointed by Governor Patrick Henry to govern the county, with full instructions for carrying on the government.

The French settlements remained under Virginia jurisdiction until March, 1784.

## CHAPTER XI.

### Illinois County.

ILLINOIS was once the frontier county of Virginia; and Bancroft says that "Virginia was the first State in the world composed of separate boroughs, diffused over an extensive surface, where representation was organized on the principle of universal suffrage."

As the State of Illinois has never, at any time, printed in any statute or volume of session laws, either public or private, the act of Virginia organizing what is now known as the State of Illinois into the *County* of Illinois, we have here printed it in full, so that it can be seen and read of all men:

#### THE COUNTY OF ILLINOIS.

AN ACT for establishing the County of Illinois, and for the more effectual protection and defense thereof.

WHEREAS, By a successful expedition carried on by the Virginia militia, on the western side of the Ohio river, several of the British posts within the territory of this commonwealth, in the country adjacent to the river Mississippi, have been reduced, and the inhabitants have acknowledged themselves citizens thereof, and taken the oath of fidelity to the same; and the good faith and safety of the commonwealth require that the said citizens should be supported and protected by speedy and effectual reinforcements, which will be the best means of preventing the inroads and depredations of the Indians upon the inhabitants to the westward of the Allegheny Mountains; and whereas, from their remote situation, it may at this time be difficult, if not impracticable, to govern them by the present laws of this commonwealth, until proper information, by intercourse with their fellow-citizens on the east side of the Ohio, shall have familiarized them to the same, and it is therefore expedient that some temporary form of government, adapted to their circumstances, should in the meantime be established:—

*Be it enacted by the General Assembly*, That all the citizens of this commonwealth who are already settled, or shall hereafter settle, on the western side of the Ohio aforesaid, shall be included in a distinct county, which shall be called Illinois county; and that the governor of this commonwealth, with the advice of the council, may appoint a county lieutenant or commandant in chief in that county, during pleasure, who shall appoint and commission so many deputy commandants, militia officers and commissaries, as he shall think proper in the different districts, during pleasure, all of whom, before they enter into office, shall take the oath of fidelity to this commonwealth and the oath of office, according to the form of their own religion, which the inhabitants shall fully, and to all intents and purposes enjoy, together with all their civil rights and property.

And all civil officers to which the said inhabitants have been accustomed, necessary for the preservation of peace and the administration of justice, shall be chosen by a majority of the citizens in their respective districts, to be convened for that purpose by the county lieutenant or commandant, or his deputy, and shall be commissioned by the said county lieutenant or commandant in chief, and be paid for their services in the same manner as such expenses have been heretofore borne, levied and paid in that county; which said civil officers, after taking the oaths as before prescribed, shall exercise their several jurisdictions, and conduct themselves agreeable to the laws which the present settlers are now accustomed to.

And on any criminal prosecution, where the offender shall be adjudged guilty, it shall and may be lawful for the county lieutenant or commandant in chief to pardon his or her offense, except in cases of murder or treason; and in such cases, he may respite execution from time to time until the sense of the governor in the first instance, and of the General Assembly in the case of treason, is obtained. But where any officers, directed to be appointed by this act, are such as the inhabitants have been unused to, it shall and may be lawful for the governor, with the advice of the council, to draw a warrant or warrants on the treasury of this commonwealth for the payment of the salaries of such officers, so as the sum or sums drawn for do not exceed the sum of five hundred pounds, anything herein to the contrary notwithstanding.

And for the protection and defense of the said county and its inhabitants,

*Be it enacted*, That it shall and may be lawful for the governor, with the advice of the council, forthwith to order, raise, levy, either by voluntary enlistments or detachments from the militia, five hundred men, with proper officers, to march immediately into the said county of Illinois, to garrison such forts or stations already taken, or which it may be proper to take there or elsewhere, for protecting the said county, and for keeping up our communication with them, and also with the Spanish settlements, as he, with the advice aforesaid, shall direct. And the said governor, with the advice of the council, shall, from time to time, until further provision shall be made for the same by the General Assembly, continue to relieve the said volunteers, or militia, by other enlistments or detachments, as hereinbefore directed, and to issue warrants on the treasurer of this commonwealth for all charges and expenses accruing thereon, which the said treasurer is hereby required to pay accordingly.

*And be it further enacted*, That it shall and may be lawful for the governor, with the advice of the council, to take such measures as they shall judge most expedient, or the necessity of the case requires, for supplying the said inhabitants, as well as our friendly Indians in those parts, with goods and other necessaries, either by opening a communication and trade with New Orleans, or otherwise, and to appoint proper persons for managing and conducting the same on behalf of this commonwealth.

*Provided*, That any of the said inhabitants may likewise carry on such trade on their own accounts, notwithstanding.

This act shall continue and be in force from and after the passing of the same, for and during the term of twelve months, and from thence to the end of the next session of assembly, and no longer.—[Oct., 1778, 3d of Commonwealth. Chapter XXI, page 552, Vol. 9, Hening's Statutes at Large.

The name of Illinois county was changed by General St. Clair and his council, when he became governor of the Northwestern Territory, to that of St. Clair county, in March, 1790. Randolph county was established in 1795, and these two counties were continued by the Illinois Territorial Government, when Illinois was set off from Indiana Territory, in 1809, and the boundaries of these two counties were coterminous with that of the present State.

Edwards county was organized November 28, 1814, and its original boundaries were as follows: "All that tract of country within the following boundaries, to-wit: Beginning at the mouth of Bon Pas Creek, on the Big Wabash, and running thence due west to the meridian line (3d P. M.), which runs north from the mouth of the Ohio river; thence with said meridian line, and due north till it strikes the line of Upper Canada; thence with the line of Upper Canada to the line that separates this territory from the Indiana Territory, and thence with the said dividing line to the beginning."

Edwards county was cut off from Gallatin, and then White county, in 1818, was taken off from the south part of Edwards.

In its original organization Edwards county embraced an immense area of territory, extending practically from the Ohio river (for its southern boundary, Gallatin county, was but relatively a short distance from that river) to Upper Canada, including what is now a portion of the State of Wisconsin.

The following counties, or parts of counties, in Illinois, have been formed out of the territory included in Edwards county, Wabash, Clay, Jasper, Coles, Macon, De Witt, Kankakee, Kendall, De Kalb, Wayne, Richland, Effingham, Cumberland, Piatt, McLean, Grundy, Du Page, Boone, Jefferson, Lawrence, Fayette, Edgar, Champaign, Livingston, La Salle, McHenry, Marion, Crawford, Shelby, Clark, Vermillion, Iroquois, Will, Kane, Lake and Cook.

It is difficult to imagine, in the great changes that are here shown to have taken place in the civil divisions of the State, that when Edwards county was organized neither Cook county nor the city of Chicago had an existence; but that Cook county was embraced in

Edwards county, and its county seat, at Palmyra, at the falls of the Big Wabash, a town which has long since ceased to exist.

When the first constitution of the State of Illinois was formed, not a man was in the convention that framed it who lived North of what is now the limits of Madison county. All of the records of that convention have been lost.

The first governor of Illinois Territory, by proclamation, divided the whole territory into three counties, and so it remained until the 14th of September, 1812, when Governor Edwards, by proclamation, established the county of Madison, with the following boundaries, to-wit: "Beginning on the Mississippi, to run with the second township above Cahokia, east until it strikes the dividing line between the Illinois and Indiana territories; thence Illinois, with the said dividing line to the line of Upper Canada; thence with said line to the Mississippi; thence down the Mississippi to the place of beginning.

This included about three-fourths of the State.

On the 31st of January, 1821, Pike county was established, by an act of the Legislature, with the following boundaries: "Beginning at the mouth of the Illinois river, and running thence up the middle of said river to the forks of the same; thence up the south fork of said river until it strikes the State line of Indiana; thence north with said line to the north boundary line of this State; thence west to the boundary line of the State, and thence with said line to the place of beginning."

On the 28th of January, 1823, Fulton county was carved out of the above territory, and on the 13th of Jannary, 1825, the Legislature passed a law organizing and establishing the county of Peoria, with the following boundaries, to-wit: Beginning where the line between townships eleven and twelve north intersects the Illinois river; thence west with said line to the range line between ranges four and five east; thence south with said line to the range line between townships seven and eight; thence east to the line between ranges five and six; thence south to the middle of the main channel of the Illinois river; thence up along the middle of the main channel of said river to the place of beginning.

On the 7th of December, 1825, the county was divided into three election districts: One was called the Chicago precinct; and Alexander Wolcott, John Kinzie and John Baptiste Beaubien, all inhabitants of Chicago, were appointed judges of election for said precinct.

In 1778 Chicago was in Virginia, and up to 1809 was in Indiana. February 3, 1809, Indiana Territory was, by an act of Congress, divided into two separate governments. President Madison appointed John Boyle, an associate justice of the Court of Appeals of Kentucky, governor of the territory, but he declined, and Ninian Edwards, chief justice of the same court, was appointed in his stead. Nathaniel Pope was appointed secretary; Alexander Stuart, Obadiah Jones and Jesse B. Thomas, judges; Benjamin H. Boyle, attorney-general.

Under the ordinance of 1787 and the act of Congress February 3, 1809, the Governor and Judges constituted the law-making power of the territory, and as such they met for the first time at Kaskaskia, June 13, 1809, and their first act was to resolve that the laws of Indiana Territory, in force prior to March 1, 1809, which applied to the government of the territory, should remain in full force and effect. The duration of the session was seven days.

In 1821 Chicago was in Pike county; in 1823 in Fulton county; and in 1825 in Peoria county.

The act creating Cook county was passed and approved by the General Assemby of Illinois, January 15, 1831, and by that same act Chicago was made the county seat, and a ferry established at the seat of justice. It was named after Daniel P. Cook, a son-in-law of Governor Ninian Edwards, who was one of the first United States Senators from this State. He was a member of Congress from 1820 to 1827, and died during that year at the age of thirty-two.

In March, 1831, Cook county was organized. It embraced within its boundaries all the territory which now constitutes the counties of Lake, McHenry, Du Page and Will, and the only voting place in the county at the first election was Chicago.

## CHAPTER XII.

### Constitutional Conventions in Illinois.

THE State of Illinois has held already four constitutional conventions. The first was in 1818, under an act of Congress passed April 18, 1818, termed an enabling act, and was for the purpose of forming a "State Constitution and a State Government," republican in form, and in accordance with the principles embodied in the ordinance of 1787.

The next was held in 1847, the next in 1862, and the last one in 1869-70. Each of these last conventions was for the purpose of "altering, revising and amending" the then existing Constitution.

## THE CONSTITUTION OF 1818.

In 1818 the whole number of people in the State of Illinois was about 45,000. Some two or three thousand of these were the descendants of the old French settlers in the villages of Kaskaskia, Prairie Du Rocher, Prairie Du Pont, Cahokia, and Peoria. Many of these had intermarried with the Indians and lived a roving life, hunting and trapping. The American inhabitants were chiefly from Kentucky, Virginia, Maryland and Pennsylvania. Some of them had been officers and soldiers under George Rogers Clark, and were good types of the pioneer element. They were farmers, mechanics and soldiers, and skilled in Indian warfare. The settled part of the State did not, in 1818, extend much north of Edwardsville and Alton, while all the rest of the State was comparatively an unbroken wilderness. The Black Hawk war did not occur until 1832.

The first Constitution was made up in its principal provisions from the Constitutions of Kentucky, Ohio and Indiana; was adopted by the delegates and never submitted to the people—following, in this regard, the precedent set by most of the slave States. Indeed, the first Constitution, we believe, that ever was submitted to the people for its adoption or rejection, was in the case of Maine, in 1820.

It was very objectionable, in vesting the Legislature with the appointing power of most of the principal officers of the State—and this we are told arose in this way: As originally framed this power was committed to the executive, but as it was expected that Shadrach Bond would be elected governor, and that he would not appoint a particular candidate to the office of state auditor, whom the members of the convention favored, they changed the provision, and inserted this clause in the schedule: "An auditor of public accounts, an attorney-general, and such other officers as may be necessary, may be appointed by the General Assembly." At first the Legislature limited its exercise of this power to the appointment of the above designated officers, the governor appointing the state's attorneys, recorders and other officers and agents provided for by law, but whenever it happened that the governor was not in accord with the General Assembly, it would deprive him of his patronage. Thus there was a continual liability to a change of the appointing power, and the consequences were a constant pulling, hauling and intriguing, which led to corrupt combinations and the most disgraceful system of log rolling that could be imagined.

In the election of members to the convention the only questions which were agitated and discussed before the people were the right of constituents to instruct their representatives, and the introduction of slavery. It is needless to say that the Constitution bears many visible marks of the slave-holder, and the slave-holding interests were unduly, and most unjustly protected, as will appear by article VI of that instrument.

While professing to abolish slavery in the first section, by declaring that "neither slavery nor involuntary servitude shall *hereafter* be introduced into this State, otherwise than for the punishment of crimes, whereof the party shall have been duly convicted, it proceeded to recognize the validity of contracts of indenture of "persons" in several ways, especially the third section, which is in these words:

"Sec. 3. Each and every person who has been bound to service by contract or indenture by virtue of the laws of the Illinois Territory, heretofore existing, and in conformity to the provisions of the same, without fraud or collusion, shall be held to a specific performance of their contracts or indentures; and such negroes and mulattoes as have been registered in conformity with the aforesaid laws, shall serve out the time appointed by said laws. *Provided, however,* That children hereafter born of such person, negroes or mulattoes, shall become free—the males at the age of twenty-one years, the females at the age of eighteen years; each and every child born of indentured parents shall be entered with the clerk of the county in which they reside, by their owners, within six months after the birth of said child."

Under and by virtue of those provisions the famous Black Laws were passed, which disgraced the statute books of this State for years, and which established a species of slavery about as effectually as if it actually existed. Perhaps this is rather too strong language, but these laws served to annoy greatly the negroes and mulattoes, and, strange to say, were continued in force until repealed by the General Assembly, in 1867.

A still further explanation of this matter may not be amiss.

In 1807 the Indiana Legislature passed an act authorizing the owners of negroes and mulattoes more than fifteen years of age to bring them into the Territory, and to have them bound to service by indenture for such time as the master and slave might agree upon. If, within thirty days of the time he was brought into the Territory, the slave would not consent to be indentured, then his owner should have sixty days in which to remove him into any State where slavery existed. The law also permitted any person to bring slaves under fifteen years of age into the Territory, and to hold them to service—the males until the age of thirty-five, the females until the age of thirty-two years. Male children, born in the Territory, of a parent of color owing service by indenture, should serve the master until the age of thirty years; female children until the age of twenty-eight years. This act continued in force until 1810. On the territorial statute book are also found very repressive acts concerning servants. This act was continued in force by the Illinois Legislature after the division of the Territory. In 1814 the same Legislature passed a law providing that slaves might, with consent of their owners, hire themselves in the Territory for a term not exceeding one year, and that such act should not in any way affect the master's right of property in them in the State or Territory where they belonged. The preamble of this act assigns as reasons for its provisions that mills can not be erected, or other needed improvements made, for want of laborers; and, particularly, that the manufacture of salt, the supply of which should be abundant and the price low, can not be carried on by means of white men. Still further, an act passed in 1812 forbade the emigration of free negroes to the Territory of Illinois under severe penalties; and enjoined free negroes already there to register themselves and their children in the office of the clerk of the county, also under severe penalties.

When one remembers that the Northwest was covered on two sides by slave territory, from which it was separated only by the Ohio and Mississippi rivers, he appreciates the facilities that such enactments as the foregoing gave for evading the intent of the sixth compact of the ordinance. Comment is not needed to show that the ingenuity here displayed could have invented a system of enforced labor not at all inferior to that devised by some of the Southern States under President Johnson's reconstructed scheme. Moreover, these enactments explain certain provisions respecting indentures in the first Constitutions of Ohio, Indiana and Illinois that would otherwise be inexplicable.

When the resolution declaring the admission of Illinois to the Union was on its passage through the House of Representatives, Mr. Tallmadge, of New York, opposed its adoption on the ground that it contravened the sixth article of the ordinance of 1787. He felt himself constrained to come to the conclusion that the section of the Constitution described above embraced a complete recognition of existing slavery, if not providing for its future introduction and toleration. He contrasted the Illinois and the Indiana Constitutions, to the disadvantage of the former. Thirty-four votes were registered in the house against the resolution.

In the constitutional convention of 1818 there were but three lawyers, Jesse B. Thomas, Elias Kent Kane and A. F. Hubbard, so far as we know.

Thomas was a delegate to Congress from Indiana Territory in 1809, at the time it was divided, and the principal agent in securing the division. He was a lawyer of ability, of high standing, but an advocate of slavery, and in the subsequent history of Illinois was a leader of the pro-slavery party.

He was president of the convention which formed our State Constitution at the time we were admitted into the Union, and was elected the first United States Senator.

The leading member of the convention was probably Elias Kent Kane, although we can not certainly tell, owing to the loss or destruction of the records of the convention. He was born in the State of New York and was bred to the profession of the law. He removed, when a very young man, to Tennessee, and finally came to Illinois and settled in Kaskaskia in 1815, when he was about twenty years of age. His talents were both solid and brilliant, and he soon became a leader; was appointed Secretary of State under the new government in 1818, then became a member of the General Assembly and finally United States Senator, and died a member of that body in 1835.

Kane county on the Fox river was named after him.

A. F. Hubbard is chiefly distinguished for having attempted to oust governor Coles from the office of governor—while he was temporarily absent from the State—by issuing a call for an extra session of the General Assembly, and appointing one W. L. D. Ewing paymaster-general of the State militia, etc., basing his claim for so doing on a provision in the executive article of the Constitution, which reads as follows:

"In case of impeachment, refusal to qualify, resignation or absence from the State, the lieutenant-governor shall exercise all the power and authority appertaining to the office of governor, until the time pointed out by the Constitution for the election of a governor shall arrive; unless the General Assembly shall otherwise provide by law for the election of a governor to fill such vacancy."

Under this provision Hubbard claimed that he was governor *de jure* and *de facto*, having been elected lieutenant-governor at the election in 1822, but on an opposition ticket. The State at that time was considered overwhelmingly democratic, and Chief Justice Phillips was the regular candidate of that party, with Adolphus F. Hubbard lieutenant-governor. Edward Coles, a very popular and strong anti-slavery man, was brought out against Phillips, and was elected over him by a considerable majority, but both branches of the Legislature were opposed to him, and every kind of a partisan scheme was resorted to, to annoy him. Mobs were incited against him, with threats of personal violence, suits were commenced against him for bringing slaves into the territory and liberating them, and he was heavily fined. At last, while temporarily absent from the State, the bold attempt was made by Hubbard to usurp his office. The issuing of a commission to Ewing was, at the time, considered a very shrewd move, and it was thought for a time that it would succeed, but Judge Lockwood was at that time on the Supreme Bench, and he showed so clearly the ridiculous nature of the attempt, that it came to naught. The legal history of this affair may be found set forth at large in Breese's reports, and arose on an application of Ewing to compel the Secretary of State, George Forquer, by mandamus, to append his signature to this commission which had been issued by Hubbard.

We know but very little of the constitutional convention of 1818, owing to the fact that all its records have been lost or destroyed, but there is one thing that Governor Ford mentions in his history of Illinois that is quite interesting, and that is that during the session of the convention of 1818, the Reverend Mr. Wiley and his congregation of Covenanters in Randolph county, sent in a petition asking the convention to declare in the Constitution that "Jesus Christ was the head of the government, and that the Holy Scriptures were the only rule of faith and practice." This petition was either not noticed at all or was acted upon unfavorably, which so displeased the Covenanters, that they henceforth looked upon the Constitution as "an heathen and unbaptized government," and refused to vote, to work on the roads, serve on juries, hold any office or do any act showing that they recognized the government.

This state of affairs continued until the great contest commenced in 1824, whether Illinois should become a slave or a free State, when they arose in their might and voted unanimously against slavery.

As early as 1818 the State was filled with a class of politicians who were intent in controlling every office in sight, whether local, State or National, and when the Constitution was formed the governor was clothed with a large measure of the appointing power. Shadrach Bond had been fixed upon by the common barrators for the first governor, and the convention wished for some reason to have Elijah C. Berry the first auditor of public accounts; but it having been ascertained that Bond would not appoint him, the managers, at the very last moment, and just before it was adopted in the Convention, affixed this provision to the schedule: "An auditor of public accounts, an attorney-general, and such other officers of the State as may be necessary, may be appointed by the General Assembly," as above stated.

Thus "accoutered," the Constitution was adopted and "they all plunged in." By "they" we mean the whole army of hungry politicians, who were waiting the day when they could obtain access to the public crib and fatten on its stores. An inventory was taken, and who were "officers of the State" and who were not, soon became a matter of debate, and the question was asked by members of the General Assembly: Were state's attorneys of the circuits— were canal commissioners, fund commissioners, commissioners of the board of public works, bank directors, canal agents, etc.—were they State officers? And the reply came back from the General Assembly every time: Yes, they were State officers. And the General Assembly absorbed them with great alacrity and relish.

Ford says: "Some times such agents were appointed by election; then, again, the Legislature would pass a law enacting them into office by name and surname. They contrived to strip the governor of all patronage not positively secured to him by the Constitution—such as the appointment of a secretary of state and the filling of vacancies during the recess of their sessions. At first the Legislature contented itself with the power to elect an auditor and attorney-general; the governor, all the state's attorneys, the recorders of counties, all State officers and agents occasionally needed, and many minor county officers. But in the administration of Governor Duncan, he was finally stripped of all patronage, except the appointment of notaries public and public administrators. Sometimes one Legislature, feeling pleased with the governor, would give him some appointing power which their successors would take away if they happened to quarrel with him.

This constant changing and shifting of powers from one co-ordinate branch of the government to another, which rendered it impossible for the people to foresee exactly for what purpose either the governor or the Legislature were elected, was one of the worst features of the government. It led to innumerable intrigues and corruptions, and for a long time destroyed the harmony between the executive and legislative departments.

And all this was caused by the convention of 1818 in the attempt to get one man into an office of no very considerable importance.

At the time of the formation of the Constitution of 1818 the State was divided into fourteen counties, namely: St. Clair, Randolph, Madison, Gallatin, Johnson, Edwards, White, Pope, Jackson, Crawford, Bond, Union, Washington and Franklin.

St. Clair was represented by John Messenger and James Leman, Jr.

Randolph by George Fisher and Elias Kent Kane.

Madison by B. Stephenson, Joseph Borong and Abraham Prickett.

Gallatin by Michael Jones, Leonard White and Adolphus Frederick Hubbard.

Johnson was represented by Hezekiah West and William McFatridge.

Edwards by Seth Gord and Levi Compton.

Pope by Samuel O'Melveny and Ferguson.

White by Willis Hargrave and Enoch Moore.

Jackson by Conrad Well and James Hall, Jr.

Crawford by Joseph Kitchell and Ed. N. Cullom.

Bond by Thomas Kirkpatrick and Samuel G. Morse.

Union by William Echols and John Whiteacre.
Washington by Andrew Bankson, and
Franklin by Isham Harrison and Thomas Roberts.

Jesse B. Thomas was president of the convention and William C. Greenup was secretary.

The convention assembled at Kaskaskia on the first Monday of August, 1818, in accordance with the fourth section of the enabling act, and adjourned on the 26th of August.

## CHAPTER XIII.

### The Founders of the Commonwealth.

"IN the birth of societies," says Montesquieu, "it is the chiefs of the republics who form the institution, and in the sequel it is the institution which forms the chiefs of the republics." And he adds: "One of the causes of the prosperity of Rome was the fact that its kings were all great men. We find nowhere else in history an uninterrupted series of such statesmen and such military commanders.

"Historic truth ought to be no less sacred than religion. If the precepts of faith raise our souls above the interests of this world, the lessons of history, in their turn, inspire us with the love of the beautiful and the just, and the hatred of whatever presents an obstacle to the progress of humanity. These lessons, to be profitable, require certain conditions. It is necessary that the facts be produced with a rigorous exactness, that the changes, political or social, be analyzed philosophically, that the exacting interest of the details of public men should not divert attention from the political part they played, or cause us to forget their providential mission."

Illinois was fortunate in the beginning by having for her founders a race of great men. Col. George Rogers Clark, the conqueror of the Illinois country, takes rank next to Hannibal.

Governor Edwards, the first governor of the territory of Illinois and the first senator of the State, was the friend of Madison and the schoolmate of William Wirt. He was born in Maryland and was brought up under the very best educational and social influences of his native State. He early removed to Kentucky, became chief justice of that State, and occupied that position at the time that Madison selected him as governor of the Illinois Territory.

At the time Illinois was admitted into the Union the affairs of the State were wholly controlled by pro-slavery men, who seemed bent upon making the State a slave State.

Governor Edwards himself, the foremost citizen of the State and a man of commanding influence, first governor of the Illinois Territory, afterward senator, was a slave-holder, and held slaves in the territory, contrary to the ordinance of 1787—the great organic law of the Northwest Territory—and contrary to his oath of office, as will be seen by the following notice, under his own hand and signature.

"NOTICE.—I have for sale 22 slaves; among them are several of both sexes, between the ages of 10 and 17 years. If not shortly sold I shall wish to hire them in Missouri Territory. I have also for sale a full-blooded stud horse, a very large English bull and several young ones.

"Oct. 1, 1815. NINIAN EDWARDS."

Taken from the "Illinois Herald," published in Kaskaskia Oct. 1, 1815.

Governor Edwards, though by birth a southern man, and appointed from Kentucky as governor upon the organization of the territory, was yet, as William H. Brown said, in favor of a free Constitution for Illinois, and did, much to his credit, range himself on the side of the free soilers in the great struggle which took place between the contending hosts in 1824.

The Secretary of State was Nathaniel Pope, a man of great ability, refined in his manners and of scholarly tastes. He was chosen territorial delegate to Congress in 1816, and it was by and through his efforts that the northern boundary of the State was so changed as to bring Chicago into Illinois instead of leaving it in Wisconsin.

Judge Jesse B. Thomas was a delegate to Congress from Indiana Territory at the time it was divided, in 1809, and the Illinois Territory created. He removed to Kaskaskia, was elected the president of the constitutional convention of 1818, and then senator, with Governor Edwards as his colleague. He was a strong pro-slavery man, and a leader of that party in the State, but, as we have been told, regretted his course before he died. He died in Ohio. He was born in Hagerstown, Maryland, and claimed to be a direct descendant of Lord Baltimore. He is said to have been the author of the Missouri Compromise Bill of 1820.

Judge Griswold was from New England—strict as a Puritan and conscientious as a saint. Governor Reynolds says of him: "He was a correct, honest man, a good lawyer, paid his debts and sung David's psalms."

William H. Brown was the friend and companion of Lockwood and Coles, and one of the most upright men that we ever knew. He died at the "Bible Hotel," at Amsterdam, Holland, in 1867, of small-pox, while on a foreign journey, some twenty-three years ago, at an advanced age.

John Reynolds, familiarly known as the "Old Ranger" is one of the most picturesque characters that ever lived in this State. He was born of Irish parentage in Pennsylvania, February 26, 1788; removed to Illinois in 1800—lived on a farm for a time; then went to school at Knoxville, Tennessee—was ever foremost in horse and foot-racing—shooting matches—studied law, and when he hung out his shingle at Cahokia in 1814, announced his advent in the "Illinois Herald," published at Kaskaskia, as follows:

"To the poor people of Illinois and Missouri Territory. To the above class of mankind whose pecuniary circumstance will not admit of feeing a lawyer, I tender my professional services as a lawyer in all courts I may practice in, without fee or reward.

JOHN REYNOLDS."

He was great on the stump, in church, school-house, grocery, or the open air. He became judge of the Supreme Court, and governor of the State.

Among the reminiscences of the times is an advertisement in the "Missouri Gazette" of May 14, 1816, as follows:

"FIFTY DOLLARS REWARD

Will be given to any person, who will deliver to me, in Cahokia, a negro boy named Moses, who ran away from me in Cahokia about two months since. He is about sixteen years old, well made, and did belong to Messrs. McKnight & Brady, in St. Louis, where he has been since frequently, and is supposed to be harbored there or thereabout. He had on a hunting shirt when he left me, May 14, 1816.

JOHN REYNOLDS."

Governor Ford, in speaking of Reynolds, says that he had passed his life on the frontier among a frontier people; had learned all the by-words, catch-words, old and odd sayings and figures of speech invented by vulgar ingenuity and common among a backwoods people; to these he had added a copious supply of his own, and had diligently compounded them all into a language peculiar to himself, which he used on all occasions, public and private. He was a man of remarkably good sense and shrewdness for the sphere in which he was destined to move, and possessed a fertile imagination, a ready eloquence, and a continual mirthfulness and pleasantry when mingling with the people. He had a kind heart, and was ready to do a favor, and never harbored resentment against any human being.

Shadrach Bond was another great man who has left his mark on the times, and, although a pro-slavery man, was in his day and generation highly regarded and esteemed.

He was elected the first governor of the State by an almost unanimous vote. He came to the Territory from Maryland in 1794, and settled in the American Bottom, in what is now Monroe county. He was of commanding presence, noble mien, and of great dignity of character. He kept horses and hounds, and lived like one of the landed gentlemen of the eighteenth century. He was a member of the Territorial Legislature of Ohio and Indiana, a captain in the war of 1812, and was the first delegate to Congress from Illinois Territory, taking his seat December 3, 1812.

Pierre Menard was elected lieutenant-governor on the same ticket with Bond, and he also was a most remarkable man. He was of French extraction, born at St. Antoine, thirty-five miles from Montreal, October 7, 1766, and came to Kaskaskia from Vincennes in 1790, and engaged in merchandising. He was a great favorite with the Indians, became active in public affairs, was elected a member of the Territorial Legislature of Indiana, afterward removed to Kaskaskia and there became president of the council of the Territorial General Assembly of Illinois, and was the most distinguished of all the French emigrants that ever came to the West.

He was a good financier and understood its principles well. His command of the English language was somewhat limited, and once when the proposition came up in the Senate to memorialize the Treasurer of the United States to secure the bills of the bank of Edwardsville in payment of lands, believing it to be objectionable, he refused to put the question. Upon its being demonstrated to him that it was his duty to put the question, he said: "Gentlemen, if

I mus' I mus'. You who are in favor of dis resolution will say aye; but I bet you one tousand dollar Congress never make him land-office money; you are opposed will say no."

Thomas Reynolds, a younger brother of Governor John Reynolds, was an active politician in this State until 1828, when he removed to Missouri, of which commonwealth he was elected governor in 1840.

He possessed many of the original traits and picturesque characteristics of his brother. He was not only a very popular man among his associates, but he was a long-headed, shrewd and pushing man, and never allowed slight obstacles to daunt his courage or thwart his purposes.

George Flower, one of the old pioneers of whom we shall speak hereafter, writing from his personal knowledge, says: "Our influential men, and all who held office, from the governor to the constable, were from slave States. Every sheriff and every clerk of the county were pro-slavery men; every lawyer and all our judges were from slave States and pro-slavery. I know of but one exception in the whole bar that attended our courts, and that was Samuel D. Lockwood."

## CHAPTER XIV.

### Governor Coles, and his Immediate Friends and Contemporaries.

GOVERNOR COLES, Judge Lockwood and Judge Griswold occupy very conspicuous positions in our history; especially Governor Coles; and if ever any man deserves immortality it is he.

He drew around him the very best men of his time, such men as Lockwood, Birkbeck, Flower, Daniel P. Cook and William H. Brown, and threw his heart and soul into the fight against human slavery, and it was his efforts probably more than any one man's that succeeded in making Illinois forever a free State.

His life was pure and above reproach. He endured insults, reproaches, buffetings and persecutions without number, but survived them all and died peacefully at his home in Philadelphia in 1838.

His career demands something more than a passing notice.

He was born in Albemarle county, Virginia, December 15, 1786. His father, John Coles, had been a colonel in the Revolutionary War. He was fitted for college by private tutors, was sent to Hampden Sidney in 1805, then to William and Mary College at Williamsburg, but did not graduate therefrom owing to a very severe accident by which his leg was fractured in so severe a manner as to impair his health and prevent him from performing all labor. His limb was with great trouble preserved and his health finally restored. Among his classmates were Lieutenant-General Scott, President John Tyler, William S. Archer, United States Senator from Virginia, and Mr. Justice Baldwin of the Supreme Court of the United States. The Coles family was a very prominent one and allied with some of the most distinguished politicians in the State, and the family mansion was the seat of all the old-fashioned Virginia Commonwealth. It was visited by Patrick Henry, Jefferson, Madison, Monroe, the Randolphs, Tazwell, Wirt, and many others of the leading men of that time. At the age of twenty-three he became the private secretary of President Madison and so remained for the period of six years. His correspondence with Thomas Jefferson upon the subject of slavery is historic and fixed his opinion upon that matter forever. He was the owner of a plantation and many slaves and these he resolved to liberate. He visited the West in 1815 to select a place for his future abode and where he might take his slaves and liberate them. He selected Illinois, but before he could effect that object he was sent by President Madison to Russia to settle a difficulty which had arisen between the Czar and our American Consul. The trouble grew out of the conduct of the Russian Minister at Washington who had misrepresented matters there to the Czar, but when he became aware of the facts offered to make proper amends, even to sending the offending minister to Siberia.

Mr. Coles, after having finished the business which he was sent abroad to transact, returned by way of Berlin and Paris, where he was presented to Louis XVIII by Mr. Gallatin and there he met La Fayette.

In 1819, he removed to Edwardsville in this State, after having liberated his slaves on their voyage down the Ohio river. After his arrival at Edwardsville, for the better protection of the freedmen, and on the advice of the Hon. Daniel P. Cook, one of the best lawyers of the State, he gave separate papers of manumission to all his former slaves. At this time neither Governor Coles nor Mr. Cook knew anything about a law of the State that had been previously passed, but which was not promulgated till several months afterward. This law prohibited any person from bringing into the State any negroes for the purpose of emancipation unless he should give bonds in the penalty of one thousand dollars, that the negro would not become a county charge; and that if the emancipator neglected to give this bond, he should forfeit and pay the sum of two hundred dollars for every negro emancipated. Governor Coles had, as we have said, emancipated all his slaves long before they reached Illinois, but had given them certificates of manumission after his arrival at Edwardsville. This afforded a fine opportunity for the pro-slavery party to harass and annoy him on the ground of a technical violation of the law. Consequently proceedings were instituted against him in the name of the County of Madison and the writ was returnable at the March term of the Circuit Court at Edwardsville, 1824. John Reynolds was the presiding judge and after a considerable delay, every special plea having been ignored, the case came to trial before a jury on the plea of *nil debet* and resulted in their returning a verdict against him for $2,000. It appeared on the trial that three of the negroes had died before the commencement of the suit, but the judge held that that made no difference; that a grave offense had been committed and he must suffer the consequences. The late Elihu Washburne in his very interesting and valuable biography of Governor Coles, says, among other things: " From a bill of exceptions taken during the trial and spread upon the records of the court it appears that the defendant, Coles, offered to give in evidence and prove to the jury that three of the negroes of the plaintiff had departed this life before the commencement of the suit; but the astute judge would not permit the testimony to be given, thus practically deciding that it was necessary to hold the county harmless from the support of *dead men*. The defendant then offered to prove by Joseph Conway, the clerk of the County Commissioners' Court, that the defendant had never been notified or required to give bond, but the court would not permit such evidence to be given. The defendant then further offered to prove by Daniel P. Cook, the attorney under whose advice he acted, the conversation he had with him before the date of manumission, and that he, Cook advised the giving of such certificate in order to protect the negroes and to 'enable them to live themselves;' and also to prove by said Cook all the circumstances and conversation between said witness and defendant, which induced and led to the execution of said certificate, all of which was rejected."

The certificate which Mr. Coles gave, was in the following words and figures, to-wit: "Whereas my father, the late John Coles, of Albemarle, in the State of Virginia, did, in his last will and testament, give and bequeath to me certain negro slaves, among others, Robert Crawford and his sister, Polly Crawford; the said Robert Crawford being a mulatto about five feet seven inches high and now about twenty-seven years of age; and the said Polly being a mulatto woman about five feet one inch high, and now about sixteen or seventeen years of age:—

"And whereas I do not believe that man can have a right of property in his fellowman, but on the contrary, that all mankind are endowed by nature with equal rights, I do, therefore, by these presents, restore to the said Robert and his sister Polly, that inalienable liberty of which they have been deprived. And I do hereby renounce for myself and my heirs forever, all claim of every description whatever to them and their services, and I do hereby emancipate and make free the said Robert Crawford and his sister Polly Crawford. In testimony whereof the said Cole set his hand and seal on the 19th day of July, 1819."

This act of emancipation, executed by Governor Coles and spread upon the records of the court, stands out to his immortal honor and makes more conspicuous the infamy of his persecutors.

The motion for a new trial, which had been made in the case at the September term, 1824, was not decided at that term, and the case went over to the March term, 1835. At this term of the court, Judge Samuel McRoberts presided. He was a hard-hearted and most unmerciful judge. The motion for a new trial in the case which he found undecided, was promptly overruled.

Between the term of the court in September, 1824, and the March term, 1825, the Legislature (in January, 1825,) passed an act releasing all penalties incurred under the act of 1819 (including those sued for), upon which Coles was prosecuted. The law required as conditions precedent to the release of the penalties, the execution of a bond that the negroes should not become a charge upon any county in the State, and that all the costs of the suit and damages should be paid. To enable the defendant to take advantage of this act, at the June term it was moved to set aside the verdict and judgment to enable him to plead *puis darien* continuance.

McRoberts proved equal to this last phase of the case; he overruled the motion for a new trial and rejected the plea, holding that the Legislature could not make a law to bar the recovery of the penalty in the case. The judge was not able to prevent the defendant from taking an appeal to the Supreme Court of the State. This appeal was taken and heard at the June term of the court at Vandalia, 1826.

The judgment of the Circuit Court was reversed and the cause remanded with directions to receive the defendant's plea. Chief Justice Wilson gave an able and elaborate opinion. The case is fully reported in Breese's Reports, page 115, and is entitled, Coles, plaintiff in error, versus The County of Madison, defendant in error.

The case was argued in the Supreme Court by Henry Starr for Coles, and Turney & Reynolds for the county of Madison. Henry Starr was at this time residing at Edwardsville and one of the best lawyers in the State. He was a strong personal and political friend of Coles and took a deep interest in this case. After being several years at Edwardsville, he returned to Cincinnati, where he attained great eminence in his profession.

This persecution did not end here but a number of libel suits were instituted against him for his just criticisms on the scandalous conduct of the judge who tried the case against him for freeing his slaves, but he finally triumphed over all his enemies and his course and conduct were fully vindicated and his character has grown brighter and brighter with each revolving year. The tribute which Mr. Washburne has paid him in his "Sketch of Edward Coles" is worthy of all praise. He died at his residence in Philadelphia, July 7, 1868. We regard Mr. Coles like John the Forerunner, in his course and career, and we have no doubt he had more or less influence upon the life and destiny of the immortal Lincoln, who was thoroughly acquainted with his persecutions, his sacrifices and his martyrdom in endeavoring to make Illinois a free State.

Judge Gillespie, in a letter to Mr. Washburne, dated Edwardsville, February 28, 1881, speaks of Governor Coles as follows: "I knew the governor well. He lived in this place while he was a citizen of Illinois. He was a remarkable man, and devoted himself to the propagation of the sentiments of freedom. He was the most unrelenting foe to slavery I ever knew. His time, money, everything belonging to him, was expended in the cause so dear to his heart. He brought his slaves here from Virginia and liberated them, gave to each head of a family a tract of land, within four miles of this place, where they settled and lived for many years. He was unmarried while he lived in Illinois, and when in Edwardsville boarded in the family of James Mason. His character was without spot or blemish in all the walks of life."

Judge Caton, who was for many years a circuit judge and one of the Supreme judges of the State, a man who is revered by every one who knows him as one of the earliest settlers of Chicago, in a great argument made by him in 1881, in the United States Circuit Court, at Chicago, against the repudiation of certain bonds issued by the city of Ottawa, said: "In closing this reference to the past of our State, allow me to say that Illinois has produced three great men, whose conspicuous services will render their names immortal, and which should be commemorated by enduring monuments, and to whom we owe a debt of gratitude that can never be paid.

The first was Edward Coles, who was governor of the State in 1824, and who saved the State from the black curse of African slavery, then and forever. The second was Thomas Ford, who was governor in 1842, and who saved the State from the scarcely less blighting curse of repudiation; and the third was Abraham Lincoln, who saved the Union from dismemberment and the Nation from destruction. Not alone, either of them; for all were assisted and supported by other great men whose names should be scarcely less honored; but they were the great leaders in these great labors, whose talents and whose integrity led the people to these great accomplishments. In all time to come posterity should bow its head in gratitude whenever either of these names should be spoken."

His public career in the State of Illinois was practically closed in 1826, when, on the 5th day of December of that year, he sent his valedictory message to the Legislature, and soon after retired from office. This message was mainly devoted to the affairs of the State. But in it he made a most touching allusion to the deaths of Thomas Jefferson and John Adams, which occurred simultaneously, on the 4th of July preceding, "thus sanctioning by their deaths a day rendered glorious by the most important event of their lives and in the history of their country." To Mr. Jefferson, to whom he was most tenderly attached by ties of sympathy and friendship, he paid a most eloquent tribute, describing him as a "sage and a philanthropist, as a statesman and a patriot, the author of the Declaration of Independence, the great political reformer to whose strong, bold and original genius we are, in a great degree, indebted for our civil and religious freedom, and for our correct understanding of the rights of men and of nations.

In closing, he earnestly appealed to the General Assembly to repeal the "Black Code," which related to the servitude of the blacks and "indentured servants;" in order, as he said, to "make the laws in relation to that unfortunate class of our fellow-beings, the descendants of Africa, less repugnant to our political institutions and local situation;" to do which "it is requisite that provision should be made, not only for loosening the fetters of servitude, but for the security and protection of free persons of color. It is also indispensable that the law should be radically altered, and, so far from considering every colored person a slave unless he can procure written evidence of his freedom in Illinois, every man should be presumed free until the contrary is made to appear."

It will scarcely be believed that these laws, to which Governor Coles refers, and known, as we have said, as the "Black Code," actually remained on the statute books of this State for more than a quarter of a century afterward, and were not repealed until the year 1865.

On the 28th of November, 1833, he was married at Philadelphia by Bishop De Lancey, to Miss Sally Logan Roberts, a daughter of Hugh Roberts, a descendant of Hugh Roberts, of Peullyn, Wales, who came to this country with William Penn in 1682. Possessed of an ample fortune, his private life seems to have brought him every charm, and surrounded him with every happiness. Of a very happy, bright and cheerful disposition, he entered sympathetically into the pleasures of all, and promoted in every possible way the happiness of all. He was an affectionate husband, a devoted father and a kind friend.

Governor Coles was a very little less than six feet in height, of a slender build, and strongly marked features. His eyes were brilliant, and his countenance—particularly when lighted up by a smile—was one of rare beauty. He died in Philadelphia at the ripe old age of eighty-two, July 7, 1868, and lies buried in that beautiful resting-place of the dead near the city known as the "Woodland."

## COL. WILLIAM S. HAMILTON.

During Governor Coles' administration was the visit of Lafayette to Illinois in 1825. In the month of December previous, the Legislature of the State had extended to the General a most cordial and pressing invitation to visit Illinois, and as Lafayette came up the Mississippi river from New Orleans, Governor Coles, who had extended the invitation to him on behalf of the State, couched in the most respectful and cordial language, sent forward his aid-de-camps to meet him at St. Louis and accompany him to the State, with a letter in his own hand to this effect:

EDWARDSVILLE, April 25, 1825.

DEAR SIR:—This will be handed to you by my friend and aid-de-camps, Col. William Schuyler Hamilton, whom I take pleasure in introducing to you as the son of your old and particular friend, Gen. Alexander Hamilton. As it is not known when you will arrive at St. Louis or what will be your intended route from thence, Col. Hamilton is posted there for the purpose of waiting on you as soon as you shall arrive and ascertaining from you and making known to me by what route you propose to return to the eastward and when and where it will be most agreeable for you to afford me the happiness of seeing you and welcoming you to Illinois.

I am, with the greatest respect and esteem, your devoted friend,

EDWARD COLES.

GENERAL LAFAYETTE.

This Col. William Schuyler Hamilton is worth remembering, and is deserving of more than a passing tribute owing to more reasons than one. He was the son of the immortal Alexander Hamilton, and his real name was William Stephen Hamilton and not William Schuyler, as Governor Coles calls him. He lived in the State of Illinois during the administration of Governor Coles, was appointed by him his aid-de-camps, with the rank of colonel, and performed all his duties with great intelligence, dignity and decorum. He was born in New York, August 4, 1797, and was admitted to the West Point Academy in 1814 and resigned in 1817. He left his home in New York and settled at an early day in Sangamon County, Illinois. He was United States deputy surveyor of the public lands, and in that capacity surveyed the township in which Springfield now stands. In 1824 he was elected a member of the House of Representatives from Sangamon County. In 1827 he removed to the "Fever River Lead Mines" and commenced mining for lead ore at a point soon known as "Hamilton's Diggings," now Wiota, in Lafayette county, Wisconsin. Hon. Elihu Washburne, in referring to him, says: "I knew Colonel Hamilton well from 1841 to 1849, when he emigrated to California. He occupied a prominent position in Southwestern Wisconsin and was a well known whig politician. He was a member of the House of Representatives in the Territorial Legislature of Wisconsin in 1842–3. He died in Sacramento, California, October 9, 1850. For nineteen years neither stone nor slab marked the spot where reposed his ashes. When the careless grave digger threw his shovelfuls of earth on his coffin, little could he have thought he was covering the remains of a son of Alexander Hamilton, in my judgment the greatest of all American statesmen. Colonel Hamilton was brave, generous, hospitable and humane, and unusually quick in perception and decided in action." In 1879 Cyrus Woodman, Esq., of Cambridge, Massachusetts, who was long a resident of Mineral Point, Wisconsin, and a devoted friend of Colonel Hamilton, purchased a lot in the cemetery of Sacramento, and marked the grave with granite head and foot-stones. On the polished surface of the headstone he placed the following inscription:

COLONEL WM. S. HAMILTON,

SON OF

GENERAL ALEXANDER HAMILTON,

WAS BORN IN NEW YORK,

AUGUST 4, 1797.

HE WAS AN EARLY SETTLER AND PROMINENT CITIZEN

OF WISCONSIN,

COMING TO CALIFORNIA IN 1849.

HE DIED HERE OCTOBER 9, 1850.

IN SIZE AND FEATURE, IN TALENT AND CHARACTER,

HE MUCH RESEMBLED HIS ILLUSTRIOUS

FATHER.

A FRIEND ERECTS THIS STONE.

### JUDGE SAMUEL D. LOCKWOOD.

Judge Samuel D. Lockwood was a man whose life and public services are worthy of commemoration, and he will take rank next to Governor Coles. He came to the State in 1818, and died in 1874. He was elected state's attorney in 1821—was appointed Secretary of State by Governor Coles in 1822; receiver of public moneys by

President Monroe in 1823; in 1824 was elected one of the judges of the Supreme Court and remained in that position till the adoption of the Constitution in 1848, when he was appointed trustee of the Illinois Central Railroad Company.

He was born in Poundridge, Westchester Co., N. Y., Aug. 2, 1789, and died at Batavia, April 23, 1874, in the eighty-fifth year of his age. The impress that he left upon the State and the age in which he lived, we trust, will not soon be forgotten.

The part that he took in public affairs in the founding and establishing charitable and public institutions has identified his name with everything that is noble and good. When the State was in danger of becoming a slave State, he threw into the contest his soul, his conscience, his money and estate, and in connection with Coles, William H. Brown, and scores of others, fought the good fight and won the victory.

He was a great lawyer, judge and jurist, and possessed a character worthy of imitation. He was the author of the Criminal Code of the State in 1825, and considering the time and occasion, and his want of all exterior aids in the shape of books, it was and is a masterpiece. It is a curious fact that the Chicago anarchists were tried under a provision of that Code entitled "Accessories to Crime," as follows : " An accessory, is he or she who stands by and aids, abets or assists; or who, not being present aiding, abetting or assisting, hath advised and encouraged the perpetration of the crime.

" He or she who thus aids, abets or assists, advises or encourages, shall be deemed and considered as principal, and punished accordingly."

Of Judge Lockwood, Dr. Edward Beecher, who was president of Illinois College for fourteen years, says: " I can not enter into any details of the life of Judge Lockwood, nor of his legal services to the community. But I can say that during an acquaintance of over twenty years, of which fourteen associated me with him as a trustee of Illinois College, I have seen in him incorruptible integrity and wisdom as a counsellor in all things, with an unwavering devotion to sound principles and the public good in every position he held.

" His life, in all its relations, public and social, was spotless and I think he had the entire confidence and warm affection of the whole community in which he lived.

"His services to the cause of liberty in the early history of the State deserves a warm recognition."

Dr. T. M. Post, of St. Louis, himself renowned as a minister of the Gospel, as a scholar and a statesman, says: "There was in his character a rare blending of elements—a modesty, gentleness and delicacy well nigh feminine, and great general kindness, combined with intrepid firmness of principle, a large practical wisdom, distinguished judicial ability and integrity, and a personal purity and honor as stainless as a star. He was a most beneficent power in founding and shaping the early history and civilization of Illinois."

There was heroism in those men who stayed the tide of incoming barbarism and opened the springs of a high civilization—who kept out slavery with its three-fold curse on master, servant and soil, and established freedom with its three-fold blessing on mind, body and estate; who planted the seed, and cherished to a vigorous growth our educational, benevolent and Christian institutions, adorning the prairie with schoolhouses, asylums and churches. The real history of Illinois must be found in the lives of her eminent men.

### MORRIS BIRKBECK.

Next to Governor Coles, Lockwood and Mr. Peck, the man who did the most in arousing and forming public opinion to the dangers of making Illinois a slave State was Morris Birkbeck of Edwards county. He was an Englishman by birth, and was born in Wanborough, England, in 1763. He was highly educated, possessed a fine library and was renowned for his scholarship and high classical attainments. He had met Governor Coles on his visit to England a number of years before his advent to Illinois, and, probably through his influence, had emigrated to America and taken up his abode in Edwards county, where he founded a town and named it after his native town in England, Wanborough. The settlement was soon known as the "English Settlement" and is a romance in itself equal in interest to that of a fairy tale. He was a man of great experience and observation which he had improved by foreign travel; and he had prior to his coming to this country written a book of travels entitled "Notes of a Journey through France," which had attracted the attention of Thomas Jefferson and was found in his library at Monticello.

He is the author also of the well known works entitled "Letters from Illinois" and "Notes on a Journey in America." His views upon the subject of slavery may be gathered from a letter dated

July 28, 1818, written to a friend in France, in which he says: " In passing from theory to practice I have experienced no diminution of my love for freedom; but I hate tyranny more cordially and I want language to express the loathing I feel for personal slavery; practiced by freemen it is most detestable. It is the leprosy of the United States, a foul blotch which more or less contaminates the entire system in public and in private, from the president's chair to the cabin of the hunter."

When the great controversy was raging over the question whether Illinois should be slave or free, Mr. Birkbeck wrote a series of letters over the *nom de plume* of Jonathan Freeman, which were widely read and greatly admired. They were plainly written but were full of facts and figures and captivated all who read them. He was most bitterly assaulted by the pro-slavery party and denounced as a "foreign emissary," an "exile," a quaker and an infidel of the worst type, to exterminate whom would be doing God's will. He deserves, for the part he took in making Illinois a free State, immortal honor, and his memory should be embalmed in brass and marble. He was drowned while crossing a small stream called Fox river, June 4, 1825. His body was taken two days afterward to New Harmony, Indiana, and buried with every mark of respect and affection. Thus perished Morris Birkbeck, one of the ablest and most celebrated men of his time in Illinois, whose influence wielded in the cause of freedom and humanity, should always be gratefully remembered. Associated with Mr. Birkbeck in his work of establishing the English colony at Wanborough was George Flower, who was also a great man and deserves particular mention. He was an Englishman by birth, and was born in Hertford, the county town of Hertfordshire, twenty miles northeast of London. He had known Birkbeck in his youth, had traveled with him over France soon after the fall of Napoleon, and from France southward to the shores of the Mediterranean, skirting the Pyrenees and returning thence by a more easterly route to Paris.

Birkbeck dedicated his small but very interesting volume entitled "Notes on a Journey through France," etc., to Mr. Flower in these words:

To Mr. George Flower, of Morden, near Hertford.

DEAR SIR:—You were my agreeable and intelligent fellow-traveler, and I offer you this little volume as the result of our joint observations. Your faithful friend,

Wanborough, Nov. 13, 1814. M. BIRKBECK.

Flower first sailed from Liverpool for America in the ship Robert Burns in April, 1816, and was fifty days in crossing the Atlantic. He traveled on horseback across the Alleghanies to the far West; met Gen. Jackson at Nashville, Tennessee, and returning East visited Jefferson at his Poplar Forest estate, to whom he had letters of introduction and with whom he stayed, on Jefferson's invitation, for several months, passing the winter with him. There is nothing which has ever been written, which contains such a charming picture as his life-like sketch of Mr. Jefferson in the home of his family and in his domestic privacy, as he saw him in 1816.

Mr. Jefferson, it appears, was a great believer in land and his large possessions at Monticello did not seem to satisfy him and he purchased an estate in Bedford county, which he called Poplar Forest, and which was but a short distance east of Lynchburg. Mr. Flower was a man of rare intelligence, of fine literary tastes, and extensive reading, with a great knowledge of men and things in Europe, and Mr. Jefferson became very much interested in him.

Mr. Flower in his account of his visit to Jefferson, says: "We entered the State of Virginia at Abington. I found Mr. Jefferson at his Poplar Forest estate, in the western part of the State of Virginia. His house was built after the fashion of a French chateau. Octagon rooms, floors of polished oak, lofty ceilings, large mirrors, betokened his French taste, acquired by his long residence in France. Mr. Jefferson's figure was rather majestic; tall, over six feet, thin and rather high-shouldered; manners simple, kind and courteous. His dress in color and form was quaint and old-fashioned, plain and neat, a dark pepper and salt coat, cut in the old quaker fashion, with a single row of large metal buttons, knee-breeches, gray worsted stockings, shoes fastened by large metal buckles—such was the appearance of Jefferson when I first made his acquaintance in 1816. His two granddaughters—Misses Randolph—well educated and accomplished ladies, were staying with him at the time." He was delighted with the conversations of Jefferson, who gave him the minor history of events before only known to him generally in published records and publications of the times. While here he became acquainted with the Coles family, Isaac Coles, the brother of Governor Coles, being Jefferson's private secretary. His sister, Miss Coles, had just been married to Hon. Andrew Stevenson, who was afterward minister to Great Britain, and was the first American, we believe, who was ever voted the freedom of the city of London. He was present at the inauguration of James Monroe as President of the United States. He afterward met Edward Coles at the house of Madison.

A short time after this he joined the colony of Morris Birkbeck and went West with him and located at the English colony in Edwards county. The story of his life is as thrilling as a romance and is embodied in what is known as the "History of the English Settlement in Edwards County," published at the expense of Levi Z. Leiter, and constitutes the first of a series of the Chicago Historical publications. He and his wife died on the same day early in January, 1862, at the house of their daughter, Mrs. Agniell, at Grayville, White county, Illinois. Dr. Barry of the Chicago Historical Society, in a just tribute to his great and exalted worth, says: "Born in Hertfordshire, England, in affluent circumstances, after gaining some distinction in his native land by continental travel for the benefit of British husbandry, he came to America in 1817 (about thirty years of age) as the associate of Morris Birkbeck in founding the English colony at Albion, Edwards county, in Illinois."

It was no mere sordid impulse that moved either of these noble-hearted men in their scheme of colonization. Republicans from deep-seated sentiment and conviction, the great American Republic drew them hither as to a congenial home, and here they jointly established a thrifty and successful colony, transplanting on our virgin prairies the arts and improvements of the old mother country. The large wealth possessed by Mr. Flower gave him a commanding, a responsible, and we may add, a laborious position in the new colony. His spacious mansion of rare extent and finish in a new settlement was the scene of frank and elegant hospitality. Strangers of distinction sought it from afar. Improved husbandry, with the importation of the finest fleeces of England and Spain, followed the guiding hand of the master mind. The calm and philosophic wisdom of Mr. Flower, united with a rare benevolence, has left bright traces upon our western history.

In the eventful strife which accompanied the daring attempt in 1823, to legalize African slavery in Illinois, no one enlisted with a truer heroism than he. We of the present day, and amidst the dire commotions of civil war, can but poorly comprehend the ferocity and the gloomy portents of that struggle. So nearly balanced were the contending parties of the State, that the vote of the English colony, ever true to the instincts of freedom, turned the scale, a handful of sturdy Britons being the forlorn hope to stay the triumph of wrong and oppression, whose success might have sealed forever, the doom of republican and constitutional liberty in America. The failure of that nefarious plot against our young and noble State, led to an outburst of persecution against free negroes and their humane protectors, transcending even the invidious hostility of our so-called Black Laws, and constitutional conventions.

Mr. Flower was one of that class of men whose fine insight, large views and calm force, raised him above all claimants to popular favor. In his early maturity, he numbered among his friends and correspondents such personages as our American Jefferson, Lafayette, and the Comte de Lasteyrie, of France, Madame O'Connor (the daughter of Condorcet), Ireland, and Cobbett, of England. By these, and such as these, his superior tone of mind and character was held in true esteem. In the depths of our yet unfurrowed prairies, and amidst the struggle and hardship of a new settlement, a mind and heart like his might fail of a just appreciation by his contemporaries. This sad realization he doubtless felt. But now that he has passed from the scenes of his voluntary exile, let it not be said that a true and gifted manhood was here and we knew it not.

There are those now, and to come, who will keep green his memory, and take pleasure in recovering the traces of a noble mind that lived and thought and acted only for human good.

That his teachings and example bore fruit is evidenced by the fact that the records of the Indiana volunteers show that Richard Flower was among the first to enlist in the First Indiana Cavalry, at Mount Vernon, Indiana, on the breaking out of the rebellion, and he fell in the battle of Fredericktown, Missouri, on the 18th of October, 1861.

Daniel P. Cook, who was at this period a young and rising statesman, did not figure in the great contest for freedom in Illinois as conspicuously as many others, but he acted as the legal adviser of Governor Coles on many occasions and his name and fame are closely identified with this great movement.

In 1827 Hon. Daniel P. Cook, member of Congress from this State, obtained a grant of land in aid of the Illinois and Michigan Canal, and thus obtained the title of "Father of the Illinois and

Michigan Canal." At that time this project was wholly a Southern Illinois enterprise, and Mr. Cook was a representative from that portion of the State.

He was a member of Congress commencing with the second session of 1819, and served with great distinction in that body eight years. He was elected at the early age of twenty-five, served eight years and died when only thirty-three years old. He was a most remarkable man, possessed of great foresight, eloquence and sagacity and was the compeer of Clay, Calhoun, Wirt, Stevenson and McDuffie. He was chairman of the important committee of ways and means in the House, during his last term of service and bid fair to become one of the foremost men in the Nation. He was early impressed with the idea of improving the water ways of our State and of building a canal from the Mississippi river to Chicago.

In 1824, the Legislature of the State passed a law giving to a private company the practical, if not exclusive, control of the Illinois river and the power of making a canal. So averse was he to this, that he left his seat in Congress, came home to Illinois, procured the repeal of the charter and then procured the land grant which resulted in building the canal. The project of connecting the waters of the Mississippi with those of Lake Michigan was agitated as early as 1814. In 1818, Governor Bond pressed it upon the attention of the first Legislature, then sitting at Kaskaskia, and Governor Coles, in 1822, did the same.

In 1821, the Legislature appropriated $10,000 for the survey of the route of the Illinois and Michigan Canal. In 1823, canal commissioners were appointed and a tour of inspection was made under Col. J. Post and R. Paul, of Missouri. The work was commenced in 1836, and completed in 1845.

Daniel P. Cook was one of the most enterprising and far-seeing statesmen of his time. The State of Illinois and the county of Cook owe him a debt of gratitude which can never be repaid. He deserves at least a monument to his memory and it should be erected at no distant day.

# CHAPTER XV.

## The Great Convention Struggle of 1823-4 to Make Illinois a Slave State.

SIX years after the Constitution of 1818 had been adopted and before even the provisions had become known to the scattered population of the State a struggle commenced for supremacy between the pro-slavery inhabitants and those who were in favor of forever keeping the State free such as has never been witnessed in this country, except perhaps in regard to Kansas, nearly forty years afterward. It was a gigantic conspiracy which was entered into by the leading office-holders and aspirants for office in the State backed by parties in Kentucky, Tennessee and Missouri. Missouri had just been admitted into the Union under and by virtue of what is known as the Missouri Compromise, and the slave-holding population and their sympathizers resolved to keep company with their neighbors.

The times were hard. The farmer could find no market for his abundant crops. Manufactures languished, improvements were at a standstill, and the mechanic was without work. The country was cursed by a fluctuating and irredeemable paper currency, which had driven all *real* money out of circulation.

The flow of immigration to the State had in a great measure ceased, but a great emigration passed through the State to Missouri. Great numbers of well-to-do emigrants from the slave States, taking with them their slaves, were then leaving their homes to find new ones west of the Mississippi. When passing through Illinois to their destination, with their well equipped emigrant wagons, drawn by splendid horses, with their retinue of slaves, and with all the lordly airs of that class of slave-holders, they avowed that their only reason for not settling in Illinois, was that they could not hold their slaves. This fact had a very great influence, particularly in that part of the State through which the emigration passed, and people denounced the unwise provision of the Constitution prohibiting slavery and thus preventing a great influx of population to add wealth to the State.

## ATTEMPT TO MAKE ILLINOIS A SLAVE STATE.

During the years 1823-4 occurred the great controversy over the question—"Shall a convention be called to form a new State Constitution"—it being well understood that if the convention was called, Illinois would become a slave State, if it was not, it would remain a free State.

The proposition was beaten by a considerable majority after one of the most exciting campaigns ever held within our borders.

The success which had attended the admission of Missouri into the Union, under and by virtue of the famous compromise bill, encouraged the pro-slavery party in this State to believe that if a convention were called to revise and amend the Constitution, they could make Illinois a slave State, and every effort was put forth to accomplish that object. The Constitution had, it must be recollected, been in operation only about four years, and the only thing that was ever particularly complained of was the restrictions on the appointing power of the governor and the Council of Revision. But this made no difference; the fiat went forth that Illinois must be made a slave State in order to keep pace with Missouri, and the struggle commenced.

William H. Brown, in recounting his reminiscences of the period, says: "Among those who supported the convention, as a general thing, were the rank and file of the politicians of the State. Of these must be excepted a few such men as Daniel P. Cook, and Governor Edwards, even, who, according to my recollection, was absent from the State and took no part in the controversy. These politicians were dangerous opponents, because, long engaged in the struggles for power and office, they were practiced leaders and familiar with all the means and appliances for success with the people. With them were the men of wrecked fortunes and loose principles, as also the young, aspiring and ambitious, misled by the loud boasting and extravagant calculations of the party, supposing that the great majority was upon that side. The French population also, to secure more perfectly their supposed rights to the people of color then held by them in bondage, were the natural allies of the conventionists and desirous of their success. To these must be added, with very few exceptions, the poor whites from the slave States, the most vociferous and malignant of all. Their poverty and shiftlessness precluded the possibility of their becoming slaveholders if the Constitution should be changed. Their toil and zeal could only be accounted for upon the supposition that they desired a class of humanity among us more debased and ignorant than themselves."

The Constitution of Illinois made it the duty of the General Assembly whenever two-thirds of its members should think it necessary to alter or amend the Constitution, to recommend to the electors at the next election of members to the General Assembly, to vote for or against a convention for such purpose, and if it shall appear that a majority of all the citizens voted for a convention, the General Assembly shall at their next session call one to be held in time and manner specified under the provision. The agitation for a convention commenced and was favored by every pro-slavery elector in the State.

The first skirmish occurred in the General Assembly of 1820-21, when Lockwood was elected to the office of attorney-general.

The second was the election of Edward Coles governor, in August, 1822, as the second governor of the State, and was one of the most wonderful dramas ever enacted, whether State or National.

The convention party never dreamed of any other result than that in their own favor, and nominated Chief Justice Joseph Phillips. Some opposition having, however, developed against him, a faction nominated Judge Thomas C. Brown, who they thought would draw largely from Coles, but in this they were mistaken, and when the votes were counted it was found that Coles had received 2,810 votes; Phillips, 2,760; Brown, 2,543, and Moore, a fourth candidate, 522.

This gave Coles a plurality of fifty-one votes over Phillips, and he was elected. The first thing that Coles did was to appoint Samuel D. Lockwood Secretary of State, and the party squared for battle.

On the convening of the General Assembly it was found that in order to hold a convention to revise the Constitution, under the provisions of the Constitution it was necessary to have a two-thirds vote, and they were lacking one vote in the House. At first it was attempted to have the question decided by joint ballot, but as it was found that the Constitution required that the act calling the convention must be decided by a two-thirds majority in each House, that plan was abandoned and scoundrelism was resorted to.

A man by the name of Hanson had been elected to the House of Representatives from Pike county. His seat was contested by a man by the name of Shaw. Finding Hanson favorable to calling a convention, Shaw was ousted of his seat and went home. This happened very early in the session, and but little was thought about it. It was after a time, however, discovered that Hanson would not vote in favor of a convention and he was unseated and Shaw recalled. This gave them the requisite two-thirds majority and their joy knew no bounds. They indulged in the most shameful orgies and an impromptu jollification was gotten up not only to celebrate their hard-earned victory but to insult and degrade their opponents.

Governor Ford in describing this affair says: "The night after this resolution passed, the convention party assembled to triumph in a great carousal. They formed themselves into a noisy, disorderly and tumultuous procession, headed by Judge Phillips, Judge Smith, Judge Thomas Reynolds, late governor of Missouri, and Lieutenant-Governor Kinney, followed by the majority of the Legislature and the hangers-on and rabble about the seat of government; and they marched with the blowing of tin horns and the beating of drums and tin pans to the residence of Governor Coles and to the boarding houses of their principal opponents toward whom they manifested their contempt and displeasure by a confused medley of groans, wailings and lamentations. Their object was to intimidate and crush all opposition at once."

Governor John Reynolds characterized the proceeding as "a wild and indecorous proceeding by torch light and liquor," and in his history "My Own Times," says that, "this proceeding in the General Assembly looked revolutionary and was condemned by all honest and reflecting men. This outrage was a death blow to the convention."

The people soon took fire and the contest commenced. Each anti-convention member of the General Assembly contributed fifty dollars to a common fund. Governor Coles gave his whole four years salary, amounting to $4,000, to the work. Lockwood, in order to earn money to aid in the work, resigned the office of Secretary of State with its meagre fees and accepted the office of receiver of public moneys, and devoted all his surplus income to the cause. The enthusiasm kindled and men, women and children became aroused and interested, and the excitement spread through the State. Papers were bought and established, appeals were made, broadsides written, and in less than six months after the adjournment of the General Assembly the heavens glowed as if illuminated by prairie fires. The convention men formed secret clubs with grips and signals, and adopted as a pass word "convention or die," but it was of no use. There was a God in Israel. The anti-convention party became thoroughly united, and were led by men that knew no fear, and whose convictions were so strong that they would have gone to the scaffold or the stake singing hosannas to God. They belonged to that class of martyrs that have worshiped God and died for the "Old Cause," since the Redeemer was crucified on the cross and since Sidney poured out his soul for the liberty of his fellow-men.

The leaders of the convention party were politicians and schemers. They were influenced to a great extent by their ambition for office and were envious and distrustful, often angry, often overbearing and in want of respect for the opinions of others. Gov. Reynolds, an active convention man himself, says that "the convention question gave rise to two years of the most furious and boisterous excitement and contest that ever visited Illinois. Men, women and children entered the arena of party warfare and strife, and the families and neighborhoods were so divided and furious and bitter against one another that it seemed as if a regular civil war might result. The leaders of the convention were Elias Kent Kane, McLean, Judge Phillips, Judge McRoberts, A. P. Field, Governor Bond, A. Beaird, Robinson, Smith, Kinney, West, R. M. Young and others. The opposition was headed by Governor Coles, Rev. J. M. Peck, Judge Lockwood, Daniel P. Cook, William H. Brown, Judge Pope, Governor Edwards, Morris Birkbeck, George Flower, David Blackwell, Hooper Warren, Henry Eddy, George Forquer, George Churchill and others. Ostensibly the most influential and energetic public men were on the side of the convention, but the opposition was better organized and trained in the cause. The facts and arguments were the strongest on the merits of the subject in opposition to slavery, which had its effect in such long discussions before the election. The *question*, as it was familiarly called at the time, united the various denominations of religion which had never before acted together. The opposition to the convention labored with more enthusiasm and devotedness to the cause than the other side and organized better and sooner. The opposition succeeded by 1,800 votes majority, and thus ended the most important and the most exciting election that was ever witnessed in the State. The full vote stood 4,972 for the convention, and 6,400 against the convention, showing that each party brought out its full strength. The victory thus won undoubtedly saved Indiana (because the same thing was agitated there) from becoming a slave State, and set bounds to that great blighting and withering curse to every clime and country it ever reached. "The noise of the conflict has long since died away, and the actors in it all rest from their labors, but a grateful people should always remember that freedom in Illinois was secured, not by the ordinance of 1787 alone, but by the persistent energy, the noble faith and heroic enthusiasm of our honored fathers of the present century."

Those who were in favor of calling a convention to make Illinois a slave State, numbered among its champions, the ablest and most influential men of the time, among whom were ex-Governor Bond, and six gentlemen who afterward became United States senators: Jesse B. Thomas, John McLean, Elias Kent Kane, John M. Robinson, Samuel McRoberts and Richard M. Young; there were also, Chief Justice Phillips of the Supreme Court, who was characterized at the time as a demagogue of the first water, William Kinney and Zadoc Casey, subsequently lieutenant-governors of the State, Colonel Alexander P. Field, Joseph A. Beaird, Gen. Willis Hargrave, Emanuel J. West, Lieutenant-Governor Hubbard, John Reynolds, a judge of the Supreme Court, Thomas Reynolds, brother of John Reynolds, afterward governor of Missouri, and many others.

On the anti-convention side were a class of men, not so distinguished, but they were the most conscientious, intensely earnest and determined men that ever lived. The martyrs and holy men of old never surpassed them in zeal and Christian fortitude. Men, we have been told, prayed for success and the blessings of Almighty God upon their efforts and the results of their labors who never prayed before, and Christian women sang, wept and prayed, cheered and encouraged them to persevere to the end.

Governor Coles took the lead and worked night and day organizing the opposition everywhere and wielding his facile and powerful pen with great effect. He was aided and assisted by Judge Lockwood, William H. Brown, Rev. John M. Peck, Morris Birkbeck, Robert Flower, and hosts of others whose names deserve immortality.

Among the most effective and untiring workers was Rev. John M. Peck of St. Clair county. He was originally from Connecticut, possessed of a strong and comprehensive mind, well educated and with an energy and perseverance rarely surpassed. His headquarters were St. Clair county. This he organized in the most thorough manner and then extended his system, which was something like the organization of the minute men in the times of the Revolution, to fourteen other counties. He appealed to God and the consciences of men with an eloquence akin to that of St. Paul. Uniting the work of establishing Sunday schools, temperance societies and the distribution of the Bible, he preached a crusade against slavery wherever he went, equal to those who roused the masses to rescue the Holy Sepulchre from the hands of the infidels during the middle ages. He was a master of pathos and painted the trials, sufferings and sorrows of the poor and downcast creatures who were held in bondage in colors such as moved all to tears. To the humble and needy farmers he held above them a crown of glory like that of Bunyan's diadem over the toiler with the muck-rake if they did their duty, and his appeals to their wives to aid and assist them in the good work were irresistible. Bunyan's allegory was at his tongue's end and he never failed to point out the trials of Christian as those of their own, and that the sight of the Delectable mountains and Paradise itself were theirs if they would go to the polls and vote against calling a convention to make Illinois a slave State. John Bunyan had much to do with dedicating to freedom our great and glorious Commonwealth. God be praised.

Mr. Hinsdale, in his "Old Northwest," in reviewing this period and this great struggle says: "From the first the propagandists fought a losing battle. When the end was finally reached, the vote stood for a convention, 4,950; against a convention, 6,822, being a majority of 1,872 in a total vote of 11,772. In view of this large majority, the subsequent political history of Illinois for thirty years is very remarkable. The State passed almost at once into the hands of a powerful and violent pro-slavery party and thus remained until the repeal of the Missouri Compromise brought about a new combination of political forces. But the attempt to enthrone slavery in the citadel of the State Constitution was not renewed."

## CHAPTER XVI.

### The Development of Infant Industries, or how Banking can be Carried on by Politicians.

THE history of banking by politicians and the administration of State banks by boards of directors, composed of politicians, is one of the most instructive lessons ever taught a free people. The late Thomas Ford has given a most graphic account of the period of speculation in Illinois, which set in soon after the adoption of the Constitution of 1818, and which is worth recounting. "Until 1817," says he, "everything of a foreign growth or manufacture had been brought from New Orleans on keel boats, towed with ropes or pushed with poles by the hardy race of boatmen of that day, up the current of the Mississippi, or else wagoned across the mountains from Philadelphia, and from thence floated down the Ohio, to its mouth, in keel boats, and from there shoved, pushed and towed up the Mississippi, as from New Orleans. Upon the conclusion of the war of 1812, the people from the old States began to come and settle in the country. They brought some money and property with them and introduced some changes in the customs and modes of living. Before the war, such a thing as money was scarcely ever seen in the country. The skins of the deer and raccoon supplying the place of a circulating medium."

The money which was now brought in and which had before been paid by the United States to the militia during the war, turned the heads of all the people, and gave them new ideas and aspirations, so that by 1819, the whole country was in a rage for speculating in lands and town lots. The States of Ohio and Kentucky, a little before, had each incorporated a batch of about forty independent banks. The Illinois Territory had incorporated two at home, one at Edwardsville, and the other at Shawneetown; and the Territory of Missouri added two more at St. Louis.

These banks made money very plenty; emigrants brought it to the State in great abundance. The owners of it had to use it in some way, and as it could not be used in legitimate commerce in a State where commerce did not exist, the most of it was used to build houses in towns which the limited business of the country did not require, and to purchase land which the labor of the country was not sufficient to cultivate. This was "developing the infant resources of a new country." The United States Government was then selling land at two dollars per acre; eighty dollars on the quarter section to be paid down on the purchase with a credit of five years for the resident. For nearly every sum of eighty dollars there was in the country, a quarter section of land was purchased; for in those days there were no specie circulars to restrain unwarrantable speculations; but, on the contrary, the notes of most of the numerous banks in existence were good in the public and land offices. The amount of land thus purchased was increased by the general expectation that the rapid settlement of the country would enable the speculator to sell it for a high price before the expiration of the credit. This great abundance of money, also, about this time made a vast increase in the amount of merchandise brought into the State. When money is plenty, every man's credit is good. The people dealt with the stores on credit, and drew upon a certain fortune in prospect for payment. Every one was expecting to make it out of the future immigrant.

The speculator was to sell him houses and lands, and the farmer was to sell him everything he wanted to begin with and to live upon until he could supply himself. Towns were laid out all over the country and lots were purchased by every one on credit; the town maker received no money for his lots, but he received notes of hand which he considered to be as good as cash, and he lived and embarked in other ventures as if they had been cash in truth. In this mode, by the year 1820, nearly the whole people were irrevocably involved in debt. The banks in Ohio and Kentucky broke one after another, leaving the people of those States covered with indebtedness and without the means of extrication. The banks at home and in St. Louis ceased business.

The great tide of immigrants from abroad, which had been looked for, failed to come. Real estate was unsalable; the lands purchased of the United States were unpaid for and likely to be forfeited. Bank notes had driven out specie, and when these notes became worthless, there was no money of any description left in the country.

To remedy those evils, the Legislature of 1821 created a State bank. It was founded without money and wholly on the credit of the State. It was authorized to issue one, two, three, five, ten and twenty dollar notes, the likeness of bank bills, bearing two per cent. annual interest, and payable by the State in ten years. A principal bank was established at Vandalia and four or five branches in other places; *the Legislature elected all the directors and officers*, a large number of whom were members of the Legislature, and *all of them professional politicians.*

The bank was directed by law to lend the bills to the people, to the amount of one hundred dollars on personal security, and upon the security of mortgages upon land for a greater sum.

These bills were to be received in payment of all State and county taxes, and for all costs and fees and salaries of public officers; and if a creditor refused to indorse on his execution his willingness to receive them in payment of his debt, the debtor could replevy or stay its collection for three years by giving personal security.

The bill creating this new system of banking, was forced through the House by sheer brute force. John McLean, of Shawneetown, who was speaker of the House at the time, was insulted and bullied to such a degree and in such an outrageous manner, that he resigned the speakership, and opposed the bill with all his might, but it was of no avail.

The governor and judges, acting as a council of revision, objected to it as being unconstitutional and inexpedient, but it passed through both Houses by the constitutional majorities. The Supreme Court of the United States afterward decided that all the bills of such banks which were payable at a future day, were bills of credit and prohibited by the Constitution.

In 1821 the new bank went into operation. Every man who could get an indorser borrowed his hundred dollars. The directors were, as before stated, all politicians, and were either then candidates for office or expected to be. Lending to everybody and refusing none was the surest road to popularity.

Three hundred thousand dollars of the new money was soon lent without much attention to security or care for eventual payment. It first fell twenty-five cents, then fifty and then seventy cents below par. As the bills of the Ohio and Kentucky banks had driven all other money out of the State, so this new issue effectually kept it out. Such a total absence was there of the silver coins, that it became utterly impossible, in the course of trade, to make small change. The people, from necessity, were compelled to cut the new bills into two pieces so as to make two halves of a dollar. For about four years there was no other kind of money, but this uncurrent State bank paper. In the meantime, very few persons pretended to pay their debts to the bank. More than half of those who borrowed considered what they had gotten from it as so much clear gain, and never intended to pay it from the first.

By the year 1824 it became impossible to carry on the State government with such money as the bills of this bank. The State revenue varied from twenty-five to thirty thousand dollars per annum which was raised almost exclusively by a tax on lands, then owned by non-residents, in the military tract lying northwest of the Illinois river.

The resident land tax in other parts of the State was paid into the county treasuries. The annual expenditures of the State government were about equal to the annual revenues; and as the taxes were collected in the bills of the State bank, the Legislature, to carry on the government, were compelled to provide for their own pay, that of all the public officers, and the expenses of the government, by taking and giving enough of the depreciated bills to equal in value the sums required to be paid. So that each member instead of receiving three dollars per day, received nine dollars per day. The salaries of the governor and judges, and all other expenses were paid in the same way. So that if $30,000 were required to pay the expenses of the government for a year, under this system it took $90,000 to do it. And thus by the financial aid of an insolvent bank, the Legislature managed to treble the public expenses, without increasing the revenues or amount of service to the State. In fact, this State lost two-thirds of its revenues and expended three times the amount necessary to carry on the government. In the course of ten years, it must have lost more than $150,000 by receiving a depreciated currency, $150,000 more by paying it out, and $100,000 of the loans, which were never repaid by the borrowers and which the State had to make good, by receiving the bills of the bank for taxes, by funding some at six per cent. interest, and paying a part in cash in the year 1831.

## CHAPTER XVII.

### Repeal of the Black Laws of Illinois.

THE struggles which the early settlers of Illinois underwent in endeavoring to establish a free government, developed heroes who braved hardships, dangers and outrages such as have seldom fallen to the lot of mortals in this new world. They deserve to have their names handed down to posterity, embalmed by the most tender recollections.

> "Long ago was Graccbus slain,
> Brutus perished long ago;
> But the living roots remain,
> Whence the shoots of freedom grow."

Among those who made their appearance on the stage of action soon after the pioneers had retired to rest and who entered with heart and soul into the work of liberating the slaves and of ameliorating the condition of the negroes and mulattoes in Illinois was Zebina Eastman. He located at an early day in Chicago, established "The Western Citizen," and in connection with Hooper Warren, James H. Collins, Calvin DeWolf, Philo Carpenter, Dr. C. V. Dyer, L. C. P. Freer, Rev. F. Bascom and others who were indignant that a pro-slavery mob had taken the life of Elijah P. Lovejoy at Alton, and who revolted at the arrogant and cruel spirit manifested by pro-slavery men everywhere, organized the old "Liberty Party," and preached abolitionism pure and simple throughout the length and breadth of the land.

Mr. Eastman took a great interest in the movement to repeal the Black Laws of Illinois, and it is to his efforts, and to John Jones, as much, if not more, than any others, that those disgraceful laws were repealed.

In 1882, in a discourse before the Chicago Historical Society, he, among other things, said:

By the ordinance of 1787 it is provided that "there shall be neither slavery nor *involuntary servitude* in the said Territory, otherwise than in punishment of crime whereof the party shall have been duly convicted."

The enabling act of Congress, by which the people of the State might vote to put off their minority and enter into the indissoluble bonds of the National Union, required strict conformity to this condition of perpetual freedom.

The Constitution of the State, made in 1818, makes the harmonious declaration: "Neither slavery nor involuntary servitude shall hereafter be introduced into this State otherwise than for the punishment of crimes whereof the party shall have been duly convicted," indorsing and using the words of the ordinance.

One would think the temple of liberty sufficiently guarded, bulwarked by these two firm buttresses, standing on the pillars of its portal. But there is something more in this State Constitution, with only a break of a semicolon. It is this: "Nor shall any male person arrived at the age of twenty-one years, nor any female person arrived at the age of eighteen years, be held to serve any person as a servant under any indenture hereafter made, unless such person shall enter into such indenture while in a state of perfect freedom, and on a condition of a *bona fide* consideration received or to be received for their services. Nor shall any indenture of any negro or mulatto hereafter made and executed out of this State, or if made in this State, whose term of service exceeds one year, be of the least validity, except those given in cases of apprenticeship."

There seems to be a strange muddle of conditions in this language. Involuntary servitude is prohibited, yet there are certain conditions that remind us that permission is granted under prohibition.

The constitutional provisions are continued in other sections: "No person bound to labor in any other State shall be hired to labor in this State, except within the tract reserved for the salt works near Shawneetown, nor even in that place for a longer period than one year at any one time, nor shall it be allowed there after the year 1825. Any violation of this article shall effect the emancipation of such person from his obligation to service." Permission again under prohibition! There is something about this saltwork business worthy of attention. It was one of the rat-holes through which slavery crept into the Territory. Saline springs or bogs were discovered which gave to the early settlers the much needed article of salt, if properly improved. To bring over a slave from Kentucky, to make salt enough to salt his porridge, served the legal purpose of his introduction, and many a farm was fenced and worked in the southern portion of the State by slaves working in the salt works, and that process of saving slavery with salt continued till 1825.

Another section provides as follows: "Each and every person who has been bound to service by contract or indenture in virtue of the laws of Illinois Territory heretofore existing, and in conformity to the provisions of the same, without fraud or collusion, shall be held to a specific performance of their contracts or indentures; and such negroes and mulattoes as have been registered in conformity with the aforesaid laws shall serve out the time appointed by said laws; provided, however, that the children hereafter born of such persons, negroes or mulattoes, shall become free—the males at the age of twenty-one years, and the females at the age of eighteen years. Each and every child born of indentured parents shall be entered with the clerk of the county in which they reside by the owners, within six months from the birth of said child." It seems by this that children of indentured persons were constitutionally owned by their masters. By reference to the law, which will be soon quoted, it will be seen that perpetual slavery was possible under this clause of the Constitution, for none of the children were emancipated till they were of legal age; but propagation may come much earlier than legal majority.

Such were the constitutional provisions of the first Constitution of the State, looking fair on their face; but on close scrutiny it is seen to attempt to provide for a muddled condition of things, which that old muddle of muddles, the slave system, ever brought to the community and muddled the heads of our good fathers. They would prohibit it, but were required to make provisions for its continuance. The fathers of our Constitution, like Gov. Edwards and Nathaniel Pope, were among the best of our early men. It was the hardest fate ever brought upon a nation to face this perpetuated evil of centuries with the necessity that it must be ended; and it is not strange that it took the greatest war of modern times to cut that intricate knot with the sword.

We must now go back a century or more to find facts which will help to solve this muddle of the Constitution.

Notwithstanding Illinois was a part of the Northwest Territory, and under the restriction of this ordinance, and one of the States formed under it, it was nevertheless one of the old slave colonies. Slavery was introduced into Illinois in 1720, when it was a part of the French possessions of the Northwest. Philip Francis Renault formed a company in France for working mines in Upper Louisiana, which was a part of Illinois; and he started from his country, ostensibly in the mining business, with two hundred mechanics and laborers, and on his way, at San Domingo, he purchased five hundred slaves and brought them with him to Illinois. A portion of these or their descendants were afterward removed to the other French possessions on the west of the Mississippi, and helped to swell the aggregate of Louisiana slavery. Those that remained were the progenitors of the class known in our State from old time as the "French slaves," and fell in later as a part of the report of the census of slaves in Illinois, and the Frenchman Renault must be set down as the first Illinois slave-holder.

The importation of blacks made a distinct class and the occasion of a distinct order of the slave-holders about Kaskaskia and the American bottoms, and where now descendants of both masters and slaves reside in a common Illinois citizenship. At that time slavery was legalized in all Christian countries—that is, if making a system which the law did not create be legalizing it. If there is any law that created American slavery I have not yet found it. These slaves that Renault brought to Illinois were under French jurisdiction at that time and for nearly half a century, till the Northwest was ceded to Great Britain in the treaty of 1763. They then came under the English law of bondage (if there was any such); and when the territory was captured by George Rodgers Clark, in 1778, which was done in the name of the sovereignty of Virginia, if they continued slaves under any law it must have been under the slave code of Virginia. When that State ceded the territory to the Nation these slaves must have been perpetuated in a bondage under United States law; and yet the United States had no such law. From the cession of Virginia to the Nation in 1784 till 1790, when Gov. St. Clair organized the county which took his name, the people who resided in this territory had no legislative or judicial supervision, and were a law to themselves, holding the slaves with the grip which they had previously obtained. But the ordinance for the cession declared that "there shall be neither slavery nor involuntary servitude in the said Territory." Why this ordinance was inoperative in this essential point to the slavery then in existence, is something similar in character to the later Dred Scott decision—virtually, that not to have slavery was unconstitutional. But the action of the ordinance of 1787 was said to be prospective, and the courts never so decided. It was not until 1845 that the Supreme Court of this State settled this question of "vested rights," deciding that the slave descendants of Renault's importation of 125 years previous were free; and the Constitution of this State of 1848 put an end to involuntary servitude of every form in Illinois.

In 1800 there was probably a population in the section that became Illinois of 3,000 persons. At that time there were reported in the census, including Indiana as well, 133 slaves. These must have been in the main in Illinois, and the descendants of the "French slaves." In 1810 Illinois had 168 slaves; in 1820, 917—a vast increase in the course of twenty years, showing that the increase must have come, if genuine slaves, from smuggling in from the border slave States, and held under the inherited vested rights as laborers in the salt works, or from the "indentured servants system," which was a dodge upon the restrictive clause of the ordinance. In 1820 the population of the State was 43,919 whites, 1,476 blacks, 917 of which were slaves; total, 50,345. There came a habit of disregarding this prohibition in bringing slaves into many parts of the Territory, and even reporting them in the census. This was done in Wisconsin as late as 1830, the marshal reporting a number of slaves in the said Territory. Dr. E. G. Dyer, of Burlington, Wis., father of the United States Judge, C. E. Dyer, of Racine, attacked the marshal for this illegal report, and disclosed the fact that these reported slaves were held generally by persons in responsible official positions in the United States Government. Considerable commotion was created soon after this report of 1840 by the disclosure of the fact that Elder John T. Mitchell, a Methodist preacher, and once a presiding elder in Chicago, had brought a slave into Wisconsin, and held her as such, and afterward removed her to Missouri, still retaining the woman as his property, and therefore gained the reputation of being a clerical kidnaper. Such were some of the early assumptions of the doctrine of squatter sovereignty, that a man had the inalienable right to take his slave with him into a Territory into which he chose to remove. These facts are a little ahead of the logical events of history. But it suits the symmetry of the subject to bring them in here. It is best, however, to state here that the prohibition of slavery in the Northwest Territory was a bid, like "free Kansas," for its settlement by a hardy and indus-trious class, who thrived by the labor of their own hands, and for its settlement by a class of men from the south who were conscientiously opposed to slave-holding. It was emphasized as a free country, and free men felt invited to make here their homes. The early population of the Northwest was composed of the mingled character of such men, and those who believed that prosperity came from one man having the power to compel some other man to work for him for nothing.

There came, then, from this condition the incipient conflict of ideas of the past generation. The anti-slavery sentiment of the revolution was then pervading as a live principle. There was dissatisfaction by interested persons on the other side at the restriction in the ordinance. The first petition on the subject to Congress came in 1796 from four persons in Kaskaskia, in this State, the seat of this inherited French slavery, asking that slavery might be tolerated there. It seems that they felt they were holding their chattels on a feeble tenure. At that time we were all in one common Northwest Territory. Ohio became a State in 1800; then all the territory west and north of the Ohio river, from the mouth of the Kentucky, became the Territory of Indiana, with William Henry Harrison, governor. In 1804 a convention was held at Vincennes, of which Gov. Harrison was president, to deliberate on territorial interests, and from this convention went up a memorial to Congress which was referred to a committee, which reported recommending the suspension of the sixth article of the ordinance of 1787, "in a qualified manner for ten years, so as to permit the introduction of slaves born in the United States." This report was not adopted, neither was the previous prayer of the Kaskaskians heeded.

At the session of the Indiana Territorial Legislature in 1806-7 a series of resolutions were adopted and reported to Congress by the delegate of the territory, requesting the suspension of this restrictive article of the ordinance. We were then a part of that Territory. Jesse B. Thomas was speaker of the House, and Pierre Menard president of the Council, both citizens of Illinois, the latter a French slave-holder and the former intermarried with such. This report was lost in Congress also. These early efforts to establish slavery aroused the people, and an issue was made similar to that which was made afterward in our State called the "convention question." Jonathan Jennings, an anti-slavery man, was elected delegate to Congress, which position he held till Indiana was admitted as a State. It is known that Gen. Harrison was in favor of introducing slavery into the Northwest Territory.

These facts prepare us for the introduction of the "The Black Code of Illinois." Some of the people, if they could not have slavery legitimately, would have it illegitimately, for the infamy which fell upon us was conceived in sin and brought forth in iniquity, a half-parented progeny.

The Indiana Territorial Legislature passed an act, dated September 17, 1807, which is the nucleus of our Black Code, with this title: "An act concerning the introduction of negroes and mulattoes into this Territory."

There are five sections in this act, and it permits the owner of any negro or mulatto, above the age of fifteen, to bring such person into the Territory, and within thirty days take him before the clerk of the court, and there make an agreement for service, which is to be recorded. If the slave should refuse to make such contract, then the owner may return him back to slavery within sixty days. Such slaves should be held to service—males until thirty-five years old and females until thirty-two. The master was required to register such slaves and the children with the clerk; and these children should be owned by the master and held to service until the age of thirty, and females until the age of twenty-eight.

This continued to be the law of the Territory of which Illinois was a part. In 1809, Indiana became a State, and Illinois inherited the Territorial condition and laws, and re-enacted the above. It is the law referred to in the Constitution. Such continued to be the law until remodeled after the Constitution of 1819.

But the iniquity was not yet fully matured. Another law was

passed in 1829. These were codified, so to speak, in 1833, in the revised laws.

There are twenty-five sections in the law of March 30, 1819. It prohibits any black or mulatto person coming into the State without producing a certificate of freedom. It was the first blow to free negroes. It followed the precedent of slave State legislation, and was aimed to keep Illinois from being an asylum for fugitives from oppression. Free negroes having such certificates were required to register their children. It forbids any person bringing slaves into the State for the purpose of emancipation. Under this act Gov. Coles was fined for emancipating his slaves July 4, 1819. It forbids slaves leaving plantations, and provided that if they be found away from their plantations without a pass they might be whipped by order of a justice to the extent of thirty-five lashes; the owner of a plantation finding such negro on his premises might flog him ten lashes. The assembling of negroes to a number more than three was to be regarded as a riot, and such assembling, seditious speeches, etc., might be punished by a justice at his discretion by flogging. A white person was fined $20 for allowing any such assemblage. It was made the duty of all judges, coroners, justices, etc., to arrest those found in any such assemblage and put them in jail till next day, and then flog thirty-nine lashes on the bare back, unless it should occur on Sunday; then the flogging was to be piously done on Monday.

This law seems to be a transcript of the slave codes of Louisiana or South Carolina. This act was passed under the administration of Shadrach Bond, our first governor. Hooper Warren, editor of the first anti-slavery paper of the Nation, printed at Edwardsville, said that a party had already been formed in the State called the Slave party. This party attempted to nullify the Northwest ordinance by passing an act in 1823 to call a convention to alter the Constitution so as to admit slavery. Gov. Coles had, however, been previously elected by a small majority, and he was an anti-slavery man of the Jefferson school. The convention project was voted down by the people. The people were anti-slavery and the Legislature pro-slavery. Senators in Congress voted to admit Missouri with slavery, and the people condemned the act. They elected Daniel P. Cook, after whom Cook county was named, who voted against Missouri, and the people continued to re-elect him while the Legislature made senators of the candidates he defeated at the polls. Free people of color humbly petitioned the Legislature for the repeal of the burdensome Black Laws, but their petitions were unheeded, and heavier burdens were laid upon them.

So, in 1829, ten years after the previous elaborate Black Act, and four years after the slave party met with its rebuff in the defeat of the call for the convention, the legislators attempted to do by legislation what the people had forbidden them to do by the Constitution. The act was approved January 7, 1829. It prohibits any black or mulatto person, being a citizen of any one of the United States, coming and residing in Illinois until he produces a certificate of freedom and gives bonds of $1,000 that he will not become a charge to the county as a pauper, and that he will obey all laws enacted, or which may be enacted, and $500 fine is imposed on any person who will give employment or sustenance to any such black person who does not give the bond. Any person who can not furnish a certificate shall be deemed a runaway slave, and he may be taken up by any inhabitant and brought before a justice, who shall commit him to the sheriff, who shall commit him to jail, and advertise him, and, if no master comes, sell him for time of service to pay the expenses of his arrest. The law forbids, under penalty of fine and whipping, the marriage of any colored person with a white person. It also provides that if any negro who is the property of any person shall come into the State for the purpose of hiring out, and shall institute proceedings for his freedom, the case shall be thrown out of court and the presumptuous negro thrown into jail.

These two laws of 1819 and 1829, and the act of February 16, 1833, in the criminal code, were the main pillars of the Black Code. The criminal code enacts that if any person shall secrete any escaped slave, or shall hinder or prevent the lawful owner from retaking him, he shall be fined $500 and be imprisoned not exceeding six months. Another section forbids any person who holds any indentured servant from taking him out of the State for sale, or otherwise kidnaping him, under the penalty of a fine of $500. The crime of kidnaping is punished the same as the crime of protecting the fugitive, less the imprisonment. The testimony of no colored or mulatto person can be taken in evidence against a white person. No colored child is permitted to attend school with white children. Indentured servants and slaves were by law made property, and could be attached for debt, sold as property, devised in wills, and sold to settle estates; and in taxation ranked with cattle, "jennies," and jackasses as property.

In 1845 there was another revision of the laws, and these were all compiled, boiled down, and made available for handy use in the administration of justice. But this was not the end of legislation. Two or three years after the passage of the National Fugitive Slave Law there was another act passed, dated February 12, 1853, which would seem to be a supercrogation, as it seems to be a repetition of all that went before, with this difference, that it made the act of any colored person coming into the State, or any person bringing such a one in, a high misdemeanor. That was coming up to the climax and apex of crime over and under the color line. This act was to be enforced by pains and penalties and fines and imprisonments of the most severe and elaborate character. These acts were the laws of the State for more than a generation, and by the friends of the anti-slavery agitation were attempted in many sections to be rigidly enforced. Then came a period of the operation of the underground railroad, the attempted enforcement of these laws, kidnaping, lawful and unlawful arrests and rescues and trials before the courts for harboring, secreting and delivering the slave from his master or from the officers—all occurring with many rich scenes of humor, in which the "black brother" played the prominent part.

The Supreme Court in 1855, in the case of Joseph Jarrot, a colored man, v. Julia Jarrot, made a decision that the inherited slavery from the old French import was unconstitutional. Joseph was a descendant of the French slaves and Julia of the slave-holders. The Constitution of 1848 made all slavery unconstitutional in accordance with the decree of the ordinance of 1787. But the Black Code, in the main, remained a part of the law till the close of the slaveholders' rebellion. In 1864 John Jones, a noted mulatto of Chicago, who had been free born, and had deposited his freedom papers with the Historical Society, carried a petition through the streets of Chicago asking, since his race had been made free, that all these laws that made distinction on account of color might be erased from our statute book. He went to Springfield and engineered the enterprise. Senator Lansing introduced the bill early in the session of 1865, for their repeal, and they went out as the smoke flies upward.

This account of the repeal of the Black Laws by Mr. Eastman, is so full and complete that we have availed ourselves of his labors in this regard. Mr. Eastman was one of the most loyal and patriotic citizens that ever lived in our midst, and on the accession of Mr. Lincoln to the office of President was rewarded by him for his faithful services to his country, by appointing him United States Consul to Bristol, England, where he remained for several years. He died at Chicago, greatly honored and respected, some three years since.

## CHAPTER XVIII.

### Mason and Dixon's Line in Illinois.

THE hostile feelings which were aroused among the slave-holding and free State advocates during the great convention struggle of 1823-4 never were allayed, and gradually led to a wide separation in all political matters.

Almost from the establishment of the seat of government at Kaskaskia, the ancient capital of the French of the "Illinois Country," an imaginary, yet dividing line, has existed between the northern and southern half of the State. It has moved forward as the capital has been changed, like that of the center of population, but always northward. The first parallel was at Kaskaskia, next at Vandalia, but when the "long nine" moved the capital from that ancient seat of empire to Springfield, they carried with them "this sign of the Zodiac," as if it was the ark of the covenant, and it has ever since been "like a pillar of fire by night" and "a cloud by day," to all the various tribes within this State.

Among politicians the rule was, as old General Linder once said, like that which governed the followers of Cortes. "After the battle every excess of rapacity was sufficiently vindicated by the plea that the sufferers were unbaptized. Avarice stimulated zeal. Zeal consecrated avarice. Proselytes and gold mines were sought with equal ardor." In all political campaigns the men of the North were most convenient and useful allies to draw on to help defray party assessments and furnish the sinews of war, but it would never do to allow them to direct the policy of the party.

In the exciting times of election the Yanks were good enough to swell the majorities, but at all other times their wants and necessities went unheeded. When the inhabited parts of the State extended a little north of Alton, then the people of Randolph, Monroe, St. Clair and Madison, now southern counties, were as anxious for a canal as the people of La Salle and Hennepin. When the seat of government was removed to Vandalia and afterward to Springfield, those living between these two places immediately became Southerners and ever after opposed a canal with all their power and might.

Time, it is true, has somewhat modified this feeling, but still "the Cooks" are distrusted and the representatives of portions of the State greatly fear "the Trojans bearing gifts." We think, however, that it is about time that this "Mason and Dixon's line" business should be obliterated, and the interests of the people be considered strictly upon their merits, whether those wanting public improvements happen to live in Chicago, Cairo, Springfield or Quincy.

There has never been a free zone in Illinois and no neutral ground, but from the very earliest times there has been a north and south party and the prejudices of each against the other have been manifested in almost every constitutional convention; at every session of the General Assembly and in every deliberative body ever called for any purpose whatever. Governor Ford in his "History of Illinois" refers to it in these terms: "Obstructions to the success of wise policy which would relieve the State from multiplied evils, were to be found in the character, varieties and genius of the masses of the people, and in the motives, aims and enterprises of politicians. The shape of the State naturally divided the Legislature into representatives from the south and representatives from the north, and under any circumstances a State so long in proportion to its breadth, must contain much and many elements of discord.

The southern portion of the State was settled principally by people from the slave-holding States; the north principally from New York and New England. The southern people were generally poor; they were such as were not able to own slaves in a slave State and who came here to avoid slavery. A poor white man in a slave State is of little more importance in the eyes of the wealthy than the negro. The very negroes of the rich call such poor persons "poor white folks."

The wealthy immigrant from the slave States rarely came here. He moved to some new slave State, to which he could take his negroes. The consequences were, that our southern settlements presented but few specimens of the more wealthy, enterprising, intellectual and cultivated people from the slave States. Those who did come were a very good, honest, kind, hospitable people, unambitious of wealth and great lovers of ease and social enjoyment.

The settlers from the North, not being debarred by our Constitution from bringing their property with them, were of a different class. The northern part of the State was settled in the first instance by wealthy farmers, enterprising merchants, millers and manufacturers. They made farms, built mills, churches, schoolhouses, towns and cities, and made roads and bridges as if by magic, so that, although the settlements in the southern part of the State are twenty, thirty, forty and fifty years in advance, on the score of age, yet are they ten years behind in point of wealth and all the appliances of a higher civilization. This of itself was cause enough of discord between the two ends of the State. The people of the South entertained a most despicable opinion of their Northern neighbors. They had never seen the genuine Yankee. They had seen a skinning, trafficking and tricky race of peddlers from New England, who much infested the West and South with tin ware, small assortments of merchandise and wooden clocks, and they supposed that the whole of the New England people were like these specimens.

They formed the opinion that a genuine Yankee was a close, miserly, dishonest, selfish getter of money, void of generosity, hospitality or any of the kindlier feelings of human nature. The Northern people formed equally as unfavorable an opinion of their Southern neighbors. The Northern man believed the Southerner to be a long, lank, lean, lazy and ignorant animal, but little in advance of the savage state, one who was content to squat in a log cabin, with a large family of ill-fed, ill-clothed, idle, ignorant children. The truth was, both parties were wrong. There is much natural shrewdness and sagacity in the most ignorant of the Southern people; and they are generally accumulating property as fast as any people can who had so little to begin with. The parties are about equal in point of generosity and liberality though these virtues show themselves in each people in a different way. The Southerner is, perhaps, the most hospitable and generous to individuals. He is lavish of his victuals, his liquors and other personal favors. But the Northern man is the most liberal in contributing to whatever is for the public benefit. Is a school house, a bridge or a church to be built, a road to be made, a scholar, a minister to be maintained or taxes to be paid for the honor or support of government, the Northern man is never found wanting. This misconception of character was the cause of a good deal of misunderstanding. The great canal itself, from Lake Michigan to the Illinois river, was opposed by some, at an early day, for fear it would open a way for flooding the State with Yankees; even as popular a man as the late Lieutenant-Governor Kinney opposed it, in a speech in the Senate, on this ground. He said the Yankees spread everywhere. He was looking daily for them to overrun the State. They could be found in every country on the globe; and one strong proof to him that John Cleves Symmes was wrong in his theory of the earth was, that if such an opening at the north pole as that theory supposed really existed, the Yankees would have had a big wagon road to it long before its discovery by Mr. Symmes.

In this manner, and by constant appeals to the prejudices of the masses, ill-feeling was engendered, and almost any public enterprise which was proposed by the people of one section of the State would be opposed by the other. It was exactly such a feeling as existed between the people of the Southern States and the people of the Northern States before the war.

Another thing: The State of Illinois has, from the beginning, been cursed by politicians. They have infested the country, and from the time when Jesse B. Thomas became a delegate in Congress from the Indiana Territory, down to a period within the memory of men still living, northern and southern politics have swayed and ruled the hour.

All local questions became subordinate to national questions, and consequently men did not seem to take much interest in the development or improvement of the State, but the great and absorbing question always was, what would be for the best interests of the party, and how this and that would affect the party. All candidates for office were selected with reference to their ability to control the masses and draw votes, and not with reference to their ability to devise a system of public improvements, or establish a sound system of finance or build up manufactories. Stump oratory was of greater importance than the wisdom of Solomon, and the gift of gab greater than the philosophy of Plato or Aristotle.

It is true that the annals of this State have been adorned by men who will forever take rank with those of the greatest orators of any age and any nation, and the cultivation of eloquence is not to be despised or undervalued, but the ability of a man to harangue the mulitude and carry the crowd is one thing, statesmanship is entirely another. Politicians know a great deal better how to obtain an office than how to perform its duties when they have obtained it. Political science ought to be studied with reference to the best interests of the government, and not for the best interests of any given party. Education should be more universally diffused, knowledge made more abundant, and, above all, the people must be taught the power of thinking for themselves and not permit others to do it for them.

The time has come for wiping out Mason and Dixon's line in the State of Illinois and including the entire State in a free zone.

## CHAPTER XIX.

### The Period Preceding the Calling of the Constitutional Convention of 1847.

THE period preceding the calling of the convention of 1847, had, through a series of years, been a period of unrest and excitement and, at times, of great turbulence. Politics seemed to absorb the attention of everybody and there was a greater amount of partisanship to the square rod than was ever found in the history of States. The principal business of the lawyers and the people generally, seems to have been politics.

Commencing with the contest over the appointment of Secretary of State in 1838, by Governor Carlin, to take the place of one Alexander P. Field, who had been appointed by Governor Edwards some ten years before, all the politicians in the State became involved until it reached the Supreme Court, and soon a war broke out upon the judges of the Supreme Court which furnishes as disgraceful a chapter as ever occurred in our local annals, with the exception of the efforts of the slave-holders to make Illinois a slave State. Field was a most striking character. He was a native of Kentucky, a nephew of Nathaniel Pope, who was secretary of the

Territory of Illinois, afterward delegate in Congress and then judge of the United States District Court for the State of Illinois. He was perhaps the innocent cause of more bad blood and of more political intrigues than almost any man of his time. He was a member of the Lower House, or General Assembly, from Union county, from 1822 to 1828, and from 1828 to 1830 he represented Union, Johnson and Alexander counties. He was Secretary of State from 1828 to 1840. He had, by a process of evolution, gradually become a whig, and the democrats wanted to get him out of the way and obtain the office.

After several years of strife and turmoil, in which the late Judge Douglas, Judge Trumbull and McClernand became conspicuous, he was legislated out of office and was then appointed secretary of Wisconsin Territory. Then he moved to New Orleans, where he became distinguished as a criminal lawyer, was elected a member of the 48th Congress and on the 7th of December 1863, he, in conjunction with his colleague, Thomas Cottman, was put on the roll of the House as a member of Congress from Louisiana. They both voted on preliminary questions and for speaker, but after the organization was perfected, the House refused to swear them in as members, and subsequently decided that they were not entitled to seats. After the war was over he became attorney-general for the State of Louisiana, and died in 1877, at New Orleans, after a long and painful illness. He was a man of great ability, but somewhat erratic, as he appears to have been a "convention man" in 1823-4, and made the motion to unseat Hansen against all parliamentary usages, in order to carry the call for a convention by a two-thirds majority. We met him at Springfield, in 1870, where he came on a visit, while the constitutional convention was in session, and he was most cordially received by his old acquaintances. It is not necessary to go into details in regard to Field's claim to office, for there are scores of people still living who know all about it.

The Field controversy had hardly closed, however, before a much greater one arose, and which led to an open and direct attack upon the Supreme Court, and which finally led to its complete reorganization.

## CHAPTER XX.

### The Partisan War on the Supreme Court and the Reorganization of the Same.

THE Constitution of 1818 provided that "the justices of the Supreme Court," as they were called, should be appointed by the Legislature, and hold office during life; provided, however, that the justices first appointed should hold office only five years. The selection by the Legislature was a bad feature, but when we consider the character of the men who were actually appointed, the provision that those first appointed should only hold for five years was a wise one. The court consisted of a chief justice and three associate justices. John Phillips was chief justice; William P. Foster, Thomas C. Brown and John Reynolds associate justices.

Judge Phillips appears to have been a lawyer, but came to the State, in 1812, a captain in the regular army. Although a soldier, politics was his best hold.

He was nominated by the pro-slavery party for governor in 1822, was defeated by Coles, when he resigned in disgust and left the State. He went to Tennessee.

Judge Brown was a large man, affable, yet somewhat stately, with but little industry and possessed of but few of the qualifications for a judge. He was assigned to the northern circuit; was laughed at and despised by many lawyers, who sought to impeach him for unfitness, but he remained on the bench until 1848, when the new Constitution took effect.

The selection of John Reynolds—afterward known as the Old Ranger—was at that time regarded with derision and as a farce, for he had studied law only a few months, had had no experience or practice whatever, and was absolutely without any of the qualifications requisite for judge of the highest court in the State.

But the climax was capped in the selection of a man by the name of William P. Foster, who had not been in the State much more than three months. Nobody knew it at the time, but he afterward proved to be a consummate scoundrel and swindler, and no lawyer at all. He had never studied law and had no license, yet he contrived to stay in the State for about a year, never offering to perform any of his duties, yet drawing his salary regularly. He suddenly decamped and was heard of several times afterward in connection with numerous crimes and villainies.

Thomas Reynolds succeeded Judge Phillips as chief justice, and William Wilson to succeed Foster. Wilson was a man of considerable ability and proved to be a sound judge and commanded the respect of the bar.

At the session of 1824-5 the Legislature, under the provisions of the Constitution, re-organized the judiciary by creating five Circuit Court judges, who were to hold all the Circuit Courts in the State; and the Supreme Court, composed of four judges, was to be held twice a year at the seat of government. William Wilson was elected chief justice; Thomas C. Brown, Samuel D. Lockwood and Theophilus W. Smith, were elected associate judges of the Supreme Court. John York Sawyer, Samuel McRoberts, Richard M. Young, James Hall and James O. Wattles, were elected judges of the circuits, and James Turney to be attorney-general.

The appointment of Judge McRoberts was one not fit to be made. He was always a most bitter and relentless partisan. He removed Joseph Conway and appointed Emanuel J. West, one of his particular friends, to the office of clerk of Madison county. The people resented this to such an extent that they immediately elected Conway to the Senate and kept him there for eight years.

The salary of these judges was fixed at $1,000 per year, payable, however, in depreciated currency, which reduced it to about $400. The Missouri Compromise measures had stirred up the country so that judges and everybody else had taken sides; the movement to make Illinois a slave State had engendered a great deal of bad feeling in which Judge Smith had engaged in an open street brawl with one Hooper Warren, whom he undertook to cowhide for personalities in the streets of Edwardsville. Then came the triangular contest for the presidency between Henry Clay, Andrew Jackson and John Quincy Adams in 1824, in which it was charged that Wilson, Lockwood and Brown indorsed the action of Daniel P. Cook in giving the vote of the State to Adams, while Smith was for Jackson.

The public seemed to make no discrimination or allowance for the opinions of judges any more than anybody else. Wilson, Lockwood and Brown, it is said, maintained strict silence, but Smith, who was one of the most pestiferous demagogues that ever lived, was "blatant mouthed."

The very fact that the judges were appointed for life made them more and more unpopular and the whole system was attacked and declared a fraud and an imposition. But this was not all. The Constitution made them a council of revision, and required that all bills which should have passed the Senate and House of Representatives, shall, before they become laws, be presented to said council for their revision and consideration, and if they disproved of the same they could not become laws without receiving the votes of a majority of the whole number of members elected.

The provision was a wise one in many respects, but as it gave the judges of the Supreme Court a *quasi* veto power on the acts of the Legislature, it exposed the judges to the most severe criticisms every time they acted contrary to the Legislature, and they were often misrepresented, vilified and threatened with impeachment and a reorganization of the judiciary was resolved upon. In the reorganization in the first instance, the State was divided into five circuits, and five circuit judges were appointed, leaving to the supreme justices only appellate jurisdiction with no circuit duties.

At the session of the Legislature of 1826–27, four of the circuit judges were legislated out of office and their duties assigned to the four Supreme Court judges.

The reason assigned for this change was economy; but that was not the true reason at all, and every one knew that it was not.

The combined salary of all the nine judges was only $6,200, and the saving was ostensibly $2,400, but it proved such an injury to the public in consequence of delays and postponement of cases, and was found so deleterious, that there was a universal outcry to return to the old system. The democratic Legislature was unable to starve the whig justices out of office or compel them to resign by any species of petty persecution, and for a time they ceased to badger the judges. But this state of things was short-lived, and in 1840–41, matters reached a climax.

The Supreme Court decided against McClernand, who instituted the suit against Field, and

> The war which for a space did fail
> Now trebly thundering swelled the gale.

The democrats resolved to reform the judiciary.

The Constitution of the State provided that all free white male *inhabitants*, over the age of twenty-one years, who had resided in the State for six months, should be entitled to vote at all general and special elections.

The whigs contended that this did not authorize any but citizens to vote, while the democrats contended that it included aliens as well as citizens.

There were in the State at this time about 10,000 alien votes, nine-tenths of which were democratic, and this matter assumed great importance. A case came up to the Supreme Court from Galena, in December, 1839, and had been argued, but the democratic lawyers discovered, as it is said, by the aid of Judge Smith, that a date was wrong in the record and a continuance was had until December, 1840. This was thought at the time to have been one of the sharpest things ever done, because people believed that the majority of the judges had determined to decide against the aliens and they could in this way be secure for at least one more election.

"The plan of campaign," as it is now called in Ireland, which was agreed to, was broad and comprehensive. They would abolish all the circuit courts, repeal or legislate the judges out of office, and create five additional judges of the Supreme Court, all of whom were required to hold circuit courts in place of the circuit judges legislated out of office. A long and violent struggle ensued, but the bill was finally passed through both Houses and returned by the council of revision, with their objections, by a considerable majority in the Senate, and by one majority in the House. By this means, Ford says, the new Secretary of State was secured in his office, and the democratic party were secured in the continued support of the alien vote; for all the new judges elected at this session were as thoroughly satisfied of the right of each governor to appoint his own Secretary of State, and of the right of the alien inhabitants to vote, as the whig judges could be to the contrary.

During the pendency of this question before the Legislature the whig judges decided the alien case from Galena, but did not decide the main question, and it was charged by the democrats that the whig judges had hunted up on purpose a trivial point to evade responsibility, in the hope that when the dominant party could see that they were no longer threatened with a decision contrary to their wishes, they would abandon their reform measure.

Stephen A. Douglas, who had been one of the counsel for the aliens, had, it appeared, been in constant and daily communication with Judge Smith, who had long aimed to be United States Senator, and one evening, in a speech in the lobby of the House, boldly affirmed that the judges had at one time all their opinions written and ready to deliver, and that all but Judge Smith were against the aliens, and they would have so decided if a defect in the record had not been discovered. He affirmed this in the most positive manner, and stated that he knew exactly what he was about; that he had the information upon authority that could not be denied, and nobody dared deny it; and he therefore proceeded to denounce the whig judges in the strongest language at his command. His statements attracted great attention, and were reiterated by John A. McClernand in the House.

John A. McClernand was at that time a member of the House of Representatives and in the heat of debate also made the most direct and specific charges against the judges, charging them with misconduct, with violations of their oaths of office and of their attempt to disfranchise thousands of inhabitants of the State, and suggesting that they had committed high crimes and misdemeanors enough to warrant their impeachment and removal from office. The judges had before this been repeatedly assailed by speeches in the lobby, by anonymous newspaper articles and unsigned handbills, which had been circulated everywhere in the city and around the capital and posted on the corners of the street, but they had, much to their credit, maintained a most dignified silence.

But the time came at length for them to break silence, and John J. Hardin, who was a member of the House of Representatives immediately addressed a note to the judges, asking them if the statements which had been made by Douglas and McClernand were true. To this communication they returned the following reply:

SPRINGFIELD, Jan. 26, 1841.

*John J. Hardin, Esq.,*

DEAR SIR:—Your letter of to-day has just been received and we proceed to answer it without hesitation. In doing so, we can not, however, but express our great astonishment at the character of the statement to which you refer. You say that Mr. McClernand, a member of the House of Representatives, has asserted in debate: " I am authorized to say and I do say on my own responsibility, if any such responsibility is needed, that the judges of the Supreme Court prepared an opinion against the right of foreigners to vote, at the last June term of that court, but on account of objections made by counsel to a mistake in the record, they withheld their opinion but did so most reluctantly. The opinion has gone abroad that these judges made the decision, recently delivered, on the subject of the right of foreigners to vote, in order to defeat the bill under consideration, and to prevent these judges going on the circuit."

To this statement we give the most unqualified denial in all its points; neither of the members of the court having ever prepared or written any opinion against the right of aliens to vote at elections. As to the insinuations that the decision of any case was made at the time to defeat the judiciary bill we reply, it is in all its parts equally unjust and without a pretense for its justification.

We have thus promptly complied with your request and we can not close this communication without remarking the great injustice done to ourselves, not only by the statement referred to, but the numerous other slanders, which in our situation we have no means of repelling. We have the honor to be

Your obedient servants,
THOS. W. SMITH,
SAMUEL D. LOCKWOOD,
WM. WILSON,
THOMAS C. BROWN.

This communication was a stunner and created a great sensation.

Douglas and McClernand were called to account in both Houses of the Legislature and it was demanded of them to give their authority, and they gave Judge Smith as their authority, and they were backed up in their assertions by several very prominent men who had heard Smith say the same thing. Judge Smith now became very unpopular, was accused of hypocrisy and prevarication and denounced by men in his own party as a liar, an intriguer and utterly unworthy of confidence or belief. He lost caste and never regained it.

The history of this man Smith has never been written, but if it should be, it would furnish one of the most striking examples of the demagogue on the bench, that was ever presented to the people of this country. He had, as one of the old pioneers once told me, always a penchant for politics, was always scheming and plotting, and greatly desired to be United States Senator, and if he could not be that, he wanted to be governor; but having obtained a seat on the Supreme Bench, he was reluctant to give it up, and undertook to use it as a stepping stone to something else. His devices and intrigues to this end were, according to all accounts, unceasing. In fact, he never lacked a plot to advance himself or blow up some other person. He was laborious, indefatigable and untiring in his scheming; but his plans were too complicated and intricate to be successfully executed. He was always unsuccessful, and as misery loves company, he was delighted alike at the mishaps of friends and foes, and "was ever chuckling over the blasted hopes of some one else." He was impeached by the House of Representatives in 1833 on several charges of gross misdemeanor in office, and only escaped conviction by the Senate by that provision of the Constitution which required a two-thirds vote of that body to sustain the charges.

It is no light thing for a man like Judge Smith, who was called to occupy one of the highest positions in the State, to be thus summoned before the tribunal of posterity and have judgment passed upon him. But men must not trifle with justice or with a high and holy office. The generation to which he belonged has disappeared, and the time has come when the rash and indiscriminate judgments which his contemporaries passed upon his character may be calmly revised by history; but in the interest of justice, and as a warning to all demagogues who may seek to prostitute a high judicial position to their own purposes and their own aggrandizement, we have been compelled to make this note, and this shall be our excuse for disturbing his consecrated mould.

Of him it may be said, in the words of Hudibras:

> Our State-artificer foresaw
> Which way the world began to draw,
> For as old sinners have all points
> O' th' compass in their bones and joints,
> Can by their pangs and aches find
> All turns and changes of the wind.
> And better than by Napier's bones
> Feel in their own the age of moons;
> So guilty sinners in a State,
> Can by their crimes prognosticate,
> And in their consciences feel pain
> Some days before a shower of rain;
> He therefore wisely cast about
> All ways he could to ensure his throat.

The Council of Revision which still existed and which still retained a shadow of authority did not approve the bill and returned it to the House with their objections. The bill was, however, repassed by a majority of one, and that one vote was given by a member who opposed the bill on its passage and who immediately after was appointed clerk of the Supreme Court as newly organized, the five new judges, without any consultation whatever with their associates, turning out the old clerk and putting this very conscientious and reformatory member in his place. But this was not all. The old judges, it mattered not where they lived, were assigned to circuits as far removed from their homes as possible, and they were treated with every mark of discourtesy within their power.

Old Judge Brown, whose home was in Shawneetown in the extreme southern part of the State, was assigned to the Galena district. This was done in order to secure his resignation, but it proving unsuccessful, an attempt was made to remove him by impeachment on the following charges and specifications, to wit: "That he had not the natural strength of intellect and lacked the legal and literary learning requisite and indispensable to the high and responsible duties devolving upon him as a judge of the Supreme Court; that his opinions delivered in that court were written and revised by others and that his decisions on the circuit had been the mere echo of some favorite attorney; and that by nature, education and habit he was wholly unfit for his high position."

It is probable that never since the impeachment of Warren Hastings for high crimes and misdemeanors, had there been an instance like this, of an attempt so degrading. His office was wanted for another, and so eager were the applicants that they could not wait for the old man to pay the debt of nature. They were more rapacious and merciless in their demands than the Mahrattas, for *they* had some respect for the rules of justice and the sentiments of humanity. But the common sense of mankind, which, in matters of this sort, seldom goes wrong, will always recognize a distinction between crimes which originate in an inordinate zeal for the commonwealth and crimes which originate in selfish cupidity. Indeed, if a man is honest and upright, the community is quite apt to overlook transactions which may even be characterized as indelicate and irregular. It is quite likely from what we know and what we have heard of Judge Brown, that he had long since outlived his usefulness and would have commanded the respect of the community had he voluntarily retired to private life and enjoyed the closing hours of a serene old age in the perusal of the classics like "De Senectue," or even Bunyan's Pilgrim's Progress, but he was reluctant to be driven from his post of duty or have his effects administered upon before the appointed hour. An impression got abroad that the weak old man was being persecuted and the impeachment proceedings which had barely been initiated, were dropped and came to nothing.

All these things that we have narrated, however, did not have the effect to stay the tide of reform which now set in. The democrats were determined to teach the judiciary a lesson and to give them to understand and be informed that if they undertook to thwart " the will of the people " they must take the consequences. The reform bill passed, and five additional judges of the Supreme Court were forthwith elected, consisting of Thomas Ford, Sidney Breese, Walter B. Scates, Samuel H. Treat and Stephen A. Douglas. Some of these newly appointed judges applied themselves with great diligence to the discharge of their duties and afterward became distinguished as jurists, notably Judges Breese and Treat.

Judge Douglas was far better fitted for the stormy scenes occurring in the halls of Congress than in the consultation chamber or in listening to dry and uninteresting arguments on the bench, and in a short time resigned and entered upon a career in that great world of politics that is almost without a parallel. Judge Douglas wrote but very few opinions while on the bench, but there is one that was written by him that is quite famous and that is the opinion in the case of Penny v. Little, 3 Scam. 301. It shows great research; shows how Illinois adopted the common law, how it is still in force, and then proceeds to show that a landlord has a right to distrain for rent where the rent is due and no power is contained in the lease, the same being authorized by the common law. This is the leading case upon this subject in this State and has been often cited in this and other States. His name and fame are indubitably linked with that of his great rival, Lincoln, like that of Pitt and Fox.

History owes to him this attestation: that in an hour of peril, when this Government was threatened with overthrow by the most gigantic conspiracy which the world ever saw, he cast to the winds every consideration except his country. He declared that there were but two parties left, namely patriots and traitors, and he unhesitatingly ranged himself on the side of his country and with his dying breath besought the people to stand by the Government. He was possessed of genius of a very high order, of strong passions, of quick sensibility, of magnetic power and vehement enthusiasm which in a good cause could carry everything before him.

All men and all parties have united in decreeing to him posthumous honors although he was gravely criticized while living. If Lincoln was the great representative of the people in their contest for liberty—and acted as its guardian, Douglas acted as the great commoner and steadying power of the State when the crisis came. If he was forced into the position that he finally assumed, it was not unnatural, and the language that he made use of was not the cant of patriotism. He died suddenly amid the fiery paroxysms of malcontents, some of whom thought that he should have still held out in his opposition to his great rival; but time has decreed that Lincoln and Douglas occupied co-ordinate positions in an undivided empire, and while posterity takes note of his errors it deliberately announces that among the eminent men of this generation scarcely one has left a more stainless and a more splendid name.

At the same session, when the Reform Bill was passed, and as a reward for unexampled services to the party while occupying the bench, Samuel McRoberts was nominated and elected United States Senator. He was known at that time, and ever will be known, as the maligner and oppressor of Governor Coles, before whom a part of the litigation took place relating to penalties incurred for bringing slaves into the State and liberating them here.

The violent and unjustifiable attacks which at this period were made upon the judiciary, were disgraceful to all those engaged in it, and will always be regarded as a dark shadow cast over our judicial annals. The part which Judge Theophilus W. Smith took in this matter is certainly entirely inexcusable and he may be regarded as one of the arch conspirators against his brethren on the bench and an aider and abetter of those off the bench, to degrade the majority of judges composing the highest tribunal in the land, and among whom may be reckoned some who were the purest and most upright and conscientious men that ever lived. But decency and common sense finally triumphed.

> "And sovereign law the States collected will
>   O'er thrones and globes elate,
> Sits empress-crowning good, repressing ill,
>   Smit by her sacred frown
> The fiend, Discretion, like a vapor sinks,
>   And e'en the all dazzling crown
> Hides his faint rays and at her bidding shrinks."

## CHAPTER XXI.
## The Constitutional Convention of 1847.

TWENTY-FIVE years after the Constitution of 1818 had been adopted, a general movement was started for calling a convention "to alter, amend and revise" that instrument. It was claimed that it was not to be a party measure at all, but in the sequel, both parties, whigs and democrats, nominated delegates upon strictly party lines, with the exception of Morgan county. The special election for delegates was fixed for the third Monday of April, 1847, and the convention was to meet in Springfield, on the first Monday of June following.

Morgan county was entitled to four delegates, and there, by an agreement of parties, Judge Samuel D. Lockwood, William Thomas, James Dunlap and Newton Cloud were elected. This circumstance was of such an unusual and extraordinary character, politics having been carried into every election of every sort, character and kind, from the formation of the State down, that it gave these delegates, aside from their merits as men, a high rank at once. Newton Cloud was elected president of the convention, and the others assigned to prominent positions, Judge Lockwood being chairman of the executive committee.

There were many men in that convention of great ability, some of whom afterward acquired a national reputation, among whom may be mentioned Judge David Davis, John M. Palmer, Stephen T. Logan, and others. The names of the delegates are herewith appended.

The proceedings were reported for the public press, in part by the late James Sheahan of Chicago, the well known newspaper writer who came on from Washington for that purpose, and from him we learned that every question was discussed from the institution of human governments and the birth of republics down to the last ward caucus. The chief topics, however, next to State sovereignty and National union, which engaged the attention of that body, was the appointing power, the re-organization of the judicial department—limiting the right of suffrage to citizenship, repudiation of the State debt and tax titles.

When the constitutional convention met in 1847, the financial condition of the State was at a very low ebb. The interest on the State debt was greatly in arrear. The State banks had gone down with a crash, and bankruptcy had overtaken many of the best men in the State, and Illinois was charged with repudiation and was in great danger of becoming "a stench in the nostrils of the civilized world." The governor of the State said: "The people at home began to wake up in terror; the people abroad who wished to settle in a new country avoided Illinois as they would pestilence and famine; and there was great danger that the future emigrants would be men who, having no regard for their own characters, would also have none for that of the State where they might live. The terrors of high taxation were before all eyes, both at home and abroad. Every one at home wanted to sell his property and move away, and but few, either at home or abroad, wanted to purchase. The impossibility of selling kept us from losing population, and the fear of disgrace or high taxes prevented us from gaining materially."

After a considerable discussion and great opposition the following article was introduced into the convention: "There shall be annually assessed and collected a tax of two mills upon each dollar's worth of taxable property to be applied as follows, to wit: The fund so created shall be kept separate and shall annually, on the first day of January, be apportioned and paid over *pro rata* upon all such State indebtedness, other than the canal and school indebtedness, as may, for that purpose, be presented by the holders of the same to be entered as credits upon and to that extent, in extinguishment of the principal of that indebtedness." This was a very wise measure but strange to say, so bitterly was it fought that it had to be submitted to the people as a separate article and was only adopted by a vote of 42,017 to 30,586, whereas it should have been unanimous.

It was a great reform measure, and was, we believe, originally suggested by Governor Ford, and was advocated with all his power and wisdom. The next great measure was that relating to tax titles, which was introduced by Judge Lockwood, and appears in full in Section 4, Article 9 of the Constitution. Before this time, the *onus probandi* of showing irregularities in the proceedings leading up to the issuing of a tax deed rested upon the owner, and the deed was *prima facie* evidence that the land was subject to taxation, that the taxes were unpaid, that the lands were unredeemed, that it had been legally advertised, that it was sold for taxes, that the grantee was the purchaser, and that the sale was conducted in the manner required by law. It was possible for a man to lose title to his land, although residing on it and having paid the taxes.

The next thing that the convention did was to wipe out completely and entirely the provision in the Constitution of 1818 relating to the Council of Revision. That was especially odious, and was hated and reviled and denounced without stint or measure. But much can be said in its favor, and such a mode of revision of the laws, before going into effect, seems to be based upon considerations of the highest wisdom, and in any State where the greatest perfection is sought after and desired, ought not to be objected to. In a country, however, where every man takes rank with Solon and Lycurgus, there can be but few restraints imposed upon a "fierce democracie," and even the veto power, upon hasty legislation, has often been declared odious and undemocratic.

Our legislation seems to proceed upon the theory of rectifying present defects and providing for present necessities, no matter how the same may be brought about, nor how it may affect the future condition of the people, nor what the results may be. If such laws are ever submitted to the Supreme Court for construction, after being put in force, and the various conflicting provisions are weighed and compared, the decision arrived at is based upon an equation of errors, and they soon become obsolete and of no force and effect. The only consolation about the whole matter is, that the Supreme Court of the State does, in spite of everything, constitute a standing committee of revision, and first and last passes upon almost every law that is enacted.

There is one thing, we think, in connection with the Constitution of 1847, not generally known, and which is particularly referred to in Coffin's biography of Judge Lockwood, and that is this: the manner in which God is recognized in the Constitution. It will be recollected that the Covenanters had in 1818 petitioned to have some mention of the Supreme Being made in the Constitution, but their petition was rejected and they opposed its adoption with all their might and main. Judge Lockwood, knowing this fact, wrote out, and on motion of William Thomas, the colleague of Lockwood, the preamble was amended as follows: "We, the people of the State of Illinois, grateful to Almighty God for the civil, political and religious liberty which He has so long permitted us to enjoy, and looking to him for a blessing upon our endeavors to secure and transmit the same unimpaired to succeeding generations, in order to form a more perfect government, establish justice, insure domestic tranquillity, provide for the common defense, promote the general welfare and to secure the blessings of liberty to ourselves and our posterity, do ordain and establish this Constitution for the State of Illinois." And there it remains as a part of the organic law to this day.

The Constitution which was then framed was a great improvement over that of 1818, but proved to be subject to abuse in many ways—notably that of special legislation and the granting of private charters, which encouraged the greed of politicians and others to such an extent as to almost absorb the time and attention of the members, and to such an extent as to sacrifice all public interests. It also fixed irrevocably in the Constitution itself the salaries of all the officers of the government, which, in a few years, proved a great evil, because, with the change of the times and the increased cost of living, the salaries fixed in the Constitution were wholly inadequate to pay officers for their services. The judicial system proved inadequate, and, as a matter of fact, the State increased in population so fast, and the development of the various complicated interests was so rapid, and there were so many things which came to pass that nobody anticipated or thought of, that the Constitution became almost obsolete. The people had outgrown it, and it was so defective in so many particulars that a new constitutional convention became imperative.

This convention numbered among its members many men of great experience and of the highest integrity, as will be seen by referring to the list of the same hereto appended; they served their country long and well, but very few are now left to tell the tale.

## CONVENTION OF 1847.

Adams County—William Laughlin, Wm. B. Powers, Jacob M. Nichols.
Adams and Highland Counties—Archibald Williams.
Alexander and Pulaski Counties—Martin Atherton.
Bond County—Michael G. Dale.
Boone County—Daniel H. Whitney.
Brown County—James W. Singleton.
Brown and Schuyler Counties—James Brockton, Alexander McHatton.
Bureau County—Simon Kinney.
Calhoun and Jersey Counties—William Bosbyshell.
Carroll and Ogle Counties—Garner Moffet.
Cass County—Henry F. Dummer.
Campaign and Vermillion Counties—Thompson R. Webber.
Christian and Shelby Counties—D. D. Shumway.
Clark County—William Tutt, Justin Harlan.
Clark, Edgar and Coles Counties—Uri Manly.
Clinton County—Benjamin Bond.
Coles County—Thomas A. Marshall, Thomas Trower.
Cook County—Patrick Ballingall, Francis C. Sherman, Reuben E. Heacock, E. F. Colby.
Crawford County—Nelson Hawley.
Cumberland and Effingham Counties—William H. Blakely.
DeKalb County—George H. Hill.
DeWitt County—George B. Lemon.
DuPage County—Jeduthan Hatch.
DuPage and Will Counties—Samuel Anderson.
Edgar County—William Shields and George W. Rives.
Edwards and Wayne Counties—Alvin R. Kenner.
Fayette County—John W. Edmonson and Joseph T. Eccles.
Franklin County—John W. Akin.
Fulton County—David Markley, Hezekiah M. Wead, Isaac Linley, George Kreider.
Gallatin County—Albert G. Caldwell, Jacob Smith.
Greene County—Franklin Witt, L. E. Worcester, D. M. Woodson.
Grundy and La Salle Counties—George W. Armstrong.
Hancock County—Thomas C. Sharpe, George S. Moore, Robert Miller, Thomas Geddes.
Harding and Gallatin Counties—Andrew McCallen.
Henderson County—Gilbert Turnbull.
Henry and Knox Counties—Joshua Harper.
Highland County—Lewis J. Simpson.
Iroquois and Will Counties—Jesse O. Norton.
Jackson County—Alexander M. Jenkins.
Jasper and Crawford Counties—Richard G. Morris.
Jefferson County—Franklin S. Casey.
Jefferson, Marion and Franklin Counties—Zadok Casey, Walter B. Scates.
Jersey County—A. R. Knapp.
Jo. Daviess County—Thompson Campbell, W. B. Green, O. C. Pratt.
Johnson County—John Oliver.

Kane County—Alfred Churchill, Augustus Adams, Thomas Judd.
Kendall County—John West Mason.
Knox County—Curtis K. Harvey, James Knox.
Lake County—Horace Butler, Hulbut Swan.
La Salle County—William Stadden, Abraham Hoes.
Lawrence County—John Mieure.
Lee County—John Dement.
Livingston and McLean Counties—Samuel Lander.
Logan County—James Tuttle.
McLean County—David Davis.
Mason County—F. S. D. Marshall.
Macoupin County—James Graham, John M. Palmer.
McDonough County—James M. Campbell.
McDonough and Warren Counties—John Huston.
McHenry County—John Sibley, Peter W. Deitz.
Madison County—Cyrus Edwards, E. M. West, Benaiah Robinson, George T. Brown.
Marshall and Stark Counties—Henry D. Palmer.
Marion County—George A. Pace.
Macon and Piatt Counties—Edward O. Smith.
Massac County—Thomas G. C. Davis.
Menard County—Benjamin F. Northcott.
Mercer County—Frederick Frick.
Montgomery County—Hiram Rountree.
Montgomery and Bond Counties—James M. Davis.
Moultrie and Shelby Counties—Anthony Thornton.
Morgan County—Newton Cloud, James Dunlap, William Thomas.
Monroe County—James A. James, John D. Whiteside.
Ogle County—D. J. Pinckney.
Perry County—H. B. Jones.
Perry, Washington and Clinton Counties—John Crain.
Peoria County—William W. Thompson, Lincoln B. Knowlton.
Peoria and Fulton Counties—Onslow Peters.
Pike County—William R. Archer, Harvey Dunn, William A. Grimshaw.
Pope County—William Sim.
Putnam County—Oaks Turner.
Randolph County—Ezekiel W. Robbins, Richard B. Servant.
Richland County—Alfred Kitchell.
Rock Island County—John W. Spencer, John Dawson.
Sangamon County—James H. Matheny, Ninian W. Edwards, Stephen T. Logan.
Scott County—N. M. Knapp, Daniel Dinsmore.
Schuyler County—William A. Minshall.
Shelby County—Edward Evey.
St. Clair County—William W. Roman, Wm. C. Kinney, John McCully, George Bunsen.
Stephenson County—Seth B. Farwell, Thomas B. Carter.
Tazewell County—William H. Holmes.
Union County—John Canady, John W. Vance.

Wabash County—Charles H. Constable.
Warren County—Abner C. Harding.
Washington County—Zenos H. Vernor.
Wayne County—James M. Hogue.
Whiteside County—Aaron C. Jackson.
White County—S. Snowden Hayes, Daniel Hay.
Woodford County—Samuel J. Cross.
Winnebago County—Selden M. Church, Robert J. Cross.
Williamson County—John T. Louden.
Williamson, Franklin and Jackson Counties—Willis Allen.
Will County—Hugh Henderson, William McClure.

## CHAPTER XXII

### Constitutional Convention of 1862.

FIFTEEN years after the adoption of the Constitution of 1848 another convention was called " to revise, alter and amend " that, but as its work was not indorsed by the people, we shall not enter very much into details concerning it. It was termed a " High Rolling Convention," and assumed such powers that it soon disgusted the people and brought its work into disrepute.

It spent a great deal of time over the question whether the members should take an oath to support the Constitution, and frittered away much valuable time in the discussion of the question whether it could pass ordinances—whether it could legislate—appropriate money out of the public treasury—and indulged in a vast amount of buncombe and wearisome platitudes involving the policy of the war, and insisting that instead of the same being conducted according to Hardee's tactics, Generals Scott's, Halleck's or Grant's tactics it should be conducted according to the Constitution. Many had never heard of the war powers of the Constitution and were greatly surprised to find that war meant war, and that "unconditional surrender" was a very impolite way of treating rebels in arms, who were endeavoring to overthrow the government. In short, the use of gunpowder was very offensive and the din of battle greatly interfered with profound thought and deep meditation.

But there is one thing which it is well to remember and that is this: "If there be any truth by the universal experience of nations, it is this, that to carry the spirit of peace into war is a weak and cruel policy. The time of negotiation is the time for deliberation and delay. But when an extreme case calls for that remedy, which is in its own nature most violent, and which in such cases is a remedy only because it is violent, it is idle to think of mitigating and diluting. Languid war can do nothing which negotiation or submission will not do better, and to act on any other principle is not to save blood and money, but to squander them."

At this period there were many who were in favor of languid war, but the people generally were not. Time proved that the science of politics was incompatible with the science of war, and that those who were great in the forum and on the hustings, were powerless before belching batteries and the shot and shell from parks of artillery.

Politics and partisan feelings followed us from the field of politics to the hall of our assemblage and marred if they did not ruin the objects and purposes of our deliberations. The mouth disease was prevalent and in many instances proved fatal.

The majority of the delegates to the Illinois Convention of 1862 affirmed in substance that the act of the General Assembly under and by virtue of which it was convened, was no longer binding upon the convention after we had assembled and organized. It assumed and claimed all governmental powers, and while it proceeded on that theory, as one witty member said on its adjournment, " it has still left us in doubt when the functions of a constitutional convention ends, and when revolution begins."

The time at which we convened was not propitious. The war was then at its height, and every member was deeply interested in it. There was marching and counter-marching throughout the land. There were camps of recruits, camps of instruction forming everywhere, and the railroads were loaded with soldiers hastening to the front. The great campaign in the West and in the Mississippi valley had been in progress for some time, and Grant had ascended the Tennessee, and had commenced his march on Forts Henry and Donaldson.

We had members who had volunteered, and one at least left the convention to take charge of his company, and arrived in time to take part in the storming of the forts. I recollect at one time our convention suspended business and flocked to the windows to see Col. Robert Ingersoll march out of Springfield at the head of the 12th Illinois Cavalry.

Grant was charged with great rudeness by General Buckner, his former classmate at West Point, when in response to a communication asking for delay, he responded with the laconic reply "Unconditional surrender; we propose to move immediately upon your works." He moved, and General Buckner moved, and the next thing that we knew was the arrival of some ten thousand prisoners in our midst, "clad in their Joseph coat, of many a dye." Many were thinly clad, with straw hats on, sick, sore and diseased, sad at heart, and were marched to temporary cantonments and entered upon a new life as prisoners of war in camps a short distance out of Springfield. Train load after train load arrived in quick succession, and United States soldiers swarmed everywhere. Many prisoners were afterward transferred to Chicago, and many died of disease, of homesickness and exposure. The minds of men were naturally more absorbed with the progress of the war, than in altering, amending, revising or forming a new constitution.

The policy of the war had been challenged long before the election of delegates, and when the convention assembled, the majority were overwhelmingly against the republican party, and partisan proclivities soon became manifest.

The convention was composed of seventy-five delegates, and numbered among its members many men of distinction, as will be seen by reference to the list of delegates hereto attached. Some afterward attained national renown. One at least now fills the next highest office in the republic, the office of Chief Justice of the United States. There was Benjamin Edwards, the son of the great Ninian Edwards, the first governor of the Illinois Territory. There was John Dement, one of the early pioneers, William J. Allen, now United States District Judge, George Wall, now on the Appellate bench in this district, each of whom were afterward members of the convention of 1869–1870. There was also ex-Governor French, Anthony Thornton, O. B. Ficklin, Judge Purple, and the gifted orator Joel Manning, from Peoria, General Orme, Porter Sheldon, afterward a member of Congress, E. P. Ferry, now Governor of the State of Washington, and one of the early governors of the Territory, and many others too numerous to mention. My colleagues were Melville W. Fuller, now Chief Justice of the United States Supreme Court, John Wentworth and John H. Muhlke. Hon. William H. Hacker was elected president of the convention, and Hon. William M. Springer, commonly known at that time as "Bill Springer," was elected clerk. He has for many years been engaged in doing missionary work at Washington as a member of the House of Representatives. The convention was lively and at times boisterous. We might as well have undertaken to form a constitution on the battlefield.

There were many members who had become infused with the doctrines of State sovereignty and the omnipotence of the convention—and it went to excesses. It claimed to have all the powers of the people if they were assembled together and were bodily present, and were acting in their original and primary capacity. It was at a time when a great deal was said in the newspapers about ordinances, and that was a term which was well known throughout the South. Ordinances were made use of then to accomplish secession, and they were odious.

Our people did not like the nomenclature and did not like their purpose, and denounced them without stint or measure. Notwithstanding this, ordinances of one kind and another were introduced and passed, and the people began to find fault, and the soldier element greatly excited. It was rumored that some of the leading men in the convention were "Knights of the Golden Circle," and were hostile to the government.

This feeling of hostility reached its climax when, on the arrival of news of the capture of Fort Henry, we introduced some high sounding, yet patriotic resolutions, rejoicing over the great victory which had been achieved by our soldiers over "the rebels and traitors," and which, instead of being adopted by a rising vote, as we demanded, were referred to a select committee, and after some delay were reported back shorn of all their beauty and symmetry—cold and lifeless as if they had been subjected to a refrigerating process. This aroused the people greatly, and responses soon came from the army and Illinois soldiers in the field, and the usefulness of the convention was at an end. It was foredoomed, and several times the minority threatened to retire in a body.

It was at this juncture that Mr. Manning, of Peoria, on the fall of Fort Donaldson, in a paroxysm of patriotic zeal, introduced, and the convention passed, an ordinance commencing: "Be it ordained by the People of the State of Illinois, represented and assembled in constitutional convention, That the sum of five hundred thousand dollars, or so much thereof as may be necessary, be, and the same is hereby appropriated out of the treasury of the State of Illinois, for the exclusive purpose of relieving the wants and sufferings of the brave sons of Illinois who have been or may be wounded in the battles fought by them and their brothers in the defense of the Union and Constitution." Sections two and three authorized the issue by the governor, auditor and treasurer of Illinois, of State bonds for that amount, and provided for the disbursement of the money by those officers, jointly, with a committee to be appointed by the convention.

There never was a more praiseworthy object; but as the ordinance was introduced, as all who were members of that convention know, as a bluff, and to silence all hostile criticisms of the action of those who were in the majority, it is needless to say that it never amounted to anything; but it does illustrate most clearly the pretensions of those who held to the doctrine that the people of the State of Illinois were not only "represented" there on that day, but were actually "assembled in constitutional convention," and could legislate to any extent and on any subject, precisely as if every individual voter were bodily present and then and there voting.

When it was perceived that the work of the convention was being so severely criticised, a reaction took place among the "high rollers," and a partial restoration of good feeling took place, and a great effort was then made to frame a Constitution that would be acceptable to the people, and if it had not been for the hostile feelings which had been so injudiciously engendered, the Constitution would have been adopted. As finally prepared, it was really a good Constitution, and a great improvement over the then existing Constitution, but nothing would suffice. It was, on a popular vote, overwhelmingly defeated, and matters left in their condition until peace was restored, and all national issues had been settled by the dread arbitrament of war.

Many of the discussions which took place were characterized by great ability, but the two speeches which we recollect with great distinctness, and which were probably the two ablest speeches, all things considered, made upon the floor of the House, were those by Melville W. Fuller, now chief justice, and that of John Wentworth, on the death of Stephen A. Douglas. Judge Douglas had died some months before, and this was the first deliberative body which had assembled in the State after his death; and very early in the session Mr. Fuller had introduced a resolution calling for the appointment of a special committee to report suitable resolutions in regard to the same, and was, of course, made chairman of the committee; on the report coming in at a fixed day, some weeks afterward, the convention was given up to a consideration of the same and to speech-making. Mr. Fuller had made the most thorough preparation for the occasion, and his effort was not disappointing. It was a master-piece, and gave him almost a national reputation. Mr. Wentworth's speech was of a somewhat different character from that of Fuller's, and abounded in reminiscences of Douglas and his contests for recognition in Illinois, his great contest for the House of Representatives with John T. Stuart, his opposition to Buchanan, and closed with a magnificent tribute to his patriotism, his honesty and the position that he would assume in the future annals of this State. Mr. Wentworth was on this occasion at his best and carried all before him.

No finer tributes were ever paid to the memory of Douglas than those two speeches, and we have often wondered that they were not resurrected and published.

And here we would say, as many may be interested in knowing, that Mr. Fuller, while going with his party on party questions, was not a "high roller" in the convention, but was most eminently fair and considerate in everything. He was always a gentleman and was distinguished as a scholar. The abilities that he then displayed were a sure promise of what he afterward became.

THE NAMES OF THE DELEGATES TO THE CONSTITUTIONAL CONVENTION OF JANUARY 7, 1862.

Alexander, Pulaski and Union Counties—William A. Hacker.
Pope, Hardin and Massac Counties—George W. Waters.
Williamson and Johnson—William J. Allen.
Gallatin and Saline Counties—Milton Bartley.
Franklin and Jackson Counties—Andrew D. Duff.
Randolph County—Daniel Reiley.
Washington and Perry Counties—George W. Wall.
Jefferson, Marion and Hamilton Counties—H. K. S. Omelreny, T. B. Tanner.
Wabash and White Counties—Thomas W. Stone.
Wayne and Edwards Counties—R. P. Hanna.
Monroe County—Thomas W. Morgan.
St. Clair County—Augustus C. French, James B. Underwood.
Clinton and Bond Counties—Samuel Stevenson.
Madison County—Solomon Koepfli.
Fayette and Effingham Counties—Isaac L. Leith.
Richland, Clay and Jasper Counties—James H. Parker.
Lawrence and Crawford Counties—Harmon Alexander.
Cumberland and Alexander Counties—Anthony Thornton.

## CONSTITUTIONAL CONVENTION OF 1862.

Montgomery and Christian Counties—Horatio M. Vandeveer.
Macoupin County—Lewis Solomon.
Greene County—John M. Woodson.
Edgar County—James A. Eades.
Coles, Moultrie and Douglas Counties—Orlando B. Ficklin.
Sangamon County—Benjamin S. Edwards, James D. Smith.
Morgan and Scott Counties—Joseph Morton, Albert G. Burr.
Pike and Brown Counties—Alexander Starne, Archibald Glenn.
Adams County—James W. Singleton, Austin Brooks.
Schuyler County—John P. Richmond.
Hancock County—Milton M. Morrill.
McDonough County—Joseph C. Thompson.
Fulton County—Lewis W. Ross, John G. Graham.
Cass and Minard Counties—Thompson W. McNeeley.
Logan and Mason Counties—E. L. Austin.
Macon, Piatt, DeWitt and Champaign Counties—T. R. Webber.
Vermillion and Ford Counties—Elias S. Terry.
McLean County—William W. Orme.
Tazewell County—Robert B. M. Wilson.
Henderson and Warren Counties—Jonathan Simpson.
Peoria County—Julius Manning.
Stark County—Norman H. Purple.
Marshall, Woodford and Putnam Counties—John Burns.
La Salle, Livingston and Grundy Counties—Alexander Campbell, Perry A. Armstrong.
Kendall County—Thomas Finnie.
Will, DuPage, Kankakee and Iroquois Counties—Francis Goodspeed, J. W. Paddock, Henry C. Childs.
Kane and De Kalb Counties—Stephen B. Stinson.
Bureau County—Robert T. Templeton.
Mercer, Henry and Rock Island Counties—George W. Pleasants.
Lee and Whiteside Counties—John Dement.
Ogle County—Charles Newcomer.
Jo Daviess and Carroll Counties—Wellington Weigley, Henry Smith.
Stephenson County—Williard P. Naramore.
Winnebago County—Porter Sheldon.
Boone and McHenry Counties—William M. Jackson, Luther W. Lawrence.
Lake County—Elisha P. Terry.
Cook County—John Wentworth, Melville W. Fuller, Elliott Anthony, John H. Muhlke.
Madison County—Samuel A. Buckmaster.
Jersey County—William A. Allen.
Kane County—Adoniram J. Joslyn.
Knox County—W. Sheldon Gale.

## CHAPTER XXIII.

### Constitutional Convention of 1869-70.

SEVEN years after the constitutional convention of 1862 had adjourned another was called together and entered upon the task of revising the Constitution which had been in existence since 1848. The war was then over and when the convention assembled, the delegates were in a chastened mood. The grave lessons which had been taught us during that long period which preceded and accompanied the war had not been forgotten, but all entered upon their duties with the ripe experience of men who had given to the subject of government the most profound study. Many had taken part in the war and had at various times been connected with the government, had filled high and honorable positions in the National and State government, had had long experience and great observation in local affairs, and knew the wants and requirements of the State thoroughly. We met in the Hall of the House of Representatives of the old State House on Monday, the 13th of December, 1869, at 2 o'clock in the afternoon, and the final adjournment took place on the 13th of May, 1870.

The delegates were nearly equally divided in politics and an occurrence happened in regard to the selection of a permanent chairman of the convention, very similar to that which took place on the assembling of the constitutional convention of 1847. The delegates from Cook county had been elected as non-partisans and on a citizens' ticket. It was composed of Joseph Medill, editor of the Chicago Tribune, William F. Coolbaugh, S. S. Hayes, Daniel Cameron, Charles Hitchcock and myself. We held the balance of power and we concluded to assist in the organization of the House on as nearly a non-partisan basis as possible; and as the State was overwhelmingly republican, we thought of course that the permanent chairmanship should be given to a republican, and as Mr. Hitchcock was a republican lawyer of great learning and distinction we selected him. The minor offices were all about equally divided. A slight skirmish occurred at the opening of the convention between the opposing forces, as to who should be made temporary chairman, which imparted zest to the occasion. The friends of William Cary, of Jo Daviess, and the friends of John Dement, of Lee, were both proposed by parties at one and the same time, and they were both declared elected, both ascended the platform at the same moment and each "assumed the chair;" and on motions being made each would alternately put the motions and sometimes one would declare the same carried, while the other would declare them lost. The scene was so ludicrous and laughable that we were kept in an uproar nearly all the afternoon. On the adjournment of the convention for the day a consultation was had, and as it was shown that Mr. Dement had the greatest following, was an old pioneer, and had been in the constitutional convention of 1847 and 1862, it was decided that it would be no more than right to confer the honor of temporary presiding officer upon him, and expunge from the record all that had taken place under the auspices of the double-headed convention. This was agreed to, and the record of the convention as made up, shows nothing of the dual order of proceedings, but shows that Mr. Dement was elected temporary presiding officer by a vote of 45 to 38.

Col. Dement was a most worthy man, had been long connected with the State, and had been a member—as we have said—of the constitutional conventions of 1847 and 1862, and on taking the chair referred to these things in a most happy manner, as follows:

"*Gentlemen of the Convention:*—Usual as I know it is, for persons indicated as presiding officer for the mere temporary purpose of organizing a deliberative body to make a response in return to their friends, I certainly, under the peculiar circumstances by which I occupy this position, would not act in accordance with my feelings if I did not adopt some form of expressing my thanks to you. While there has been something that at first appeared as though unpleasant results might occur, my obligations and gratitude are eminently increased by what I firmly believe to be a harmonious conclusion of this little episode, as I shall please to call it. I am proud of it on account of the kindness and good feeling that I believe exists between the gentleman who was proposed for the same position as myself, and when I cast my vote for him, there was something more intended than a mere exchange of courtesies.

I respect the gentleman.

I respect those gentleman that cast their votes in his favor.

The compliment that I have received at your hands is greatly enhanced by the circumstances that have been mentioned already; nevertheless, without adopting these compliments and sentiments, I must say that I regard *this* compliment as high as it is possible for me to regard any, for the reason that there are so many here who are my seniors and superiors.

But l have another reason to feel grateful to you.

There are gentlemen here with whom I have been associated in the conventions of 1847 and 1862, and others here who are my friends of more than forty years standing.

These circumstances renew to my mind scenes of my life that are dear to me. They carry me back to that period when I explored the then wilderness territory of Illinois, and you will allow me, with yourselves, to express my gratitude, admiration and wonder at the great change which we experience in comparing these two periods—that, when our State contained probably not over twenty thousand white people, and the present, when we estimate its population by millions. We all recognize the fact that we occupy our present positions at the call of the great people in the exercise of the most conservative and liberal spirit, and also the obligations that these circumstances impose upon us of framing a constitution and a fundamental law, under the provisions of which the affairs of our State shall be administered for the prosperity and happiness of the millions of our general population as well as for their welfare in the future."

No address was ever conceived in better taste. It was well received, and coming from one so well known and respected, and from one who was so nearly connected with the pioneer period of the State, we all looked upon it as a happy augury and a most graceful ending to what at first bid fair to be an unpleasant beginning to our labors.

Hon. William Cary, who was brought into prominence by the occurrence above referred to, was a lawyer of prominence, who lived at Galena and who was elected a delegate from Jo Daviess county. He afterward became United States District Attorney for Utah Territory, then removed to Deadwood in Western Dakota, where he has resided ever since.

The men who composed that convention were many of them distinguished in their chosen walks long before their fellow-citizens selected them to assist in framing a fundamental law, under which our civil institutions have been ennobled, and our beloved commonwealth has attained the front rank in the galaxy of States. There, on that day, the 13th of December, 1869, were assembled men, venerable in years, who had adorned the Senate of the United States, men who had been members of Congress, distinguished jurists who had presided over the highest tribunal within our borders, men renowned in the marts of commerce, great bankers and merchants, the editors of great newspapers, leaders of public opinion, men who were authority in finance, representatives of the hardy yeomanry and tillers of the soil, who understood well the interests of the rural population, men who had traveled far and learned much, men who were masters of experimental science, physicians of renown, men of great classical attainments, men of native eloquence, ornaments of the Senate, the pulpit and the bar, and we will add, no one of whom ever presumed or had the temerity to believe that he was legislating for all time, or that when he died all wisdom in framing the laws and the Constitution of the greatest of our commonwealths, would die with him.

Hon. John M. Palmer was the Republican governor of the State at that time. His politics were sound, his instincts good, and he was one of the most intelligent public officers that ever occupied the executive chair.

He was frequently called upon by members of the convention for his advice, and so highly was he regarded that we caused to be published for our use all of his veto messages, which were quite numerous and very able, among which was his veto message of the famous Lake Front Bill, which was a master-piece of logic and one of the most important documents of the kind which ever emanated from the hand and brain of a lawyer in this State. He assisted by his advice in the framing of the executive article, and we will not withhold our tribute of respect and meed of praise, although strange vagaries may have since passed over his mental vision, and the lurid flames of the Chicago fire warped his judgment as to what constitutes the true limitations of the police power of the United States Government and that of the State in attempting to deal with unforeseen calamities and untold woes in the midst of a conflagration which had never been equaied since the destruction of Jerusalem in the days of Titus.

He took a prominent part in putting down the war of the Rebellion—was among the first to liberate the slaves while stationed in

Kentucky, and was a leader of public opinion. We trust that he will some day tell us why he became a democrat. He yet lingers on the stage of action as powerful as Ajax, as invulnerable as Achilles, in the full enjoyment of unimpaired energies, gloriously awaiting his apotheosis.

And right here we fall into reverie. The metamorphosis which political parties and many of our public men have undergone in relation to many public questions since the close of the war, is astonishing to us. It is not unlike that which took place in the times of George the First, as described by Macaulay in his review of the life and times of "The Earl of Chatham."

"Dante tells us that he saw in Malebolge, a strange encounter between a human form and a serpent. The enemies, after cruel wounds inflicted, stood for a time glaring on each other. A great cloud surrounded them, and then a wonderful metamorphosis began. Each creature was transfigured into the likeness of its antagonists. The serpent's tail divided itself into two legs; the man's legs intertwined themselves into a tail. The body of the serpent put forth arms; the arms of the man shrank into his body. At length the serpent stood up a man and spoke; the man sank down a serpent and glided, hissing, away. Something like this was the transformation which, during the reign of George the First, befell the two English parties. Each gradually took the shape and color of its foe, till at length the tory rose up erect, the zealot of freedom, and the whig crawled and licked the dust at the feet of power."

The lesson which this teaches is one of sad and solemn import, like the fall of Adam, and is attended with all of its consequences.

We entered upon the discharge of our duties with alacrity, and held an inquest upon all existing institutions, systems and departments of the government, and we let nothing escape us. We voted for every resolution of investigation in regard to all created things, from the days of the "mound builders" down to the construction of the Illinois and Michigan Canal. We pondered over all forms of government and all methods of exercising the elective franchise, and ended by adopting minority representation, which has, it is claimed, proved to be a great check on the tyranny of majorities, and like carrying a lighted lamp into regions heretofore black with darkness and surrounded with gloom. Hon. Joseph Medill, the veteran editor of the Chicago Tribune, was the great apostle and champion of this system of voting, and is to-day its warm defender.

It seems to have worked very well and has been the means of introducing those differing in politics to each other, and toning down in many instances the views of those who could never before see any good coming forth from Nazareth.

Minority representation was, at the time of its introduction, a novelty in political science, and was regarded as an experiment, and of it, it may be said: "There is no more hazardous enterprise than that of bearing the torch of truth into those dark and infected recesses in which no light has ever shone."

It was the choice and pleasure of Mr. Medill to penetrate the noisome vapors, and to brave the terrible explosion. He took his stand upon the popular parts of his political creed with firmness and decision, and defended them with an ability rarely equaled. He was like Milton when he stood up for divorce and regicide. He attacked the prevailing system without scruple, and bore down on it without let or hindrance. "His radiant and beneficent career resembled the god of light and fertility." He pushed through minority representation, and there it remains a monument to his foresight and an educator of the highest order. It astonished all the Bourbons and old-fashioned Andrew Jackson democrats, and moss-backed politicians of both parties, and they have never ceased to wonder at it till the present hour. We do not think that it has effected all that has been claimed for it, and the system is still open for debate.

What the delegates did on that occasion was by no means a finality, and it may be that in the rapid changes which have taken place, and are now taking place, much of their work may have been found useless or impracticable, and should be superseded by other systems and other provisions that we thought not of, but we doubt it. Men who have neither looked into the history of the past, nor yet troubled themselves to learn what happens year by year, will often be surprised to find what changes take place in a few months or years, and it is asserted that neither men nor measures can remain for an hour unchanged. This statement is partly true and partly false in its application to fixed governments, and changes in systems are not as rapid as they are sometimes thought to be. The members of that convention did the best that they knew how, and many now sleep from their labors and are at rest. The great majority of them have long since passed over into the better land.

A few of us still remain, but
> "When I remember all
> The friends so linked together,
> I've seen around me fall,
> Like leaves in wintry weather,
> I feel like one who treads alone,
> Some banquet hall deserted,
> Whose lights are fled,
> Whose garlands dead,
> And all but he departed."

LIST OF DELEGATES TO THE CONSTITUTIONAL CONVENTION OF 1869 AND 1870.

*First District.*—Alexander, Pulaski and Union Counties—William G. Allen.
*Second District.*—Massac, Pope and Johnson Counties—George W. Brown.
*Third District.*—Hardin, Saline and Gallatin Counties—W. G. Bowman.
*Fourth District.*—Lawrence and Wabash Counties—James M. Sharp.
*Fifth District.*—Franklin and Jefferson Counties—William B. Anderson.
*Sixth District.*—Jackson and Williamson Counties—James M. Washburn.
*Seventh District.*—Clinton and Washington Counties—Harvey P. Buxton.
*Eighth District.*—Monroe, Randolph and Perry Counties—J. H. Wilson, George W. Wall.
*Ninth District.*—Marion County—Silas L. Bryan.
*Tenth District.*—Wayne and Hamilton Counties—Robert P. Hanna.
*Eleventh District.*—Jasper and Crawford Counties—James C. Allen.
*Twelfth District.*—Clay and Richland Counties—James P. Robinson.
*Thirteenth District.*—Fayette and Effingham Counties—Beverly W. Henry.
*Fourteenth District.*—Edwards and White Counties—Charles E. McDowell.
*Fifteenth District.*—St. Clair County—William H. Snyder, William H. Underwood.
*Sixteenth District.*—Madison and Bond Counties—Charles F. Springer, Henry W. Billings.
*Seventeenth District.*—Clark and Cumberland Counties—John Schofield.
*Eighteenth District.*—Shelby County—George R. Wendling.
*Nineteenth District.*—Christian and Montgomery Counties—Edward Y. Rice.
*Twentieth District.*—Sangamon and Logan Counties—Milton Hay, Samuel C. Parks.
*Twenty-first District.*—Macoupin County—John W. Hankins.
*Twenty-second District.*—Jersey and Calhoun Counties—Robert A. King.
*Twenty-third District.*—Green County—James W. English.
*Twenty-fourth District.*—Pike and Scott Counties—William R. Archer, John Abbott.
*Twenty-fifth District.*—Cass and Brewer Counties—William S. Vandeventer.
*Twenty-sixth District.*—Menard and Mason Counties—O. H. Wright.
*Twenty-seventh District.*—Morgan County—Henry J. Atkins.
*Twenty-eighth District.*—Adams County—Orville W. Brown Onias C. Skinner.
*Thirtieth District.*—Schuyler County—Jesse C. Fox.
*Thirty-first District.*—Hancock County—David Ellis.

*Thirty-second District.*—Henderson and Mercer Counties—James S. Poage.
*Thirty-third District.*—Warren County—A. G. Kirkpatrick.
*Thirty-fourth District.*—Knox County—Alfred M. Craig.
*Thirty-fifth District.*—Fulton County—Lewis W. Ross, Samuel P. Cummings.
*Thirty-sixth District.*—Peoria and Stark Counties—Henry W. Wells, Miles S. Fuller.
*Thirty-seventh District.*—Tazewell County—Jonathan Merriam.
*Thirty-eighth District.*—McLean and DeWitt Counties—Reuben M. Benjamin, Clifton H. Moore.
*Thirty-ninth District.*—Coles, Douglas, Edgar and Vermillion Counties—John L. Trucker, Henry P. H. Brownwell, Richard B. Sutherland.
*Fortieth District.*—Champaign, Macon, Moultrie and Piatt Counties—Charles Emmerson, Abel Howard.
*Forty-first District.*—Kankakee County—Original delegate—Wm. H. Patterson, deceased; to fill vacancy, John P. Gamble.
*Forty-second District.*—Iroquois and Ford Counties—Addison Goodell.
*Forty-third District.*—Will and Grundy Counties—Wm. C. Goodhue, W. P. Pierce.
*Forty-fourth District.*—La Salle and Livingston Counties—George S. Eldridge, Joseph Hart, Nathaniel J. Pillsbury.
*Forty-fifth District.*—Bureau, Putnam, Woodford and Marshall Counties—S. D. Whiting, Jas. G. Boyne, Peleg S. Perley.
*Forty-sixth District.*—Henry County—George E. Wait.
*Forty-seventh District*—Rock Island County—Calvin Truesdale.
*Forty-eighth District.*—Whiteside County—James McCoy.
*Forty-ninth District.*—Lee County—John Dement.
*Fiftieth District.*—Ogle County—Joseph Parker.
*Fifty-first District.*—De Kalb, Boone Counties—Westel W. Sedgwick, Jesse L. Hildrup.
*Fifty-second District.*—Kane and Kendall Counties—Charles Wheaton, Henry Herrell.
*Fifty-third District.*—Lake County—Elijah M. Haines.
*Fifty-fourth District.*—McHenry County—Lawrence S. Church.
*Fifty-fifth District.*—Winnebago County—Robert J. Cross.
*Fifty-sixth District.*—Stephenson County—Thomas J. Turner.
*Fifty-seventh District.*—Jo Daviess and Carroll Counties—William Cary, David C. Wagner.
*Fifty-eighth District.*—Du Page County—Hiram H. Cody.
*Fifty-ninth District.*—Cook County—Joseph Medill, John C. Haines, Snowden S. Hayes.
*Sixtieth District.*—Portion of Cook County—William C. Coolbaugh, Charles Hitchcock.
*Sixty-first District.*—Portion of Cook County—Elliott Anthony, Daniel Cameron.

## CHAPTER XXIV.

### Is a Constitutional Convention Needed.

BUT death never interrupts the continuity in the life of governments or nations. And this brings us at length to the consideration of the question which we have been requested to discuss by the Bar Association of the State, to wit: "The needs of a Constitutional Convention." The form in which the question is presented would seem to imply that the matter had been already settled, and that all we had to do was to enumerate those needs or various topics or subjects which such a convention would be called upon to deal with, and then our task would be done. But we are assured that in propounding the question in this form, it was not intended that those who should be called upon to discuss the same, should assume the affirmative side instead of the negative, but that we should be left free to discuss the same as we see fit, and it is with this understanding that we now enter the lists as a "free lance."

The visionaries of this world we are conscious we can not satisfy, for we have no time and no inclination to meet their vague and declamatory asseverations. What we are concerned with is the science of government, and, as a practicable being, what form of government is best adapted to promote the happiness and secure the rights and interests of the people upon whom it is to act.

The American forms of government, both National and State, are in many respects the most intricate and complex of all forms of government since they deal with all the various concerns and relations of man, and must perpetually reason from the imperfect experience of the past for the boundless contingencies of the future. The most that we can hope to do under such circumstances is to make nearer and nearer approximations to truth, without our ever being certain of having arrived at it in a positive form. Government, however it may be defined, is nothing more nor less than the science of *adaptations*, variable in its elements, dependent upon circumstances and incapable of a rigid mathematical demonstration.

The men who insist that government is a matter of great simplicity, that its principles are so clear that there ought to be no mistake, and that any persons of ordinary skill ought to be able to frame a constitution for any State that will last at least a hundred years, are so devoid of all sense or reason that they are beyond our influence and beyond our hopes of salvation this side of the resurrection morn. If there is any one thing that has been demonstrated it is that in proportion as a government is free, the more complicated it is. "Simplicity belongs to those only where one *will* governs all, where one mind directs all and all others obey; where few arrangements are required, because no checks to power are allowed; where law is not a science, but a mandate to be followed and not to be discussed; where it is not a rule for permanent action, but a capricious and arbitrary dictate of the hour."

Burke, who during the last century, discoursed with great force and vigor in regard to the perfection of government, declared that whenever men have a right to do everything they want everything, and that in republics great vigilance is necessary to guard against the captivations of theories as well as the approaches of more insidious foes. And this is true, for government may be overthrown by indirect means as well as direct and open assaults.

"A thousand years scarce serves to form a State,
An hour may lay it in the dust; and when
Can man its shattered splendors renovate,
Recall its virtues back and vanquish Time and Fate."

The greatest engine of moral power known to human affairs is an organized, prosperous State. All that man in his individual capacity can do, all that he can effect by his private fraternities, by his ingenious discoveries and wonders of art, or by his influence over others—is as nothing compared with the collective, perpetuated influence on human affairs and human happiness, of a well-constituted, powerful commonwealth.

"It blesses generations with its sweet influences; even the barren earth seems to pour out its fruits under a system where rights and property are secure, while her fairest gardens are blighted by despotism."

In this country no State exists or can exist without a government organized under a constitution with which the people themselves have had something to do in framing and adopting. But the value of a constitution is relative as well as possible, and no nation is to perish that a political theory or political abstraction may strive vainly for realization. The life of a people can not be sacrificed for a political form or a political dogma. That is admitted. Was the Constitution that we made good or bad? Have its theories proved delusive and has its system of government become impracticable? Have things so changed that it is now necessary to discard it and make another one that shall conform to a changed order of things? Wherein, let us inquire, has this Constitution failed? what are the changes that are demanded, and in what respect shall it be amended?

Amendments are provided for in the Constitution; are the changes which are demanded so radical in their character they can not be met by amendments to be submitted to the people in the manner provided for in the instrument itself? Is a constitutional convention necessary, and if so, what are its needs?

The subject of "Needs of a Constitutional Convention" may be considered either affirmatively or negatively. You may, if you please, assume that the objections to the present Constitution are so numerous, so well known and widely admitted as to do nothing more, as we have said, than enumerate them and thereby avoid all discussion whatever. On the contrary, if no such state of things exists, if no such assumption can be indulged in, and if everything alleged is controverted, then the question becomes still more interesting. Let us see.

The Constitution was submitted to the people for adoption or rejection at an election which was held on the first Saturday in July, 1870, and was adopted by a most overwhelming vote.

It required a considerable legislation to put the Constitution into operation, and it was over a year before many of the laws were passed and went into effect, so that, while the Constitution has been in force twenty years, the reform measures passed in accordance with the same, have not been in operation that length of time.

We have, during the period which has intervened, been a somewhat close observer of its workings, and we have yet to learn that it has proved so unsatisfactory as to require many very radical amendments, although expressions have reached us now and then to that effect. Those who have gone to the extreme of declaring that we have outgrown the Constitution, and have denounced the slow method of amending the same, have not, we think, bestowed very much thought upon the subject, and have exercised but very little discrimination as to whether the reforms that they wish to bring about, could be effected by the ordinary methods of legislation or otherwise.

It is true that two years ago this matter was given some attention by the General Assembly. A resolution was introduced in favor of the calling of a convention, but it was defeated by a considerable majority. At that time the House resolved itself into a committee of the whole and indulged in general debate. It did not, however, as it appears from the records, limit the discussion to its own members, but invited outsiders to participate. Among those who were called upon to take part was a distinguished member of the bar, a resident of the city of Chicago, and a gentleman of large experience and observation. His remarks were published at the time, and as they have since been frequently referred to, we will briefly call attention to them. He reviewed at considerable length the present condition of things, and gave his experience of the difficulties and delays which ensued in endeavoring to legislate under the present Constitution; that evils had already developed that he considered of such magnitude as to be difficult, if not impossible, to be remedied by ordinary legislation; that corporations seemed to be multiplying to an alarming extent, and that, too, without check or limit; that the entire judicial system was defective in its organization and administration; that the Supreme Court is behind the age or rather the needs and the reputation of this State, because of its nomadic character; that its reputation suffered because of the division of its work, and the numerous places where it is held, and the small attention given by the united court to the business that comes before it—a thing which should be corrected in a new Constitution; that the idea of uniformity of laws, which was one of the chief characteristics of the Constitution, was impracticable when applied to counties, towns and townships, which varied so diametrically in many of their wants and necessities, that the legislation which was required for Chicago and Cook county was entirely inadequate; that local self-government was interfered with; that the provisions in the present Constitution in regard to amendments were too cumbersome, and were attended with too much delay; and ended by declaring that " It (the Constitution) is a document, prepared by men who thought they combined, not only the wisdom of the years in which they made it, but the wisdom of all the years to come. In a broad way, in a wide sense, that general suggestion covers my objection to the Constitution of 1870." His specific objections were immediately answered by Mr. Schuwerk and Hon. James Miller, of Stark county, lately deceased, and who was, we believe, at the time of his death, speaker of the House, and as we believe, fully and completely. They showed, at the time, that there was not one of the things that were complained of but what could be remedied by the General Assembly, or by submitting to the people amendments to the Constitution itself, and that a constitutional convention was entirely unnecessary. Since that time the matter has been discussed to some extent in the public press, and two entirely different views have been presented which are quite interesting.

## CHAPTER XXV.

### Radicalism and Conservatism.

ON the fifth day of January of this year (1891) there was published in one of the leading journals of Chicago, the "Chicago Herald," an editorial, reiterating the same ideas in substance as those put forth by Mr. Jewett, in which a direct appeal is made to the present General Assembly to take steps to call a convention to revise the Constitution, as the present Constitution had long ago been outgrown; that it answered its purposes for a time, but it was hedged about by so many obstacles to the free expression of the public will, it was so completely fortified against reasonable and necessary amendment, and it was drawn by men who had such an overpowering confidence in their own wisdom and ability to regulate human government for all time, that it long since ceased to be useful, and became merely a brake upon the wheels of progress.

The entire article is as follows:

"A CONSTITUTIONAL CONVENTION.

The great need of the State of Illinois at this time is a new Constitution. The instrument of 1870 was long ago outgrown. It answered its purpose for a time, but it was hedged about by so many obstacles to the free expression of the public will, it was so completely fortified against reasonable and necessary amendment, and it was drawn by men who had such an overpowering confidence in their own wisdom and ability to regulate human government for all time, that it long since ceased to be useful, and became merely a brake upon the wheels of progress.

It has been stated in 'The Herald' that all good citizens should combine this winter in favor of the submission of one amendment—only one being possible at any general election—that would strike out of that instrument the absurd clause which provides that only one section of the Constitution can be amended at a time; but a careful examination of the organic law and due consideration of the needs of the city and the State will convince most people that to attempt to whip the Constitution into shape by amendment would be a task involving years of delay and labors almost superhuman. It would be better for all concerned to call a constitutional convention, and to prepare an entirely new instrument for submission to the people. In no other way can our fundamental law be brought down to date and the egregious mistakes of 1870 be corrected.

When the present Constitution was submitted, Chicago was a city of 300,000 inhabitants, and not a man in Illinois dreamed that within a score of years there would be a million and a quarter of people within its limits. The Constitution is peculiarl oppressive to this great city, whose needs have outgrown the limitations placed upon it, but it is also obnoxious to the people of the State at large. This is true in particular in the matter of revenue. Under existing law the corporations of the State escape just taxation, and the burdens of government fall with greatest severity upon the poor. The system of minority representation is also a fraud and a disgrace to an intelligent people. It makes the effective expression of their will at the polls a matter of accident, and not infrequently defeats the very objects that it was ostensibly designed to serve. In almost every direction it blocks with mandatory prohibition every avenue of escape from wornout ideas, and conclusively bars the way to useful and necessary reforms born of human progress and the growing demands of city and State. It is antiquated, narrow and cranky, and it must soon give place to something that will meet the requirements of an enterprising people.

The General Assembly, which meets this week, will fail of its duty if it shall neglect to do its part toward calling a convention empowered to prepare and submit to the electors of the State a new organic law."

This was followed by several other articles of a similar character, to which the "Chicago Tribune" replied by a series of broadsides in the following vigorous manner:

### NO NEW CONSTITUTION WANTED.

Again the tax-devourers through their organs and other agencies are howling for a new constitution, and are urging the General Assembly "to do its part toward calling a convention, to prepare and submit to the electors of the State a new organic law." The existing Constitution it appears is not satisfactory to the tax-devourers, the beneficiaries of the mortgage bonds, the lobbyists, special bill venders, and all the tribe of public plunderers and leeches of the kind that utilized the old Constitution to the full extent of their opportunities and their greed. The existing Constitution was not framed as the organs of the tax-devourers would have it, by " Men with an overpowering confidence in their own wisdom," but by men who had the sound judgment to carry out the wishes of the people who elected them in devising an instrument of fundamental law, which would prevent the knavish and evil practices of unfaithful legislators, carried on under the constitution which it replaced—the selling of special franchises and special charters, the taxing and bonding of the people to an oppressive degree, the granting of special privileges to corporations without consulting the wishes and the interests of the people. The existing Constitution was framed in accordance with the desires of the people of the State, who wanted protection from corrupt and mercenary members of the Legislature, and their decision was arrived at after ample discussion by themselves and the mature deliberation of their freely chosen representatives, who were all fully aware of the evils they had to contend against.

The Constitution of 1870 has admirably fulfilled the purpose of its adoption by an almost unanimous vote. It has done away with the unendurable abuses that were practiced in all the Legislatures prior to 1870.

The present agitation for a new convention and a new Constitution is intended to help the tax-devourers, while placing responsibility for complicity with their schemes on the people at large. This plan will not succeed. The honest people of the State outside of Chicago who are well satisfied with the Constitution and the honest people of the city who object to more taxation for the benefit of professional tax-eaters will not submit to a new convention in which the lobbyists, the sharpers, and the Chicago Tammanyites might, through the agency of political machines, have a majority. A new convention might be called, but the people would not ratify the product of its deliberations. There is no occasion to incur the expense.

If necessary the provision of the Constitution preventing the submission of more than one amendment at any one general election may be repealed. Thereafter as many amendments as may seem proper may be submitted for popular approval or rejection. If certain provisions of the present fundamental law are objectionable the people will have the power to rescind or to eliminate them. But let us not risk the taking down of all the bars that have been put up to keep the tax-devourers, special charter venders, and corporation agents in their proper places.

### AGAIN THE WOLFISH HOWL FOR A NEW CONSTITUTION.

A few tax-eaters and certain newspapers, organs of officeholders, are clamoring for a new Constitution. But the people of the State of Illinois are making no such demand. They are holding no meetings to ask for a constitutional convention. They are making the question an issue at no election. The papers which represent them say nothing on the subject or speak only to denounce the proposition. Among the grievances of the farmers set forth in their platforms and resolves the Illinois Constitution finds no place. No city workingmen have said a word against it.

It is evident that the masses are not troubled by the assertion that they "tied their hands" when they adopted their present fundamental law and now "want them unbound." Of course they are not, for they do not believe it. They know it to be untrue. They have a better idea of the nature of State Constitutions than certain editorial writers who set themselves up as guides of the multitude, though ignorant of the subjects concerning which they give raw advice. When "The Tribune" sees papers posing as public instructors, and yet unacquainted with the fundamental principles of the matters they write about, it confesses that it does feel exasperated and would be glad to see a law passed which would keep such sheets from making fools of themselves and perhaps befooling their readers.

The Constitutions of States which have a representative form of government are not limitations of the powers of, and do not tie the hands of, the people who make them, but of the representatives, State and municipal, to whom the people intrust from time to time legislative functions. If it were certain that Legislatures would be composed of the wisest and most honest men in the community, who would never boodle, steal or otherwise abuse their trust, there would be no need of a Constitution more than a few lines long. All that would be necessary would be to fix the number of members of the Legislature and their term of office, and to make brief provision for the executive and judicial departments of the government. But the experience of every State has proved that legislators will abuse their trust, and that they can be bought or influenced to do things which the people, if they could come together, as in town-meeting, would never vote to do. Hence, the steady evolution of American State Constitutions, with their increasing restrictions—not on the people, but on those agents whom the people, unable to meet in a primary body, select as their representatives and administrators to act for them.

Such has been the experience of Illinois. The Constitution of 1818 gave large powers to the Legislature. That body abused them by plunging headlong into a vast wildcat scheme of internal improvements for the benefit of contractors, which bankrupt the State. The result was the Constitution of 1848, which stripped the Legislature of its power to abuse its trust and betray the people by running up a crushing State debt. But the men who made that Constitution were not far-seeing. They did not perceive that it was as important to protect the minor political divisions of the State from financial wreck and ruin as it was the State itself. The legislators elected under the organic law of 1848 were even more false to their trust than those chosen under that of 1818. Their professions to their constituents before election were admirable; their practices after election, when they got to Springfield, were villainous. They empowered the city council of Chicago to issue millions of bonds for all sorts of schemes without consulting the people. They put it in the power of the speculators of smaller municipalities to fasten mortgages on the taxpayers to help railroads, rolling mills, grist mills, coal mines, glass factories, woolen mills, and every variety of private enterprise. These corrupt members enacted, with the aid of the lobby, and sold to corporations, charters granting them special privileges and immunities. They were given by the Constitution authority to pass general laws on the subject of corporations, but they refused persistently to do it, for it would have deprived them of the boodle made from the sale of special charters. They extended the terms of officers without consulting the people, and increased their fees and salaries, though already too high.

The people stood this misconduct on the part of their agents for many years, for they promised before every election to do better "the next time." Finally, unable to stand it any longer, they ordered a convention and adopted the Constitution of 1870, and limited still further, not their own powers, which are still as sovereign as they ever were, but those of their representatives. For their own protection they put a curb not merely on members of the General Assembly but on county boards, city councils and township officers. They took from them, large and small, the power to blanket-mortgage the property of their constituents and to tax them till they staggered.

The people of Illinois are not dissatisfied with those restrictions on representatives. To them they owe low taxes and arrest of debts, and they do not wish to untie the hands of their agents and let them again plunder at their sweet will in partnership with the vultures of the lobby. On the contrary, they are, if anything, in favor of drawing the constitutional strings a little tighter. The people have not been pleased altogether with the conduct of their representatives in the General Assembly for the last few years. They have seen on the part of too many of them a disposition to abuse the powers they have, and are inclined to think they could be curtailed judiciously.

Thus it will be seen that those who are working for a new "free-and-easy, go-as-you-please" Constitution are not trying to "untie the hands of the people" but of their agents. They want to secure for the latter the same unlimited power of attorney that they had under the Constitution of 1848. They want to revive the profitable industry of drawing up charters by the hundred, granting special franchises, and then lobbying them through the Legislature. They want to give again to the General Assembly its power to create monopolies for a price. They hanker after the old days when public taxes and public funds could be diverted to private uses. They wish to see the wealth which has been saved up during twenty years of low taxes and arrested mortgages handed over to the unchecked control of the tax-eaters. They want to let down the bars so that the thieves and speculators may get into the fat pastures they have been kept out of so long.

This is what they want, but they dare not confess it. The people see through their little game, and neither in the Legislature nor at the polls can they get the necessary number of votes. The people will not untie the hands of their agents, knowing well that the first use they would make of their freedom would be to abuse their power and to plunder their constituents, as was done under the Constitution of 1848.

The "Chicago Herald" says that it is useless to prepare bills giving the Chicago justices fixed salaries instead of fees, because such legislation would be in violation of the Constitution. It says:

"Any legislation touching justices of the peace, police magistrates, and constables must apply to the entire State, and it is highly improbable that while this stupid enactment remains in force an amendment consistent with it can be devised which will satisfy the General Assembly, for there is little dissatisfaction throughout the interior with the working of the justices' law as it stands."

This sweeping assertion is based on that clause of the Constitution which forbids the Legislature to pass special laws "regulating the jurisdiction and duties of justices of the peace, police magistrates, and constables." But no bill which has been drafted as yet violates this provision. The pay of justices has nothing to do with their jurisdiction or duties. The subject of pay of public officers is touched on elsewhere in the Constitution, where it is provided that the fees of public officers shall not be increased or diminished "during the term for which said officers are elected or appointed." The terms of the present Chicago justices are about expiring. This is just the time, then, to fix the pay of their successors.

The "Herald" does not seem to be aware of—or suppresses—the fact that while the fees of justices of the peace are uniform throughout the State the Constitution does not require it. The Legislature is given power to divide the counties of the State into three classes and fix the fees for county and township officers in each class. It has done so in the case of many officers. Thus the fees Cook county constables are permitted to charge are smaller than those of other constables throughout the State. As Cook county is a county of the third class the Legislature can give the justices of the peace therein just what pay it pleases.

But the power of the General Assembly to give Chicago justices salaries does not rest on this classification of counties, but on the fact that these justices are a class by themselves and that the Legislature is nowhere forbidden to provide for their payment in a different way from that of other justices. It can not give them broader or narrower jurisdiction than other justices. It can not provide that business shall be carried on in their courts in a special way, but when it is their payment which is concerned the discretion of the Legislature is unlimited—except that there must be no change during a man's term of office.

All this is so simple, so plain, that the "Herald" must know it. But for some reason that paper is dissatisfied with the present Constitution and wants a convention called to frame a new one. It will not accept the suggestion of the "The Tribune" that provision be made for the submission of many amendments at the same time, instead of but one, as now. It says:

"The Constitution of 1870 is a nuisance to the commonwealth. It bars the people's way in every direction. It locked all the doors of progress and reform and put the keys in the pockets of a number of conceited cranks who fancied that when they got through tinkering a Constitution the State would cease growing, and we should live according to the code of rules they had agreed upon. The time has come for Illinois to break its bonds. The Constitution of 1870 is not worth amending. It must go."

And it has much more to say of the same kind. But there is a remarkable absence of specific objections to the present organic law. There is no enumeration of the things which ought to be done, the doing of which it prevents. The allegation that under it Chicago justices of the peace can not be paid by salaries is the only definite complaint yet made. If that were true—which it is not—it would not justify a constitutional convention.

There is something suspicious in these vague accusations, in this assertion that changes are necessary, without specifying the changes. Can it be that the change which these gentlemen hanker after but dare not state, relates to the beneficent provision preventing municipalities plunging into unlimited expenditures and wrapping themselves in mortgages as in a blanket? For years many have been trying to let down the bars which have kept the tax-eaters out of the pasture. They understand perfectly that an amendment repealing the debt-limiting provisions of the Constitution would be beaten by 200,000 votes, but they hope that if a convention were called to frame a new Constitution it might be handled so skillfully as to slip in a clause which could be interpreted so as to give every municipality the power to borrow as long as it could find lenders.

Unless the "defects" of the present Constitution are stated more specifically than they have been, it must be assumed that the wish to repeal it is confined to the tax-grabbers."

## CHAPTER XXVI.

### Limitations and Restraints are Necessary in all Free Governments.

AS indicators of public feeling or public opinion the views here presented may probably be taken as fairly representing two theories of State government and two sets of opinions which are entertained by those differing in politics and in regard to the various economic questions now agitating the country.

On the one side are found those who resent all interference on the part of the State with local self-government and who are for removing all restraints upon legislation in every form, either by the State or by municipalities, and who are especially indignant at those who, in framing the Constitution, undertook to set bounds to the levying and collecting of taxes and the debt power of city councils; while on the other are ranged those who are of a more conservative character, and who believe that it is not only judicious for the people to have some *fixed rules* in regard to these subjects, but it corresponds with the most advanced and enlightened views of all civilized governments, that *the people ought in many things to limit themselves.* The experience of our own State has, we think, not only demonstrated the wisdom of such a course of procedure, but every other State will substantiate it.

It is necessary to regulate the association of men with each other to prevent the invasion of their liberties and rights, and to promote that good which society is willing to do for its members.

There is a class of men who consider it a great hardship that the Legislature, and counties, cities, villages and all kinds of municipal corporations, are not permitted to do just as they please, and incur debts to any extent, and for any purpose that speculators and schemers may devise, but everybody knows that if *the people* were not protected from the lawlessness and extravagance of their own representatives, that they would be ruined, and general insolvency ensue. It is very easy to cry out against what is termed paternal governments, against public guardians, and against every form of restraint on legislation, as an infringement of the liberties of the people. But there never was a voluntary organization of men associated together to carry on *any* great enterprise in which each and every one had an interest, but that they voluntarily agreed to, and entered into certain contracts and undertakings, and adopted rules and regulations for their government and guidance. Any other course would be simply to inaugurate chaos and invite anarchy.

The individuals who compose a State are not all of the same mind, and in the nature of things can not be; therefore it is, as all who have given the subject any study know, that there must be restraints and limitations in all free governments.

And this is the more necessary when we consider the varied and diverse character of the people composing the State, and who would, if left to their own notions, engage in every conceivable enterprise, from the establishment and support of a State church down to running all railroads at State expense, and carrying the people for nothing.

As the discussion has proceeded we have observed a considerable advance in the positions of those who think that we ought to have a constitutional convention, and they have grown more bold and aggressive. The Legislature is now in session, and they demand that all restrictions on legislation must be removed, and they now say: "The people want a constitutional convention. The State urgently demands that relief be had from the rusty shackles of a code, worthy only of the unprogressive and unintelligent. They demand the right to make their laws *freely*, according to changed conditions. The old Constitution must retire with its ancient predecessor."

Now it may be that "the State" or the people, are prepared to eliminate from the present Constitution all restrictions on special legislation, special charters and special privileges, and return to the old order of things as they existed under the Constitution of 1848. If they are ready to do this, we are perfectly willing that they should indicate it by their votes. The people adopted the present Constitution, and they are responsible, of course, for its longer continuance. If they say, after a full and fair consideration, that the time has come to change it, to throw it off and strike off all restraints, "shackles" or "fetters," if you please to call them so, then we shall be content. It is not a personal matter with those who framed the Constitution, for most of them are already in their graves. It is, we repeat, a matter to be determined by the people, in their sober senses, and not by the "high rollers," who are swinging their hats and crying "hoop la," before the winning post is reached. If the experience of the past amounts to nothing, then let its lessons go unheeded.

We stand upon the threshold of the mighty future, and all the events of the past seem to dwindle in their dimensions and appear insignificant.

We stand in the midst of events which may result in a catastrophe or a revolution. What is in store for us in the near future, no one can tell. Let us wait and see.

The State of Illinois has during its brief existence of not quite seventy-three years held four constitutional conventions, and it has been our fortune, good or bad, to have been a member of two of them, and on several occasions before, we have heard the charge, that those who engage in the business of framing a constitution act as if they thought that they possessed all of the wisdom of the past, the present and the future, and acted as if they thought that when they died all wisdom would die with them. Now the charge of having the "big head," for that is what it all amounts to, is a charge easily made and may be hard to answer, especially if those who are charged with the offense are arraigned before a tribunal that they can not attend, and before judges that refuse to heed their mute appeals. But as it is a charge entirely personal in its character, we submit that it would be far more prudent on the part of those making such charges, to husband their resources and proceed to answer their arguments, rather than "carp at their presence."

The dervise in the Arabian tale did not hesitate to abandon to his comrade the camels with their load of jewels and gold, while he retained the casket of that mysterious juice which enabled him to behold at a glance all the hidden riches of the universe. Surely it is no exaggeration to say that no external advantage is to be compared with that purification of the intellectual eye, which gives us to contemplate the infinite wealth of the mental world, all the hoarded treasures of its primeval dynasties, all the shapeless ore of its yet unexplored mines. A constitution maker ought, we have no doubt, in order to come up to the proper standard, to have the cunning and discernment of the Arabian dervise, so that nothing could escape his observation. He ought to be able, not only to discern "the signs of the times," but to look forward far into the future, and prepare a way for the coming generations, so straight, that a wayfaring man though a fool may not err therein.

To avoid this charge of arrogating superior wisdom, he must, it appears, legislate with a halter around his neck, and be prepared in case of failure to be arraigned before that tribunal of posterity, where no excuses are tolerated and no errors are condoned.

The impetuous and appalling rush with which the human intellect has moved forward in the last fifty years in the career of truth and liberty, and in the development of the physical resources of the country, has been such that leaders of public opinion have, it appears, become impatient, and cry faster and faster, even though the world should be endangered by the increased velocity. A constitution should not, we submit, be made a foot-ball of, or be degraded to that of an ordinary statute, which may be enacted to-day and repealed to-morrow.

## CHAPTER XXVII.

### The Power and Scope of a Constitutional Convention.

"CONSTITUTIONS are in politics what paper money is in commerce. They afford great facilities and conveniences. But we must not attribute to them that value which really belongs to what they represent. They are not power, but symbols of power, and will, in an emergency, prove altogether useless, unless the power for which they stand be forthcoming."

The real power by which the community is governed, is made up of all the means which all its members possess of giving pleasure or pain to each other.

The word "Constitution," as employed in modern times, means a system of government in which the people have some share in making the laws—and a constitutional convention, in American political grammar, means that special agency which the people select to transact the business of fundamental legislation, and to draw up for them, and on their behalf, their organic laws.

This agency is something akin to that of the school of the philosophers or amphictyonic council where only sovereigns are delegates, and where not only the fundamentals of human society are considered, but where the formation and arrangement of all the functions and powers of government are defined, marked out and limited. In its true sense a constitutional convention sustains a close and intimate official relation to the State, and is charged with definite and not discretionary, indeterminate or unlimited functions. "It always acts under a commission for a purpose ascertained and limited by law or custom. Its principal feature as contradistinguished from the revolutionary convention, is that at every step and movement of its existence, it is subaltern—it is evoked by the side and at the call of a government pre-existing and intended to survive it for the purpose of administering to its special needs. It never supplants the existing organization and never governs." And here we will remark that, although this agency is as well known in the United States as almost any other institution connected with the government, yet there was scarcely ever a constitutional convention convened, but what its powers and prerogatives were sought to be amplified and magnified in the strangest manner, and the claim put forth that whatever it does is done by the people "in their primary and sovereign capacity," and that it is clothed with an omnipotence so transcendent and far-reaching that nothing can control it. This claim was put forth in a most marked manner in Pennsylvania at an early day, in Massachusetts in 1852, was advocated in this State in 1862, and in 1869-70, and was the prevailing doctrine in most, if not all, of the Southern States, up to the time of the war of secession; and acting upon this idea and this theory, constitutional conventions were made use of as among the most efficient organizations ever devised to bring about secession, because upon a simple vote of the majority secession could be carried, and was carried. To effect it there was needed but a vote of a few conspirators, sitting as a constitutional convention, pretending to utter the voice of the people and refusing to submit their ordinances to the test of a popular vote, under the false plea that neither the theory of the convention system nor the practice of the fathers made such a submission necessary.

With the close of the war the extreme notions of State sovereignty, and the powers inherent in constitutional conventions have, we trust, passed away, and we would not have referred to it here if the same theories had not been put forward and adhered to in the recent constitutional convention held in the State of Mississippi, and which convention adopted a constitution that it had framed without submitting it to a vote of the people.

Theoretically, it seems to be a very simple matter to establish a perfect government; but practically, it is not so simple. Selfishness, greed, ignorance and passion are found to be constantly disturbing forces, and what is simple in theory is difficult in practice. Fortunately the governing genius of the people is equal to almost any emergency, and whenever a tendency to recklessness and extravagance has shown itself, the people have stepped forward and either checked it or put an end to it.

The practical statesman takes cognizance of fixed facts, and is on his guard against hypocrisy, ignorance, humbugs, incapacity, dishonesty, corruption, frauds and defalcations, and no constitution which opens wide the door for such practices either on the part of Legislatures, city councils, county commissioners or school boards, ought to be upheld or tolerated. Constitutions are in these modern times made by the people, and if they select a few of their fellowmen to draw them up for them and propose them, then their responsibility ends; it is the *people* who adopt them. The aggregate will of the people is usually better than the average intelligence of the individuals composing the people, because they accept the judgment of men wiser than themselves.

Bad men may deceive, mistakes may be made, but the evil will be temporary and will be reformed in obedience to the right feeling of the greater numbers of the people. We do not worship the Constitution as a fetish or cling to it like the Twelve Tables. We do not look upon conventions as an earthly providence and we do not think that a constitution should be looked upon as a sceptre over a free people in the hands of dead men. The true office of a constitution is to determine the order but not the course and destination of the people. "It is not providence nor destiny. The years and what they bring are withdrawn from the gaze of conventions as well as of men. They have no more a horoscope to forecast the future in the lives of nations than of individuals, nor can they outmaster time, nor wrest the secret from the years. The Constitution is to provide that the people shall stand together and march together, but their line of march is hidden from it. The nation is formed in the changing conditions of history. It must pass through conflicts which the prescience of no assembly can anticipate and they will not regulate their coming by the action of any convention, nor conform to its project, nor abide in its provision.

The aim of the Constitution is to leave each generation free to do its own work, to which it is called, but in the continuity of the nation and in its normal process, and therein it becomes the assertion of the unity of law with the realization of the freedom of the nation in its being in history."

This is, indeed, the teaching of true philosophy, but, like all general statements, is subject to certain limitations. It does not contain all the truth, for there should be some stability in our Constitutions or else we will be constantly engaged in the process of experiment and change, which all students of political science and the wisest statesmen regard as public calamities akin to revolutions. The Constitution which provides for its own amendment furnishes the most ample means for permanence and progress and for setting aside the inconsistent and incongruous, the vague and the incomplete.

We see no sense whatever in calling upon the people at the present time to assemble and rehearse anew the fundamentals of government, and we do not believe that the people are so dissatisfied with the workings of the Constitution as to demand any radical revision anywhere.

Constitutional conventions, in our American political grammar and in our American system of government, belong, as we have said, to the *genus* Legislature. The consequence is that they often contain vast aggregates of ignorance and inexperience, like ordinary Legislatures, and indulge in immeasurable platitudes and endless debates over matters long since thoroughly settled in political science and in the science of government.

No constitutional convention should, in my judgment, ever be called without selecting in advance a committee of the wisest men in the State to carefully consider the defects in the existing Constitution which it is proposed to amend, and to point out the remedies, and provide in advance the changes to be made and the reforms to be inaugurated; not that what may be proposed should bind anybody or limit the sphere of the investigations or action of those called upon to act, but that the convention may have something to act upon at once, and not waste valuable time by discussing impracticable and incoherent theories of government. If government is a science, and if written constitutions are necessary to the well-being of society, then it is due to the people that they should approximate as near perfection as the skill of man can make them and the lot of humanity will allow.

## CHAPTER XXVIII.
### Legislative Provisions in Modern Constitutions.

THE constitutions which have been framed by the various States in modern times differ very materially from those that we meet with in the early days of the republic. The earlier constitutions were confined to outlining the general structure of the government and did not undertake to enact laws and prescribe the conditions under which laws might be made and executed. Now you can find in them whole statutes, from those regulating freight bills, warehouse charges and homestead exemptions, down to those forbidding the sale of intoxicating liquors and the practice of law.

Some of our modern constitutions are getting to be little better than caricatures and are overloaded with legislation, the most notable instances of which are California and Mississippi. California especially is but very little better than a volume of State statutes and Mississippi falls but little behind it.

It will compare favorably with the "Svod Zakonof" or collection of Russian laws of which that part relating to the police alone contains five thousand sections. The Constitution of the United States is a model in many respects for all States, because it confines itself to a clear sketch of fundamentals and leaves as much as possible to be developed by circumstances. It is this feature of it which gives it flexibility and leaves so much to be developed by circumstances.

There is considerable legislation to be found in the Constitution of 1870; but if any one will take the pains to examine the list of committees who had in charge the various subjects in that convention, they will find that it was composed of men of very great experience in our State affairs, and they declared it was absolutely necessary to provide the restraints upon the General Assembly in order to bring about any of the reforms that the people demanded, and they were inserted for that purpose.

Many of the things which are there enumerated would, ordinarily, we admit, be absolutely within the jurisdiction of the Legislature, but what people ever suffered as we have done from special legislation and special charters and the enactment of private laws and the grant to individuals of special privileges?

(143)

Our legislatures had also from time to time been disgraced by unseemly struggles between contending political parties over the organization of the General Assembly. This we provided for. The forms to be pursued in the style of laws, methods of revision and enactment of the same, the appropriation and expenditure of public moneys, prohibiting special legislation upon a number of subjects which are particularly enumerated and set forth.

This legislative feature extends to counties and the removal of county seats, homestead exemptions, the organization of banks and corporations and of railroads and warehouses, which in these modern times almost dominate the State itself, and which we deemed it necessary for the State to absolutely govern and control.

Men say in answer to all these things that those who framed a constitution on such a theory, acted as if they considered the people utterly incapable of self-government, and as if they thought that they embodied "all of the wisdom of the present and of future generations."

Such remarks betray a most superficial knowledge of the condition of society and that they have bestowed but very little thought upon the subject; for, as Daniel Webster once said: "It is a fundamental rule in the structure of human society, that mankind must not only limit the powers of their rulers, but must limit themselves." No body of any sense undertakes to bind posterity to anything; but human governments do have a continuity, and in order that they may not degenerate into chaos, or society resolve itself into its original elements, rules must be provided for cohesion and continuance, although mankind may rise up to-morrow and overthrow the same. No government that was ever yet formed provided for its own dissolution.

## CHAPTER XXIX.

## An Examination of Some of the Objections Which Are Urged against the Present Constitution.

LET us now briefly examine a little more in detail, some of the objections which have been urged against the Constitution, and see if they are sound and reliable and based upon proper foundations. We enter a general denial to each and every one of them, and call for the proofs.

We plead the general issue. Those who make charges hold the affirmative and should prove them. And when anybody asserts that any given thing can not be accomplished under the provisions of a constitution, it is his duty to show wherein and why it can not be done, because, as we have already said, in the absence of a limitation on the Legislature, or a prohibition against doing any given thing, the Legislature, or as we term it in our Constitution, "the General Assembly," is as omnipotent as that of the British Parliament. The narrow constructionists will receive no encouragement from the example of Chief Justice Marshall, who expounded the Constitution with the wisdom of the sage and the prescience of the seer. In the case of New York v. Miln, 11 Peters, 139, the Supreme Court of the United States say: "A State has the same undeniable and unlimited jurisdiction over all persons and things within its territorial limits as any foreign nation, where that jurisdiction is not surrendered or restrained by the Constitution of the United States; that by virtue of this, it is not only the right, but the bounden and solemn duty of a State to advance the safety, happiness and prosperity of its people, and to provide for its general welfare by any and every act of legislation which it may deem to be conducive to these ends, when the power over the particular subject, or the manner of its exercise, is not surrendered or restrained by the Constitution and laws of the United States."

The rule, in regard to the construction of the provisions of a constitution, is very often violated both by courts and lawyers; but Chief Justice Marshall declared long years ago that the rule was to construe all such instruments liberally, and as common men would adjudge the meaning of words used by them in expressing themselves in the ordinary transactions and business of life—not technically, and in such a manner as to defeat the intention of the framers, which was to be gathered from the instrument itself, and from the facts and circumstances surrounding them at the time.

When there is no ambiguity in the words themselves and the intention is plain, then there is no room for construction, for there is nothing to construe.

A constitution has no inherent power and no abstract quality to deliver any people from all of their distresses. It is not for the individual nor for the nation to be saved by any system, however complex, nor any dogma, however subtle. The Constitution may become itself only the mark which hides from an age its degeneracy or as the mausoleum which conceals its decay. But let us treat this subject fairly. Let us commence with the preamble and trace its outlines and provisions, article by article and section by section till the end, and see wherein it falls short of providing a system adequate to all the wants of the people. It was not drafted by one man and it was not designed to provide for everything, and in that respect differs from a statute, completely and entirely. That inconsistencies may sometimes be found and incongruities may be noticed, does not militate against the instrument as a whole, if there still exists sufficient to furnish adequate remedies for wrongs and abuses.

The true scope of a constitution is that of a framework of government and not a complete and completed structure. All that is ever required, and all that ever should be presented, is a proper sketch, skeleton and framework and not a rounded whole. The fact that the Supreme Court of the State leads a nomadic existence is due to the Legislature; for the 4th section of the 6th article of the Constitution expressly provides that "judicial decisions may be altered or diminished in number and the times and *places* of holding said court may be changed by law."

Here the remedy is with the Legislature, and if the change is not made from three places to one, it is wholly the fault of the General Assembly. There was a time in the history of this State when "court days" and "cattle fairs" were great attractions, and that custom still prevails to a considerable extent, we believe, in Kentucky; but if this ever did have any application to the Supreme Court where the great amount of work is performed in retirement and not in "the show ring," the sooner the custom is dropped the better. The Supreme Court ought to be held like that of the old Court of Common Pleas in England, "in *certum loco*," in one place and that place the capital. Originally, it does appear that the cider men and petty chapmen did receive great gains from the annual recurrence of court days, and the advent of the great dignitaries that accompanied the judges as in the days of *Aula Regis;* but that time is past, and "boarding around" should cease. It is simply disgraceful that this thing should longer be tolerated, and the sooner the ancient practice of going in eyre should cease, the better. The Supreme Court ought to hold its sessions at the capital and nowhere else.

That there should be any inconvenience arising from the ease, and facilities afforded for obtaining charters of incorporation under our laws, is a matter wholly within legislative control; for, instead of inaugurating the system of dropping a dime into the slot, and receiving a charter of incorporation for the same, the Legislature have only to adopt a fee or charge for the same *sufficient in amount* to defray the expenses of employing a corps of clerks to register and record and issue the same, and this abuse would stop. In other words, no corporate charter should be issued without paying an adequate amount into the public treasury, sufficient to cover every expense, which should be, on the average, twice what it is to-day. Then there ought to be appointed by law a public examiner, such as exists in Minnesota, to examine at any time into the soundness of corporations holding franchises from the State and into all public accounts of all public officers.

The amount of money which could be realized from fees and charges for the granting of corporate charters would go far to relieve the taxpayers from their burdens, and would serve to curtail the number of the same. Our State is swarming with corporations of all sorts, characters and kinds, which seem to be almost beyond control. But it is the fault of the Legislature that it is so, and not the Constitution of this State. In Pennsylvania, and in many other States, large sums of money have been and are realized from the granting of corporate franchises under their laws; but their charges cover something beyond the cost of the paper and attaching the State seal to them.

# CHAPTER XXX.

## The Administration of the Criminal Law in the State of Illinois.

ONE of the most necessary and august functions of a government is to administer justice and it is impossible to diminish the authority of justice without taking away from the government a portion of its strength. The judicial system which has been provided by the Constitution of this State may be defective and the administration of the law unsatisfactory, but we submit that the reason for this must be looked for somewhere else than in the Constitution or the laws themselves. *Nisi prius* judges have in the State of Illinois been, by various judicial decisions, dicta and practices, deprived of almost all the powers that they ever possessed by the common law, until to-day their position in the trial of a case is but very little better than that of a moderator in an ordinary debate. They have become but little better than a nonentity, and the fault is not in the Constitution, but rests somewhere else, and entirely outside that instrument. Trace the history of a law suit in this State, and especially that of a criminal case, and see how and in what manner it is dealt with by the court of last resort.

After a criminal is tried his case is removed to the Supreme Court. For what purpose? To determine the guilt or innocence of the prisoner at the bar? No. The jury that tried him has already passed upon that. For error in law? No, that can not be, for *by the statute* of the State of Illinois, it is provided that the jury *are the judges of the law and the facts.* What then? Well, it is to determine whether the judge that tried him and the prosecuting officer that prosecuted him are guilty, whether they pursued the right methods to ascertain the facts. Was the presentation of the case fair, was there too much severity exhibited by the State's Attorney in his cross-examination of witnesses, was the jury the right kind of a jury for the prisoner? Were counsel for the defense permitted to examine them at sufficient length to ascertain whether they had any bias or had right ideas upon the subject of "reasonable doubt," would they convict upon "doubtful or unsatisfactory evidence," would they "guess a man into the penitentiary?" Were these questions answered fully and satisfactorily? What kind of a closing speech did the State's Attorney make—was it one that aroused the feelings of the jury to the highest pitch or did he proceed on a low key?

How many times was the State's Attorney interrupted in his closing speech by the counsel for the prisoner and why was it that the court did not rebuke him in language befitting the occasion?

How did the judge behave? Did he make any remarks during the course of the trial which had the effect to influence the jury? Was his bearing such as became the time and the occasion? Were his rulings fair, and were they according to law "as laid down by the jury"—or by the sages of the law? Did he place the right mark on the instructions which the counsel engaged in the case so kindly and courteously handed him just a moment before the case closed? Did he make a mistake when he wrote "given" on this instruction and "refused" on that? That is the important question. It is true that a prisoner at the bar has no right to resort to legerdemain in order to clear himself, but it amounts to exactly that and nothing more. Technical rules may be useful to guide the ignorant and unsophisticated through the mazes of the criminal law but they should never be carried so far as to produce results plainly detrimental to public repose or to a sound administration of the judicial system.

A constitutional convention may be required to confer upon judges the power to superintend the impaneling of juries and to control the trial of persons charged with heinous offenses, for almost every step that is taken seems to tend to strip them of all power in this matter. The time has come, we think, in the history of this country, when some practical rule should be adopted in regard to the competency of jurors, and that rule is the one that was provided for in the first Constitution of Massachusetts, as early as 1783, to wit: A man who commits a crime shall be "tried by a jury as fair and impartial as the lot of humanity will permit," and not by saints and angels. To require that jurors shall come to the investigation of criminal charges with minds entirely unimpressed by what they had heard in regard to them, or entirely without information concerning them, would be in many cases to exclude every man from the panel who was fit to sit as a juror. With the present means of information the facts or rumors concerning an atrocious crime are in a very few hours or days, at farthest, spread before every man of reading and intelligence within the district from which jurors are to be drawn, and over the whole country, if the atrocity be especially great. The greater the enormity of the crime the more complete is the protection afforded a villain from punishment by a jury. The opinion of Judge Lockwood in the case of McKinney v. The People, 2 Gil. 548, may be consulted always with profit.

To plead under the ancient arches of Westminister Hall, in the name of the English nobles, for great nations and kings separated from him by half the world, was to Burke the height of human glory. There are those who seem to think that if they can appear in behalf of some ideal monster, that they are justified in resorting to every species of trickery and chicanery, to overawe witnesses, browbeat courts, hoodwink juries, and if they can succeed in obtaining a verdict in their favor, that that is the acme of fame and human greatness.' If they fail, they call to their aid the court of last resort and very frequently they do not call in vain.

The whole body of the criminal law is at the present time overloaded with technicalities, subtleties, refinements, impracticable and in many instances absolutely nonsensical rules and rulings, which have no other tendency than to protect crime and criminals, and thwart public justice.

A great criminal backed by money can almost defy the public and the people, not by the use of it in corrupting courts, but by resorting to changes of venue, bills of particulars, excepting to everything under heavens, done or said in court, and out of court, and then calling upon the court of last resort for their aid and assistance in construing everything done and said against the court, prosecuting officer, judge and jury, clerks and bailiffs, and they are sure to obtain errors enough to reverse the verdict every time. Substantial justice, which is really the limit of all earthly tribunals, is wholly ignored, and absolute perfection required or else a criminal trial is erroneous. Common sense seems to be about the last thing made use of in reviewing criminal trials, and the guilt or innocence of the accused wholly ignored or forgotten.

By the law as it exists to-day in the State of Illinois, a person charged with the commission of a crime can, by resorting to changes of venue, motions for continuances and other tactics known to the law, select his judge, fix the time and place for his trial and select his own jury, if it takes months to do it. Now, this may seem astonishing to a stranger, but if it is not absolutely true in all cases it is nearly so.

A *nisi prius* judge has no discretion left in him according to its true and legal meaning as known and understood by the common law, for everything is subject to review from good morning to good night.

If we have the common law in this State will some one be kind enough to inform me what it is, and if judges have been abridged in the exercise of their powers, by whom it was done and by what means it was accomplished? Able jurists have, in Maryland and Pennsylvania, investigated this subject and determined to what extent the common law exists there. But in this State that has not yet been determined except our Supreme Court have decided that all Circuit Courts have the same powers and jurisdiction as the King's Bench, and that the common law exists as it did in Virginia prior to 1784. In addition to all these things, the statute adopting the common law is still in force and has never been repealed. Does it require a constitutional convention to enforce its observance?

Is there anything in the genius of our institutions to require absolute perfection and no errors?

A prisoner charged with the commission of a crime is entitled to a fair and impartial trial—as fair and impartial as "the lot of humanity will permit" but nothing further—and the great question should be, is *he* guilty or innocent and not somebody else.

There was a time in England when the penalty attached to almost every crime was death, and when every species of technicality and sublety was resorted to to save a criminal, but in this more liberal and enlightened age, when the administration of the criminal law has been ameliorated by just and merciful laws, and milder punishments are awarded for almost every offense, a liberal rule has obtained, and the last traces of lawyers' superstitions have been swept away and the fanciful scruples of the sixteenth and seventeenth centuries are no longer listened to.

Modern legislation ought to sweep away every vestige of those fantasies and arbitrary rules of criminal lawyers which now hinder and obstruct the administration of the criminal law, and go back to those simple principles which the untutored wisdom of our forefathers never thought of calling in question.

Finally: There are many and various conceptions of justice. The most reasonable distinction is between universal and particular justice. The first is when every duty is discharged and all right done to others, even that which could not have been exacted by force or by the vigor of the law. Particular justice is when we do that and no more, which may be strictly demanded of us. And this is again divided into distributive and commutative. Distributive justice pertains to the public, and is sometimes known as public justice, while commutative is founded upon reciprocal bargains and contracts, but partakes largely of public justice. It is the duty of a court in the administration of the law, to see that public justice has an equal chance with any other justice, either public or private.

The tendency of modern ideas seems to be to regard the public interests as of but very little consequence.

"Impartiality," says Bouvier, "is the first duty of a judge. He is bound to declare what the law is, and not to make it; he is not an arbitrator, but an interpreter of the law. It is his duty to be patient in the investigation of the case, careful in considering it, and firm in his judgment. He ought, according to Cicero, never to lose sight that he is a man; that he cannot exceed the power given him by his commission; that not only power, but public confidence, has been given to him, and that he ought always seriously to attend, not to his wishes, but to the requisitions of law and justice."

*It is the prerogative of the court,* by the common law, to absolutely determine whether a juror is biased or prejudiced for or against the prisoner at the bar or State, and his decision is final.

After a juror states that he is not sensible of any bias or prejudice in the case, it ought not to be erroneous to refuse a further examination of the juror, and it is said the mind of the court, and not of the counsel, must be satisfied that the challenged juror is free from bias and prejudice.

We can never secure from general society, as it is now constituted, a body of men entirely free from partiality, impression or bias; at best, we can only get as near to this as we can by discrimination and scrutiny. The day is fast disappearing when men are required to come into a jury box entirely and absolutely free from any impression and even opinion, as to matters of general notoriety.

We are now coming to the recognition of a fact that must have been long ago apparent—that it is preposterous to expect men moving in general society as it is to-day, to be unimpressed and uninformed as to current and striking events.

We must either recede and go back to the practice of an age when ignorance of passing events constituted a characteristic of the times, and exclude every juror who has formed an opinion, even the slightest, or we must stand abreast with the present age, when every remarkable event of to-day is known all over the country to-morrow, and exclude those whose opinions are so fixed as to be prejudgments or have been founded upon the known evidence in the cause.

It is needless to say the world moves and carries us with it, and if we lag behind we must commit the trial of the most important causes in life to those so ignorant that their dark minds have never been smitten with the rays of intelligence.

We inherited the common law, and adopted it by statute in this State at a very early period, and yet in the trial of jury cases, the true position of the court is lost sight of, and instead of being a trial by *judge and jury*, the trial is regarded as a trial by the jury alone, and the court has but very little part in it.

## CHAPTER XXXI.
### State and Federal Judges.

IT is a very common remark among lawyers and laymen that the United States courts possess many advantages over those of the State courts, but they do not stop to consider what it is that makes the difference. In the first place the permanence of the judicial office has one advantage; secondly, the limited range of their subjects, which are confined to the Federal jurisdiction, following day by day, week by week and year by year, the Supreme Court decisions; and thirdly, the power that they possess and which they exert in trying cases and summing up the facts to the jury. These are matters of great importance.

Chief Justice Kent called attention to some of these points as early as 1826, and in the first volume of his Commentaries speaks of the matter in this wise :

"There are," says he, "several reasons why we may anticipate the still increasing influence of the Federal government, and the continual enlargement of the national system of law in magnitude and value. The judiciary of the United States has an advantage over many of the State courts, in the tenure of office of the judges, and the liberal and stable provision for their support.

"The United States are, by these means, fairly entitled to command better talents, and to look for more firmness of purpose, greater independence of action, and brighter displays of learning. The Federal administration of justice has a manifest superiority over that of the individual States, in consequence of the uniformity of its decisions, and the universality of their application.

"Every State court will naturally be disposed to borrow light and aid from the national courts, rather than from the courts of other individual States, which will probably never be so generally respected and understood. The States are multiplying so fast, and the reports of their judicial decisions are becoming so numerous, that few lawyers will be able or willing to master all the intricacies and anomalies of local law, existing beyond the boundaries of their own State. Twenty-six independent State courts of final jurisdiction over the same questions, arising upon the same general code of common and of equity law, must necessarily impair the symmetry of that code.

"The danger to be apprehended is, that students will not have the courage to enter the complicated labyrinth of so many systems, and that they will, of course, entirely neglect them, and be contented with a knowledge of the law of their own State and the law of the United States, and then resort for further assistance to the never-failing fountains of European wisdom.

"But though the national judiciary may be deemed pre-eminent in the weight of its influence, the authority of its decisions, and in the attraction of their materials, there are abundant considerations to cheer and animate us in the elevation of our own local law. The judicial power of the United States is necessarily limited to national objects. The vast field of the law of property, the very extensive head of equity jurisdiction, and the principal rights and duties which flow from our civil and domestic relations, fall within the control, and we might almost say the exclusive cognizance of the State governments. We look essentially to the State courts for protection to all these momentous interests. They touch, in their operation, every chord of human sympathy, and control our best destinies. It is their province to reward and punish. Their blessings and their terrors will accompany us to the fireside, and 'be in constant activity before the public eye.' The elementary principles of the common law are the same in every State, and equally enlighten and invigorate every part of our country. Our municipal codes can be made to advance with equal steps with that of the Nation, in discipline, in wisdom and in lustre, if the State governments (as they ought in all honest policy) will only render *equal* patronage *and security to the administration of justice.* The true interests and the permanent freedom of this country require that the jurisprudence of the individual States should be cultivated, cherished and exalted, and the dignity and reputation of the State authorities sustained with becoming pride. In their subordinate relation to the United States, they should endeavor to discharge the duty which they owe to the latter, without forgetting the respect which they owe to themselves. In the appropriate language of Sir William Blackstone, and which he applied to the people of his own country, they should be 'loyal, yet free; obedient and yet independent.'"

By the organic law of the State of Illinois the tenure of office of all judges is of short duration, and all are elected by the people.

The Supreme Court judges are elected for the period of nine years, the Circuit and Superior Court judges for six years, and all other judges for four years.

In New York, by a recent amendment to their Constitution, all the judges of courts of record, like those of the circuit judges in this State, are elected for fourteen years.

By the Constitution of Massachusetts, which was adopted in 1780, it was provided as follows:

"It is essential to the preservation of the rights of every individual, his life, liberty, property and character, that there be an impartial interpretation of the laws and administration of justice. It is the right of every citizen to be tried by judges as free, impartial and independent as the lot of humanity will admit.

"It is, therefore, not only the best policy, but for the security of the rights of the people, and of every citizen, that the judges of the Supreme Judicial Court should hold their offices as long as they behave themselves well, and that they should have honorable salaries, ascertained and established by standing laws," and, we will add, not required to " board around."

Mr. Justice Gray, in deciding the case of the United States v. The Reading Railroad, 123 U. S. 114, says: "Trial by jury in the courts of the United States is a trial presided over by a *judge, with authority,* not only to rule upon objections to evidence, and to instruct the jury upon the law, but also, when in his judgment the due administration of justice requires it, *to aid the jury by explaining and commenting upon the testimony* and even giving them his opinion upon the questions of fact, provided only he submit those questions to their determination," citing Vicksburg & Meridian Railroad Co. v. Putnam, 118 U. S. 545; St. Louis Railway v. The Vickers, 122 U. S. 360. We would like for some one to define what a court is in Illinois under our practice. We think that a short definition of an Illinois court may be as follows: A court is composed of an individual called a judge, assisted by a clerk, whose chief duty and functions are to look wise and keep order. He has no power to sum up a case or explain anything to a jury and the only aid or assistance that he can render them is to mark "given" or "refused" on all instructions and conundrums presented to him by the attorneys in the case.

## CHAPTER XXXII.

### Is a Constitutional Convention Necessary to Induce the Supreme Court to Recognize and Enforce the Statutes Relating to the Common Law.

IT is well enough for us as citizens of the State of Illinois and as lawyers to remember how directly we are connected with the great expounders of the common law, and how strenuously we should uphold it when not expressly changed by statute. We all know that Illinois was once the frontier county of Virginia, and that Virginia was founded by letters-patent issued by James I, in the fourth year of his reign, to-wit, April 10, 1606, to Sir Thomas Gates, Sir George Somers and others, for two several colonies and plantations to be made in Virginia and other parts and territories, for trading and also for propagating the Christian religion "to such people as yet live in darkness and miserable ignorance of the true knowledge and worship of God, and may in time bring the infidels and savages living in those parts to human civility and to a settled and quiet government."

We think the antiquaries of the State Bar Association should investigate this matter and see if this has yet been accomplished; for if the infidels and savages living in these parts have not been reduced to "human civility," it is time that steps be taken to do so. We also know that by the fifteenth section of the charter of 1606 it was expressly stipulated by the king, "for us, our heirs and successors; and we do declare, by these presents, being our subjects, which shall dwell and inhabit within every or any of the said several colonies and plantations, and every of their children which shall happen to be born within any of the limits and precincts of the said several colonies and plantations, shall have and enjoy all liberties, franchises and immunities within any of our dominions, to all intents and purposes, as if they had been abiding and born within this our realm of England, or any other of our said dominions;" and that this planted in that colony and plantation of Virginia the common law, in all of its fullness and strength. But it is not, we think, as generally known that the first draft for the proposed first Virginia charter annexed to the petition for the same was drawn by Sir John Popham; that the charter itself was prepared and drawn by Sir Edward Coke, Attorney-General under James, assisted by Sir John Dodderidge, the Solicitor-General; that it was passed under the Great Seal by Sir Thomas Edgerton, at that time Lord Chancellor; and that the warrant for it was granted by Robert Cecil, son of the great Lord Burleigh, known as Earl of Salisbury, who was at that time the Secretary of State; and that the first drafts annexed to the petition for the second and third charters, extending the boundaries from sea to sea, and enlarging the powers of the first, were drawn by Sir Edwin Sandys; that these charters were prepared by Sir Francis Bacon and Sir Henry Hobart, and were passed under the seal also of Sir Thomas Edgerton, and the warrant issued by Robert Cecil.

By the 22d section of the second charter of Virginia, power is conferred upon the governors and those ruling and governing the colony, " full and absolute power and authority to correct, punish, pardon, govern and rule all such subjects of ours as shall from time to time adventure themselves thither," etc., "so always as the said statutes, ordinances and proceedings, as near as conveniently may be, be agreeable to the laws, statutes, government and *policy of our realm of this England."*

The third charter still further enlarged the boundaries specified in the two other charters so as to include any islands on the sea "adjoining to the said coast of Virginia and without the compass of those two hundred miles, by us so granted unto the said treasurer and company aforesaid," etc.; then it confers additional power "to punish deserters, misdoers and offenders, and those who circulate vile and slanderous reports, by summary arrest, and punishing and *proceeding* to all intents and purposes as it is used in other like cases *within our realm* of England," etc.

Hume in commenting upon the force and effect of these charters says: "Speculative reasoners during that age raised many objections to the planting of those remote colonies and foretold they would soon shake off her yoke and erect an independent government in America; but time has shown that the views entertained by those who encouraged such generous undertakings were more just and solid." In less than a generation after, the "speculative reasoners" became prophets. Hume had not evidently heard of George Washington, George Rogers Clark or the State of Illinois.

Sir John Popham was speaker of Elizabeth's fourth Parliament 1581-83, was Chief Justice of the Queen's Bench, June 2, 1592, when he was knighted and made Privy Councillor. He presided at the trial of Sir Walter Raleigh in 1603 when Coke prosecuted, and both acted like the devil. He also presided at the trial of Guy Fawkes and his associates in 1606. He died suddenly June 10, 1607. His remains repose under a magnificent tomb in the church at Wellington, Somerset, surrounded by a palisade of wood and iron.

Sir Edward Coke and Sir Francis Bacon need no introduction to the American lawyer any more than they do to the English lawyer. Bacon and Coke were at the zenith of their power when the Pilgrims sailed from England, and it was on the 22d of January, 1621, that Bacon's sixtieth birthday was celebrated with such *eclat* at York House, the ancient seat of his family, when his friend, Ben Jonson read that celebrated poem containing these lines:

"Hail happy genius of this ancient pile,
How comes it all things so about thee smile,
The fire, the wine, the men, and in the midst
Thou stand'st as if some mystery thou didst.
\* \* \* \* \*

> England's High Chancellor, the destined heir,
> In his soft cradle, to his father's chair,
> Whose even thread the Fates spin round and full
> Out of their choicest and their whitest wool."

January 27th he was created Viscount St. Albans; January 20th Parliament met, and on February 3d, Bacon, in his speech referring to the "benefits, attributes and acts of government of King James," says: "This kingdom now first in His Majesty's time hath gotten a lot or portion in the New World, by the plantation of Virginia and the Summer Islands. And certainly it is with the kingdoms on earth as it is in the Kingdom of Heaven; sometimes a grain of mustard seed proves a great tree. Who can tell?" Soon after clouds gathered around him. He was tried, convicted, fined and imprisoned—released, and died at Arundell's House at Highgate, April 9, 1626. He lies buried in St. Michael's Church, St. Albans.

In 1661-2, a sort of general revision of the laws of Virginia took place in which they expressly recognize the common law of England, and in the preamble to the code refer to the great confusion which had marked that period as follows: "Whereas the late unhappy distractions caused frequent changes in the government of this country, and those produced so many alterations in the laws that the people knew not well what to obey, nor the judge what to punish, by which means injustice was hardly to be avoided and the just freedom of the people by the uncertainty and licentiousness of the laws hardly to be preserved, this assembly, taking the same into serious consideration and gravely weighing the obligations they are under to discharge to God, the king and the country, have, by settling the laws, diligently endeavored to prevent the like inconveniences *by causing the whole body of the laws to be reviewed*, all unnecessary acts, and chiefly such as might keep in memory our enforced deviation from His Majesty's obedience, to be repealed and expunged, and those that are in force to be brought into one volume, and lest any prejudice might arise by the ignorance of the times from whence these acts were in force, they have added the duties of every act, to the end that courts might rightly administer justice and give sentence according to law for anything happening at any time since any law was in force, and have also endeavored in all things (as near as the capacity and Constitution of this country would admit) to *adhere to those excellent and often refined laws of England to which we profess and acknowledge all due obedience and reverence*," etc. 2 Hening's Statutes, p. **43.**

The charters granted by King James I, expressly provide for the administering the law according to the common law of England and the statutes made in aid thereof. We adopted the common law here when we were a Territory and finally when we were admitted into the Union as a State; now, why is it not adhered to in the impaneling of jurors and in the recognition of the powers of the court and the trial of all criminal cases?

By the express provisions of the statutes of this State, it is provided "that the common law of England, so far as the same is applicable and of a general nature, and all statutes or acts of the British Parliament made in aid of, and to supply the defects of the common law, prior to the fourth year of James the First, excepting the second section of the sixth chapter of forty-three Elizabeth, the eighth chapter of thirteenth Elizabeth and ninth chapter of thirty-seventh Henry Eighth and which are of a general nature and not local to that kingdom, shall be the rule of decision *and shall be considered* as of full force until repealed by legislative authority."

By Section 428, Chapter 38 of the Criminal Code, it is provided that "all trials for criminal offenses *shall be conducted according to the course of the common law*, except when this act points out a different mode and the *rules of evidence* of the common law *shall also* be binding upon all courts and juries in criminal cases, except as otherwise provided by law."

Now it will be observed by all lawyers in the State of Illinois, that the only things pertaining to the common law which have been expressly abolished by statute are the benefit of clergy, appeals of felony, trials by battle and trials by a jury *de mediatate linguæ*. All else remains, and yet the Supreme Court has by its rulings completely ignored these statutes for nearly forty years. They have notably ignored them by reversing case after case, because the court erred in deciding upon the competency of jurors and in many other ways too numerous to mention; whereas by the common law the impaneling of a jury and passing upon the competency of jurors was absolutely in the discretion of the presiding judge and no case can be found where it was ever sought to review this discretion. Discretion in the trial of criminal cases must rest somewhere, and to say that this discretion is liable to abuse and ought not to be vested in *nisi prius* judges is to say that there ought not to be any such thing at all; and the services of a judge might as well be dispensed with and let the lawyers for the accused and the jury control the whole trial.

By the common law all trials were by a *judge and jury;* now such a thing seems to be wholly unknown. By the common law it was the duty of the judge to tell the jury what the case was about and to *sum up* the facts; to-day all a judge can do is to mark instructions given or refused.

Why is it that the statutes relating to the common law are not recognized and enforced?

Does it require a constitutional convention, we repeat, to compel the court of last resort to recognize and enforce them?

Shakspeare must have had this condition of things in mind when he said:

> "We have strict statutes and most biting laws
> (The needful bits and curbs for headstrong steeds),
> Which, for these fourteen years, we have let sleep;
> Even like an o'ergrown lion in a cave,
> That goes not out to prey. Now, as fond fathers
> Having bound up threatening twigs of birch
> Only to stick it in their children's sight,
> For terror, not to use; in time the rod
> Becomes more mocked than feared; so our decrees,
> Dead to infliction, to themselves are dead,
> *And liberty plucks justice by the nose.*"
> —Measure for Measure, 1, 3.

## CHAPTER XXXIII.

### The Address of the Delegates to the People, Showing the Changes Made in the Old Constitution and the Reforms Proposed.

AT the time when we were called upon "to alter, revise and amend the Constitution" of this State, the Constitution of 1848 had become almost obsolete; the people had outgrown it, and great abuses existed in almost every department of the government calling for the most radical changes. When we had finished our work we gave an account of our stewardship. We issued a public address to the people, in which we recounted our labors and the reforms sought to be accomplished; and we pointed out wherein we had altered, revised and amended the Constitution. That address is as follows:

### ADDRESS IN CONVENTION MAY 13, 1870.

As your representatives in convention to "alter, revise and amend" the Constitution, it is due that we should state in brief the *most important changes* proposed, and some of the reasons therefor. Our State Constitution has been in force for almost a quarter of a century, during which time our population, wealth and interests have augmented. However wise and judicious when adopted, that Constitution has become wholly inadequate to subserve the necessities of the State, without modifications and restrictions. To secure an efficient and at the same time an economical administration of the several departments of the government, a new Constitution is an imperious necessity. It is not probable that any constitution will, in all respects, fully satisfy any one man in the State. Every one will find in it something he would exclude, and would insert something it does not contain. It must be judged all together, and if better than the old Constitution, it should be adopted. In all human institutions the good and evil are mixed and sound sense demands that we secure the greatest good attainable; and we must often be content if we get more wheat than tares. For years past the machinery of our State Government has been kept in motion only by continued violation of plain and positive constitutional provisions. Nothing can be more pernicious. By this the people lose their respect for the laws, and learn to hold them in contempt. A reverence for constitutions and laws is the best possible guaranty for the stability of the State, the peace and good order of society, and the protection of the life, liberty and property of the citizen. And whenever it becomes necessary to violate a constitution, it should be changed to meet and remove the necessity which impelled to such violation. Our State Legislatures are only restrained by the Constitution of the State and of the United States. It is therefore necessary that State Constitutions should contain many regulations and restrictions, while the Constitution of the United States may be much shorter, for that is a government of delegated powers, with only the incidental powers necessary and proper to execute the powers granted.

## BILL OF RIGHTS.

In addition to the usual guarantees of natural and civil liberty, we have declared that no person shall be denied any civil or political right or capacity on account of his religious opinions. All persons have the right to publish the truth, with good motives and for justifiable ends. Private property shall not be taken or damaged for public use without just compensation, to be ascertained by a jury. The fee of land taken for railroad tracks is to remain in the owners, subject to the use for which it is taken. All irrevocable grants of special privileges or immunities are prohibited, to protect the people against privileged orders and dangerous monopolies. Grand juries may be dispensed with. Our jails are crowded with criminals during the intervals of circuit courts, at great expense to the counties. County courts may be authorized to try, in a summary manner, many criminal cases, and thus save the counties the large expenditures of keeping prisoners for trial from term to term of the circuit courts, and persons not guilty may be promptly discharged or acquitted.

## LEGISLATIVE DEPARTMENT.

To avoid partisan injustice in representative districts, and the expense and delay of the General Assembly in making them, we have provided for districting the State, as in Ohio, by ratio and computation. To guard against undue influence upon members of the General Assembly, and to afford small counties representatives, we have increased their numbers. We have also required a stringent oath against bribery and corruption. To afford security against hasty and vicious legislation, we have required all bills and amendments thereto to be printed before they are passed. Only one subject shall be embraced in each bill, and when amendments are made to laws, or acts are revived, the sections amended and acts revived must be stated at length. The evils of special and local legislation have become enormous. The expense to the State in passing and publishing such laws, and the combinations by which private speculations have been secured and monopolies with extraordinary and dangerous powers have been created, are well known. We have prohibited the General Assembly hereafter from passing such laws, and have required general laws in all cases where a general law can be made applicable. We have forbidden the General Assembly from releasing any liability to the State or to any municipal corporation therein. We have placed additional guards against speculative contracts made with officers of the State for stationery, fuel, etc., and we have limited the amount of expenditures to be incurred on account of the State capitol now in process of construction.

We have provided for public and private roads, and for the drainage of lands. We have required the enactment of liberal homestead and exemption laws, and laws for the protection of miners; and we have submitted a separate article, designed to protect producers and shippers of grain against frauds in warehouses.

### EXECUTIVE DEPARTMENT.

We require the governor, at each session of the Legislature, and at the close of his term of office, to furnish a statement of all moneys received and paid out by him from any funds subject to his order, with his vouchers therefor. We make it the duty of the auditor of public accounts, treasurer, secretary of state and superintendent of public instruction and persons in charge of State institutions, to keep an account of all moneys received or disbursed by them severally, from all sources and for every service performed, and to make a semi-annual report thereof to the governor, under oath, to be laid before the General Assembly; thus enabling the representatives of the people to expose, and by suitable laws prevent, improvident expenditures and frauds. We have given the governor power to remove all officers appointed by him, in case they are incompetent or are guilty of malfeasance in office. We have provided a safer mode of canvassing the votes for governor and State officers, and avoided the danger of collusion in cases of contested elections. We have required the governor to submit a careful estimate of expenses and revenue to each General Assembly. This will restrain extravagant appropriations and give the people a proper understanding of the financial condition of the State. We have made the veto power as in the Constitution of the United States, only to be overcome by a vote of two-thirds in each House of the General Assembly. Had this provision been in our existing Constitution, it would have saved us from many injurious and unconstitutional acts and many chartered monopolies passed by the combinations of interested persons.

### JUDICIAL DEPARTMENT.

We have endeavored to preserve all the courts to which our people are accustomed, to avoid the evils of too great a variety of courts, and at the same time make the system sufficiently flexible to allow the General Assembly to provide for a speedy and prompt administration of justice. All the new courts indicated are left entirely in the discretion of the General Assembly to create or not, as the public wants may demand. Our Supreme Court is burdened with many unadjudicated cases, and decisions are delayed to the prejudice of suitors and the public. To enable that court to fully investigate and properly decide and write out creditable opinions, we have added four more judges to its number. We have required its judges to be elected in separate districts, and at times when no general election is held, to avoid a partisan court. Should that court be unable to dispose of its cases with reasonable dispatch, we have authorized the General Assembly to create an appellate court, which may be held in each county by the circuit judges, without additional compensation and with jurisdiction in such cases as may be prescribed by law. Such courts are said to be of great value in Ohio and New York. We contemplate continuing the old circuit court system. We have, however, authorized the General Assembly to provide for electing not exceeding four judges in a larger circuit, and to assign them to duties in its counties. The advocates of this system affirm that it has worked well in other States, and is an improvement on our present system; that it avoids frequent changes of venue and the expenses of parties and witnesses occasioned thereby; that it secures greater uniformity of practice in circuit courts, and enables the people to procure more competent judges and dispose of their suits with greater facility.

To remove the evil of frequent changes of the times of holding courts, we have provided that they shall not be altered during the terms of the judges, and to prevent the creation of too many circuits we have put restrictions upon the same. We have provided that county courts may have additional jurisdiction conferred by law, and county judges, if desirable hereafter, may be elected in districts composed of two or more counties, and probate courts may be established in counties having a population over 50,000. We have provided for the election of state's attorneys in each county, in lieu of circuit attorneys. We have established a special system of courts for the county of Cook, which, it is confidently expected, will meet her necessities. We have required laws relating to courts to be of general and uniform operation; and the organization, jurisdiction, powers, proceedings and practice of all courts of the same class, so far as regulated by law, and the force and effect of process, judgments and decrees of such courts, shall be uniform. We have made it the duty of all judges of courts of record to furnish the General Assembly with defects they may discover in our laws. The performance of this duty with fidelity will enable the Legislature to simplify and perfect our statutes.

All existing courts are continued until otherwise provided by law.

### ELECTION AND RIGHT OF SUFFRAGE.

We have made our law on suffrage conform to the Constitution of the United States, and extended that right to persons informally naturalized before courts of record anterior to January, 1870; and we have submitted a separate article on minority representation.

### COMMON SCHOOLS.

We have required a thorough and efficient system of common schools, and that all grants and donations for common school purposes shall be applied to their use with fidelity. We have forbidden the General Assembly and all public corporations from donating money or property to any church, or for any sectarian purpose, or for any school controlled by any church or sect; and we have prohibited school teachers and school officers from being interested in the sale of books, apparatus and furniture in the schools with which they are connected.

### REVENUE.

We have retained the valuable features of the revenue article in the Constitution of 1848, and have provided in addition that before sales of real estate for taxes are made, a return of unpaid taxes shall be made to some general officer of the county for collection, with authority to sell for default, on an order of a court of record, the object being to secure uniformity of sales, prevent abuses, and to provide a general and convenient mode by which persons interested may obtain information and pay assessments or taxes, or redeem from tax sales. We have forbidden the General Assembly from discharging any county, city, township or district from its proportionate share of State taxes, and prohibited all commutations for such taxes, thus securing, in State taxation, equality of burdens for common benefits, and we have repealed the two-mill tax.

### COUNTIES.

We have provided that if a portion of a county is added to another county, its inhabitants shall be obliged to pay its proportion of the indebtedness of the county from which it is taken. We have required that voters on the question of removing county seats shall, next before the election, reside in the county six months, and in the election precinct ninety days; and that the question of the removal of the county seat shall not be oftener submitted than once in ten years; and we have submitted separately the question whether less than three-fifths of the votes cast shall be sufficient for the removal of a county seat, when proposed to be moved further from the center of a county. We have provided that counties having adopted township organization, may, by vote, dispense with the same. We have provided that counties not under township organization may elect a board of three county commissioners to manage their county affairs, one of whom shall be elected every year; and we have made special provisions for Cook county. We have provided for the usual county officers and their compensation. All officers who are paid by fees, are required to make a semi-annual report, under oath, of their fees and emoluments.

### CITIES, TOWNS, ETC.

In the numerous cities and towns of this State, streets, alleys. sidewalks, etc., are indispensable to their growth and prosperity. They must be graded, paved and kept in repair. How this shall be done, how paid for, what proportion by the owners of contiguous property, and what by general contribution, the people of the particular town or city are better qualified to decide than others can be. The same system will not be suited to the wishes or necessities of all places. Under our present laws, streets and sidewalks are falling into decay, and a radical reform is indispensable. To remove this evil, we have authorized the Legislature to vest in each city and town full power and control of such improvements, and of the means best adapted to its wishes, circumstances and necessities. For all other purposes, taxation therein must be uniform. We have also prohibited the General Assembly from imposing taxes upon municipal corporations for corporate purposes. If, in all other respects, the two Constitutions are equal, these provisions alone should secure the support of every citizen of every town and city in the State.

### CORPORATIONS.

We have provided that no corporation, public or private, shall be created or have its charter amended by special law, except institutions for charitable, educational or reformatory purposes, under the patronage of the State. All grants of charters for special and exclusive privileges under which no organizations have taken place, or which shall not have been in operation within ten days after this Constitution takes effect, shall be invalid. We have prohibited the construction of street railways without the consent of the local authorities in towns and cities; and we have provided for the protection of the minority of stockholders of private corporations in the election of directors.

### BANKS.

We have prohibited the State from being interested in any banking corporation; forbidden the establishment of any bank of issue, deposit or discount without the approval of a majority of votes cast at a general election. We have declared that no suspension of specie payments shall be legalized; and we have required that banks shall deposit ample securities for the protection of their creditors.

### RAILROADS.

We have provided that railroads owning parallel or competing lines shall not be consolidated, and that a majority of the directors shall be residents of this State. We have declared railroads to be public highways, and required the General Assembly to establish reasonable maximum rates of charges, and to prevent unjust discriminations and extortions. We have asserted the right of the State, by the exercise of the power of eminent domain, to subject the property and franchises of incorporated companies to the public use, the same as the property of natural persons. We have provided against the release of the obligation of the Illinois Central Railroad to the State, thereby securing to the State nearly half a million of dollars annually.

### STATE, COUNTY AND MUNICIPAL INDEBTEDNESS.

We have prohibited the State from contracting indebtedness beyond $250,000, without submitting the law to the people. We have forbidden the General Assembly from loaning the credit of the State and making appropriations from the treasury in aid of internal improvements, and from paying or assuming the debts or liabilities of any public or other corporation, association or individual. We have prohibited county authorities from ever assessing taxes, the aggregate of which shall exceed seventy-five cents per $100 valuation, except for the payment of indebtedness existing at the adoption of this Constitution, unless authorized by a vote of the people of the county. We have forbidden cities, counties and all public corporations from creating or further increasing their indebtedness above five per cent. on the value of the taxable property within the same, and required that at the time of incurring such indebtedness, an annual tax shall be levied, sufficient to pay the interest as it falls due, and to discharge the principal within twenty years. For want of such a provision in our State Constitution, our counties, towns and cities have contracted. liabilities of over $50,000,000. We have submitted a separate article prohibiting all municipal subscriptions to railroad stock.

### FEES AND SALARIES.

Under the present Constitution it was found practically impossible to carry on the three departments of government without evading its provisions. The compensation allowed the governor, State officers, judges and members of the General Assembly, was wholly insufficient in times when the prices of all the necessaries of life were increased, and the currency inflated. By general and special laws, the fees of clerks and inferior officers afforded them much greater incomes than the salaries of governor and judges, and in the populous counties, and in Chicago, those fees afforded compensation beyond all reasonable bounds. We have inaugurated a system by which all perquisites of judges and State officers will be prohibited. We have limited members of the General Assembly to fifty dollars each per session, in addition to their per diem and mileage, in full for postage, stationery, stamps, newspapers and all other incidental perquisites. These perquisites amounted at the last session of the General Assembly to over fifty-four thousand dollars, which was about five hundred dollars to each member.

We have provided that the fees and salaries of all officers under the Constitution shall not be increased or diminished during their terms; and that, with few exceptions, such fees and salaries shall be fixed before their terms commence. We have abolished all special laws in relation to fees, and put in force the general laws in such cases; and we have required the next General Assembly, by general uniform law, to provide and regulate fees of all persons holding county offices, and their successors, so as to reduce the same to a reasonable compensation, in not exceeding three grades in the different counties; and all laws fixing the fees of State, county and township officers shall terminate with the terms of those in office at the meeting of the first General Assembly.

We have provided that State and county officers shall be paid reasonable salaries, out of the fees collected by them, and that the surplus be paid into the State or county treasury. Thus, fees and salaries may hereafter be regulated by the condition of the country; and we have allowed all officers now in office to serve out their terms.

### AMENDMENTS TO THE CONSTITUTION.

To save all controversy in the future convention to amend the Constitution, we have fixed the qualification of its members, the oath of office they shall take, the manner of filling vacancies, and provided that amendments proposed by such convention, before they take effect, shall be ratified by the electors of the State. As a means of avoiding the necessity and expense of such a convention, we have provided that two-thirds of each House of the General Assembly, may submit amendments to any one article of the Constitution; and if ratified by the people at the succeeding general election, such amendments shall constitute part of the Constitution.

Such are some of the prominent amendments we propose. They are the result of much labor, reflection and discussion, and we are confident that interest and inclination will induce you to give them that earnest, careful and candid consideration they deserve, and that you will render such a decision as will promote your own well being, and the future prosperity of the powerful, patriotic and progressive State of Illinois. And it will afford us sincere pleasure, in after years, to find that our efforts have, in some measure, contributed to such desirable consummation.

|  |  |
| --- | --- |
| W. H. UNDERWOOD, Chairman. | S. S. HAYES, |
| O. H. BROWNING, | WM. CARY, |
| L. S. CHURCH, | GEO. E. WAIT, |
| L. W. ROSS, | J. C. ALLEN, |
| J. W. ENGLISH, | M. HAY, |
| JOSEPH MEDILL, | JESSE S. HILDRUP, |
| W. J. ALLEN, | H. P. H. BROMWELL, |
| WM. C. GOODHUE, | EDWARD Y. RICE. |

# CHAPTER XXXIV.

## How State Taxes Have Been Diverted, School Lands Stolen, and Other Abuses under the Old Regime, with Some Remarks on the Value of the "Pay As You Go" Policy.

THE history of the State of Illinois shows that in the past we suffered much from the granting of special charters and hasty legislation and we did what we could to stop it. Under the then existing order of things, the public interests seemed to have been almost forgotten and just about three quarters of the time of the General Assembly was taken up in the consideration of private bills and the granting of special charters, whereas now, everybody is upon an equality, and general laws, instead of being the exception, are the rule. In our address we say: "We have provided that no corporation, public or private, shall be created or have its charter amended by special laws, except institutions for charitable, educational or reformatory purposes under the patronage of the State."

We found a condition of things existing in many parts of the State that will scarcely be believed at the present time.

We found that under the guise of assisting in the construction of railroads in new sections of the State, that towns, cities, villages and even school districts had voted large subsidies, and had issued their bonds to pay for the same, and that the people, and especially the taxpayers and property owners, were in danger of having their property confiscated. In many counties the state of affairs was such that persons avoided them, and those seeking homes in the West could not be induced to settle there. We investigated this matter thoroughly and obtained from the auditor a list of such indebtedness, and found that it was enormous. In many instances laws had been passed diverting the State taxes and appropriating them to pay the interest on the bonds of municipal indebtedness. The State Auditor was made the paymaster of these various municipalities and every effort was put forward to compel the State to assume all these debts.

As a specimen we present one single report upon this subject made by the State Auditor. This report was made by the request of the convention and in it he says:

"The American Bottom Levee Company gets the State tax on all property assessed in four (4) townships in St. Clair county for five (5) years under private laws, 1867, Vol. 2, page 795; assessed valuation of said townships in 1868, $1,534,125; estimated revenue fund tax for 1869 ............................................................ $12,273

The St. Clair and Monroe Draining Company gets the State tax on the increased valuation of subsequent years over valuation of 1859, for fifteen years from 1865 under private laws, 1865, Vol. 2, page 2, in certain districts in the counties of Monroe and St. Clair; estimated amount of State revenue tax for 1869, in surplus valuation of 1869 over 1859 .................................. 2,000

The Kaskaskia River Navigation Company under private laws, 1869, page 872, gets the State tax on all property assessed in nine (9) townships for ten (10) years from 1868 in Randolph county. Net valuation in 1868 amounts to $1,089,555; estimated amount State revenue tax for 1869 thus given ........................................ 2,400

Alexander county under public laws 1869, page 330, gets all State tax collected in said county for the years 1869–1870; estimated amount of revenue fund tax for 1869 .. 14,000

Mound City (Pulaski county) under private laws 1867, Vol. 1, page 837, gets State tax on all property in said city for ten years from 1867; estimated revenue fund for 1869 thus given ....................................... 2,500

City of Shawneetown (Gallatin county) by *its charter*, private laws 1861, page 272, gets State tax on all property assessed in said city for twenty years. Revenue fund State tax on assessment 1869, in said city, estimated to exceed ...................................................... 3,500

Wabash River and its tributaries in Allison Prairie Levee Company (Lawrence county) gets the State tax on all property assessed in six (6) townships for ten (10) years from 1866, laws 1867 (private), page 305, Vol. 2. The property in said township assessed for 1868, $418,461; estimated revenue State tax for 1869 ............... 3,000

Surplus, etc., revenue tax (State) on assessment 1869 **over** assessment 1868, *given to counties, townships, cities and towns in aid of railroads,* public laws 1869, page 316, estimated by auditor in levying rates of taxes for 1869 to amount to for 1869............................ 4,728

Total amount of revenue tax on assessment to be disposed of for *one year* by the foregoing laws............... $50,701

In estimating the foregoing amounts only the revenue fund State tax was taken into consideration. *Heretofore, it has been considered that said acts appropriated the tax levied to pay interest on the State debt;* but in a recent case that came before me, I held that said interest tax could not be so *diverted.* Should this ruling be contested in the Supreme Court, and not sustained by said court, the amounts I have given in each case, as well as the aggregate, would be increased one-eighth.

Very respectfully,

C. E. LIPPINCOTT,

Auditor."

See Vol. 1 of the Constitutional Debates, 1870, p. 413-14.

If this report of the auditor is carefully examined, and its bearings understood, it will present a most extraordinary showing, and if Cook county had thus received at any time any such magnificent *donations* for any purpose, of the State taxes, there would have been a universal outcry.

As a supplement to the above and foregoing, a most interesting chapter will be unfolded by referring to page 736 of the journal of the convention, and there examining the "statement of State taxes appropriated and diverted from the State treasury by special laws during the last ten years," together with a reference to the laws themselves, made by the auditor by request of the convention.

The amounts which, first and last, have been taken from the State treasury and appropriated for the benefit of private corporations and local improvements, and for the benefit of towns, cities and villages in the rural districts, would, if carefully collected, amount to several millions, while Cook county has never got a dollar that we are aware of.

Another thing we discovered, and it was this: that when the appetite for greed and rapacity had once been developed, it stopped at nothing and knew no bounds whatever.

We had at one time a large quantity of valuable lands belonging to the college and seminary fund of the State, located in the county of Cook. The people of southern Illinois found it out and in 1861 got an act through the Legislature incorporating an institution which they called the "Illinois Agricultural College" (a private concern—not the State Agricultural College at Champaign at all, but a private institution), came up to our county, took these lands and sold them, and soon after this high-sounding institution was found to be bankrupt and all the money which was derived from the sale of these lands was lost and squandered. We then came to the conclusion that the indiscriminate organization of private corporations by special laws, with special powers and privileges, was a great abuse and that some check ought to be placed upon the Legislature in granting them and therefore a check was placed upon the Legislature for so doing.

Under the wise and judicious lead of the late Hon. Wm. F. Coolbaugh, who had had great experience under somewhat similar circumstances in the State of Iowa, and who had a national reputation as a financier, we adopted the principle of *pay as you go*, which, if carried out, will be worth millions to this and all future generations. It is a curious thing that in this age, when wealth is so universally diffused, that so few have ever mastered the rudiments of political economy, and stranger still, that no one seems to understand the value of a dollar.

To the great mass of the people it seems to be evidence of the highest wisdom if public improvements can be made by borrowing money at high rates of interest, provided *bonds* can be issued to pay for the same, and they never bestow a thought upon how either the interest is to be paid or the principal satisfied.

The common councils of our cities and other municipal bodies beat against the barriers which protect the public treasury, like prisoners against their grated cells. Taxpayers ought to have some guaranty against improvidence and the dangers of confiscation.

We believe if it had not been for the wise and conservative policy to be pursued in the levying and collecting of taxes, and the limitations on taxation provided in the Constitution, that the city of Chicago would to-day be in debt $100,000,000 instead of thirteen or fourteen millions.

We found, in addition to the foregoing, that a system of *commutation* of taxes had been inaugurated, by which thousands upon thousands of dollars of the public revenues had been taken and appropriated to local improvements and private purposes, while the other portions of the State were supplying all the defenses. This we remedied, and we said in our address:

"We have forbidden the General Assembly from discharging any county, city, township or district from its proportionate share of State taxes, and prohibited commutation for such taxes; thus securing in State taxation, equality of burdens for common benefits; and we have repealed the two-mill tax. * * *

We have prohibited the State from contracting indebtedness beyond $250,000, without submitting the law to the people. We have forbidden the General Assembly from loaning the credit of the State and making appropriations from the treasury in aid of internal improvements and from paying or assuming the debts or liabilities of any public or other corporation, association or individual. We have prohibited county authorities from over-assessing taxes, the aggregate of which shall exceed seventy-five cents per $100 valuation, except for the payment of indebtedness existing at the adoption of the Constitution, unless authorized by a vote of the people of the county. We have forbidden cities, counties and all public corporations from creating or further increasing their indebtedness above five per cent. in the value of the taxable property within the same, and required that *at the time* of incurring such indebtedness an *annual tax* shall be levied sufficient to pay the interest as it falls due and *to discharge the principal within twenty years.* For want of such a provision in our State Constitution, our counties, towns and cities have contracted liabilities of over $50,000,000. We have submitted a separate article prohibiting all municipal subscriptions to railroad stock.

The judicial department of the government was reorganized and adequate salaries provided for and the Legislature given power to change them from time to time, to adjust them so as to allow an increase if necessary; whereas, before, they were fixed by the Constitution and made unchangeable. Uniform laws were required to be passed relating to the organization, jurisdiction, powers, proceedings and practice of the courts of the same class so far as regulated by law, and the force and effect of process, judgments and decrees of such courts shall be uniform."

## CHAPTER XXXV.

### The Organization and Government of Great Cities.

ONE of the greatest and most valuable characteristics of our Constitution is that provision which absolutely prohibits class legislation and the passage of special and private laws, and of "granting to any corporation, association or individual, any special privilege, immunity or franchise whatever by special law." This feature of our Constitution has received universal commendation, both in this country and in England, and is, as one of the members of the British House of Commons told me, one of the most valuable prerequisites that was ever appended to a fundamental law. It is a standing proclamation to the world and to the people of the State of Illinois that the contest for life here shall be that of a free fight and no favors—Queensbury rules.

The mode of "regulating county and township affairs," and of "incorporating cities, towns or villages, or changing or amending the charter of any town, city or village," it will be observed, shall be by general laws. But there is no prohibition whatever in the Constitution regarding their classification; and while it may be that the Supreme Court would hold that there could not be a law, general in its character, to apply to cities of one million and upwards, we doubt it. We think that general powers can be provided for in the organic laws of cities which would be ample for every emergency. But the Constitution does not provide or say anything *how* cities shall be organized; whether they shall be governed as a private corporation or by a mayor and common council, composed of fifty or five hundred; therefore the government of cities is an open question, and is fast becoming the great problem of the age.

The rural districts seem to be decreasing in population, while the young and rising generation seem to be struggling up from the small towns, cities and villages, and throwing themselves upon the world of the metropolis.

Hon. Andrew D. White, late President of Cornell University, one of the most cultivated of Americans, and a man who has had great opportunities for observation, both in this country and in Europe, has discussed the "Government of American Cities" in the December number of "The Forum," 1890, in a most masterly manner, and we commend it to all legislators and constitution makers as worthy of their most thoughtful consideration. He shows that we are attempting to govern our cities upon "a theory which has never been found to work practically in any part of the world."

His caution is, that, the questions in a city not being political questions, but having reference to the laying out of streets, to the erection of buildings, to sanitary arrangements, to the control of franchises and the like, and to provisions for the public health and comfort in parks, boulevards, libraries and museums, that the work of the city should be logically managed as a piece of property by those who have created it and who have a title to it or a real substantial part in it. As things are now, says he, "a city is a political organization over which a crowd of illiterate peasants, freshly raked in from Irish bogs, or Bohemian mines, or Italian robber-nests may exercise virtual control; and how they control it (speaking of New York City) we know too well."

As a compromise between the political and the corporate idea, he says, however, "I would elect the mayor by the votes of the majority of all the citizens as at present; I would elect the common council by a majority of all the votes of all the citizens, so that wards composed largely of thieves and robbers can not send thieves and robbers, and so that men who can carry their ward can not control the city; I would elect the board of aldermen on a general ticket, just as the mayor is elected now, thus requiring candidates for the board to have a city reputation. So much for retaining the idea of the city as a political body. In addition to this, in consideration of the fact that the city is a corporation, we would have those owning property in it properly recognized.

"I would leave to them, and to them alone, the election of a board of control, without whose permission no franchise should be granted, and no expenditure should be made. This should be the rule. * * * A theory resulting in a system virtually like this has made the cities of Europe, whether in monarchies or republics, what they are, and has made it an honor in many foreign countries for the foremost citizens to serve in the common councils of their cities." There is nothing in our present Constitution to prevent the trial of this theory.

The justice of the peace system might well, at the present time, be superseded by district courts, which should be courts of record, with such criminal jurisdiction as to enable them to try and dispose of, summarily, all criminal cases below the degree of felony and such cases of misdemeanor punishable by fines and imprisonment in the penitentiary, as should be provided by law.

The history of the twenty-eighth section of the judiciary article of the Constitution of the State, relating to the appointment of justices of the peace in the city of Chicago, is interesting.

For years before the constitutional convention was called to revise the Constitution, great complaint existed as to the manner in which the law was administered in the justice courts, and as to the class of persons who filled the offices. In many instances, the justices of the peace were ward loafers and bummers, and in connection with the constables who hung around their offices, perpetrated the most outrageous crimes upon the poor and defenseless who were so unfortunate as to come within their grasp. Conspiracies were found to exist, in some instances, between the justices and constables, to prefer charges against people for violation of laws and ordinances of the city; and they would then be brought before the magistrates and fined, or the suits compromised and the money divided between the justices and the constables. The whole administration of the law had become a farce, and was oftentimes attended with scenes of brutality shocking to humanity. In one instance, an ex-judge of a circuit court, while trying a case, was set upon by policemen at the command of the justice, for a fancied insult to his Majesty, and mauled to death—at least he died soon after the assault made upon him, from the effects of the beating. Public attention finally became aroused, and indictments were found against some of the justices and constables, and they were convicted and punished. It seemed as if no remedy could be offered the public under the old system of electing justices, and a universal outcry went up for an entire change in the system, and for a better class of men to fill the offices. The newspapers all took part in the discussion, and the examples of Boston and New York were cited, where district courts existed, presided over by judges who had limited jurisdiction in civil and criminal cases, and who disposed of almost all cases of misdemeanors and minor offenses without the intervention of a grand jury. Judge Russell, of Boston, we believe, long presided over one of these inferior courts and was elevated from that position to the Supreme Court. When the constitutional convention assembled, we were flooded with petitions from the people asking us to change the system from election to appointment. I introduced into that body, on January 5 or 7, 1870, the following resolution.

### AMENDMENTS OF THE OLD SYSTEM.

"There shall be no justices of the peace in the city of Chicago, but the said city shall be divided into districts, and one judge elected for each district, who shall hold his office for the term of four years and until his successor is elected and qualified. No person shall be elected a judge of the said District Court, unless he shall be an attorney at law and have been a resident of the city of Chicago at least ―――― years next preceding his election. There shall be a clerk of each of the said courts, and such other officers as may be provided by law. Said courts shall have jurisdiction in civil cases when the amount in controversy does not exceed two hundred dollars, and such criminal jurisdiction as may be provided by law. Said judges and clerks shall receive such compensation as may be provided by law, and all fees and perquisites shall be paid into the city treasury."

This section was referred to the judiciary committee, of which Mr. Hayes and myself were members. The matter was considered by the judiciary, and they finally reported it back to the convention in these words:

"SEC. 40. There shall be no justices of the peace or police magistrates in the city of Chicago, after the expiration of the terms of the existing justices of the peace and police magistrates, and the General Assembly shall, at its first session after the adoption of this Constitution, divide the city into districts, and establish courts therein, to consist of one or more judges for each district, and such officers as may be provided by law. The judges of said courts shall be appointed by the governor, by and with the advice and consent of the Senate; but no person shall be appointed except upon the recommendation of a majority of the judges of the circuit, superior and county courts, and shall hold their offices for four years and until their successors be commissioned and qualified. Such courts shall have jurisdiction in civil cases at law in said city when the amount in controversy does not exceed $200, and such criminal jurisdiction as may be conferred by law."

"The compensation of said judges shall be fixed by law, and paid out of the city treasury, and shall not be increased during their term of office. All fees and perquisites shall be paid into the city treasury. Appeals in civil cases, from justices of the peace in said county, and from said courts established in said districts, shall be allowed in the Circuit or Superior Court of Cook county, in such manner as may be provided by law." [Debates and proceedings of the Convention, 2d vol., p. 1481.]

When this came up for consideration, Mr. Hayes, under instructions from the Cook county delegation, arose and offered the following as a compromise measure, and as a substitute for the above, to-wit:

"SECTION 40. All justices of the peace in the city of Chicago shall be appointed by the governor, by and with the advice and consent of the Senate (but only upon the recommendation of a majority of the judges of circuit, superior and county courts), and for such districts as are now, or shall hereafter be, provided by law. They shall hold their offices for four years, and until their successors have been commissioned and qualified, but they may be removed by summary proceeding in the circuit or superior court for extortion or other malfeasance. Existing justices of the peace and magistrates may hold their office until the expiration of their respective terms."

The adoption of this section was most rigorously opposed by the Hon. O. H. Browning, Cummings, of Fulton, Hankins and Allen, of Crawford, and was supported by Messrs. Hayes, Wall, Underwood, Coolbaugh and myself, and was finally adopted by a vote of 46 yeas to 19 nays.

#### WHY THE CHANGE WAS MADE.

The reason why it was made from the original proposition and from the section as reported by the judiciary committee, was principally because the people in Chicago thought that if district courts were established they would become very expensive, and it was thought more judicious to provide simply for the appointment of justices of the peace rather than for judges. Great opposition manifested itself in the convention against making the innovation of appointing justices of the peace. Many thought that it was depriving the people of their rights to take away from them so precious a privilege as electing their own local magistrates. I am satisfied that if the original plan had been adopted, it would have been a great benefit to the people and would have dispensed with the grand jury in all that kind of cases which are classed as misdemeanors, and would have resulted in speedy justice. There is no reason why the law should not be administered with as much intelligence in our lower courts as in our higher courts. In Boston and in many other of our large cities the inferior courts are presided over by well-educated lawyers, and the judges compare favorably with the judges of the higher courts. The convention was assured at the time of the adoption of the present section that nobody but men versed in the law would be called upon to administer the law, and in the debate which afterward occurred on abolishing grand juries, the matter was again referred to. It was stated that the examination of criminals in the city of Chicago would take place before intelligent magistrates versed in the law, and that the great delays which now take place, in awaiting the action of grand juries, would be done away with.

I think on the whole that the system has worked well. Some of the justices at the present time are first-class men, men of culture and standing, and learned in the law, and are a credit to the city. And if they were all of the same class it would be better; and then, if vested with criminal jurisdiction, they could be of the greatest service to the people, and would relieve the Criminal Court of many trifling cases, and save the public and taxpayers thousands of dollars annually.

There seems to be a great difference of opinion about how much our justices and constables realize from fees. This matter could all be put at rest if the General Assembly would pass a law to meet the requirements of section 13 of article 10 of the Constitution, which provides as follows:

"Every person who is elected or appointed to any office in this State, who shall be paid in whole or in part by fees, shall be required by law to make a semi-annual report, under oath, to some officer to be designated by law, of all his fees and emoluments."

I think that the justice courts in the city of Chicago are of the greatest importance, and that the position should be made one of honor, and a sure guaranty that the man who is a justice of the peace in this city is a man of character and respectability. There is no difficulty whatever in finding such men. The character of these courts is, as a whole, better than ever before, and the Constitution expressly provides that any one of them may be removed by summary proceedings in the Circuit or Superior Court, for extortion, or other malfeasance.

### TO INCREASE THEIR EFFICIENCY.

If all justices of the peace in the city of Chicago could be selected for their intelligence and character, and with a view to the public good, and without fear or favor, and without regard to nationality or grounds of expediency, and then clothed with the power of trying and convicting persons charged with misdemeanors and minor offenses, I believe that it would save the city of Chicago thousands of dollars a year, and be equivalent to adding 200 men to the present police force of the city. The administration of the criminal law at the present time in this city should, if possible, be improved, and more speedy trials take place. The efforts of the police are often paralyzed by the delays attending the arrest and conviction of criminals, while the county jail is kept full and running over by persons awaiting examination by the grand jury and those awaiting trial.

So far as Cook county is concerned the problem of blending the city and county governments and abolishing township organization is more difficult; but if anything more comprehensive is required, a simple amendment regarding the same, submitted to the people, can easily be made to accomplish all that is required without calling together a constitutional convention.

The interests of the city of Chicago are such that they must necessarily engage a good deal of the attention of our Legislature.

In 1880 the population of Illinois, as we have elsewhere shown, was 3,077,877. Thirty-five per cent. of the inhabitants, or 938,620, lived in Cook county and in the thirty-eight towns, exclusive of Chicago, which had a population of over 4,000 each. In 1890, the population is returned as 3,818,536 persons of whom 1,642,732 or forty-three per cent. live in this county and the thirty-eight towns, and cities like Aurora, Elgin, Springfield, etc.

In ten years the urban population of the State has grown seventy-five per cent. The gain in the rest of Illinois has been less than 20,000.

If to the dwellers in this county and the thirty-eight principal towns were added the residents of all villages having a population of a thousand and over, they would form decidedly more than half the inhabitants of the State.

The population of Illinois to-day is 3,818,536; in 1880, 3,077,877; in 1870, 2,539,891.

Superintendent Porter, in contrasting the rural with the urban population, says: "In Ohio, Indiana, Iowa and Missouri, and in Illinois, if the city of Chicago be dropped from consideration, the rate of increase has declined decidedly. In Ohio it has fallen from 20 to 15 per cent; in Indiana, from 18 to 11; in Iowa, from 36 to 17; in Missouri, from 26 to 23, in spite of the rapid growth of St. Louis and Kansas City; and in Illinois, dropping Chicago from consideration, from 14.9 to 5.6 per cent.

It is an entire mistake to suppose that every reform that is proposed and every change in the existing order of things should be provided for in the Constitution.

The Legislature has, we assert, the power to make any changes upon any subject within the bounds of the Legislature, in all cases where it is not prohibited by the Constitution itself, and in any case where the Legislature is prohibited such prohibition can be easily removed by submitting an amendment covering the subject. Those who are so eager for a constitutional convention and who are so profuse in condemning the present Constitution, wholesale and retail, would do well to consider wherein the Legislature is so crippled, restrained and restricted as to prevent its acting. We would like to have some one point out any particular thing which is required to be done and which is necessary to be done at the present time, that can not be accomplished by the ordinary means of legislation.

No general attack on the whole instrument will suffice. We want a bill of particulars. If legislation is required for Cook county and the city of Chicago, which can not now be obtained owing to some "restraining order" of the Constitution, then we say that an amendment can be submitted which would confer all power upon the General Assembly not only to re-organize the municipal government, but regulate all its affairs in every way that may be desired. No constitutional convention is required for any such purpose.

We have heard much complaint about judges exercising functions not pertaining to the judicial office proper, such as election commissioner, or drainage commissioner, at one and the same time, and that such things ought to be prohibited by the Constitution. But why, we would like to know, should the Constitution provide for this, when it is to-day wholly within the power of the Legislature?

If there is a need of a constitutional convention for any one thing more than another, it is to enlarge the police power of the State in regard to sanitary matters in cities, and to *confer power* upon the General Assembly and *compel* that department of government to pass a law requiring owners, occupiers and abutters upon the public streets to keep their sidewalks free from dirt and filth. Our Supreme Court say that this can not be done under our present Constitution, although there is nothing in that instrument to prohibit it.

This view we do not concur in, and believe it to be unsound. The power to compel owners and abutters on sidewalks to keep them clean is a power which is exercised in every other city, so far as we know, in the American Union, and in all other civilized countries beneath the sun. We are perfectly aware of the reasons assigned by the Supreme Court for their view of the subject, and it is based upon the theory that a sidewalk is nothing but a part of the public street and you might as well compel the abutting owner to clean the street as the sidewalk; but we submit that this view is fallacious and that the analogy does not hold good in all its parts. The man who owns a house and lot, or store, has certain rights and privileges to the use of the sidewalk, which nobody else has. He may occupy certain portions of it for the display of his goods and wares; he may place machinery under the same, and use it for coal vaults and other purposes, and may even have removed any one who comes before his premises and blocks it up or obstructs it, and such persons have interests above and beyond and paramount to all others. Why, then, should not they be compelled to keep their sidewalks clean?

This matter is of such importance to the cities of this State, and especially the city of Chicago, that if we can not have it remedied short of a constitutional convention, then we are in favor of calling it to-morrow.

## CHAPTER XXXVI.

### Frequent Changes in the Organic Law of a State not Desirable.

THE tendency on the part of all young, aspiring and ambitious statesmen seems to be innovation, and to overload the people with a multiplicity of laws and to swell our Constitutions into volumes.

The experience of our State is not, we think, very much different from other States in regard to inexperienced men undertaking to frame laws for the government of the people. The record upon this subject as kept by ex-Governor Ford, and as stated by him in his "History of Illinois," is as follows: "The Assembly having organized the State government and put it in motion, adjourned to meet again in the winter of 1818–19. At this adjourned session a code of statute law was passed, mostly borrowed from the statutes of Kentucky and Virginia. Upon examining the laws of that day, it will be seen that they are generally better drawn up than those which were passed at a later and more enlightened period.

The members were mostly ignorant and unpretending men; there was then some reverence for men of real knowledge and real abilities; the world was not then filled with audacious and ignorant pretenders; and the sensible and unpretending members were content to look to men of real talents and learning to draw their bills. But in these days of empiricism and quackery in all things, when every ignorant pretender who has the luck to break into the Legislature imagines himself to be a Lycurgus or a Moses, very few good laws have been made; and those which we have, were drawn by men of talents, who were not members, for the most part.

But this code did not stand long. For many sessions afterward, in fact until the new revision in 1827, all the standard laws were regularly changed and altered every two years to suit the taste and whim of every new Legislature. For a long time the rage for amending and altering was so great that it was said to be a good thing that the Holy Scriptures did not have to come before the Legislature, for that body would be certain to alter and amend them so that no one could tell what was or was not the word of God, any more than could be told what was or was not the law of the State.

A session of the Legislature was like a great fire in the boundless prairies of the State. It consumed everything. And again it was like the genial breath of spring, making all things new." Ford's History of Ill. p. 31–2.

The moral of all this is that "the evils that inevitably flow from any fundamental change in the institutions of a country, are apt to be much more serious than the evils which the change is intended to remove. Political government is like a plant; a little watering and pruning do very well for it, but the less its roots are fooled with the better."

Change, merely for the sake of change, is unwise and unjustifiable. We should, in all of our dealings with the fundamental law of the land, exercise that true spirit of reform which animates the reformer and conservative alike, and which keeps the whole fabric standing, by repairing and improving it from time to time, instead of tearing it down and digging for relics amid its ruins. Very much will, in every country, depend upon the homogeneous elements of the people and their ideas of what enters into and constitutes a stable government. Mere theories will not amount to anything. Frenchmen in the fourteenth and fifteenth centuries had theories as magnificent as any that have been put forth in the eighteenth or nineteenth. And they had even then already learned to do deeds of blood in the name of freedom and philanthropy. Therefore French institutions have not lasted. The States-General lived but a fitful life from century to century and they perished forever in the great revolution. Since that time no French institution, no form, either of the legislative or of executive powers has been able to keep up a continuous being of twenty years. It would be hard to reckon up the number of assemblies, conventions, chambers of deputies and legislative bodies which have risen and fallen in France within the last 100 years, nor how many written constitutions they have formulated, adopted and promulgated as embodying the true and eternal principles of civilized government within the same period. At the great exposition, which was held in Paris, 1876, there were exhibited under a glass case some sixteen or seventeen constitutions finely engrossed on parchment, of their skill in providing organic laws for the government of their people, and upon reckoning up the period of their duration, it will appear that not one of them lasted beyond fifteen or sixteen years except that of the third republic, which is now but a few days beyond the twenty-first year.

We admit that the process of amending our Constitution is slow and cumbrous, but this can be most effectually done away by providing that any number of amendments may be submitted at one and the same time; in other words, remove the prohibition on the number of amendments to be submitted at any one time.

We do not insist upon the immutability of the fundamental law at all, but we do insist that it shall not be changed without some good reason and some good cause, for nothing is more deleterious than the constant upheaval and turmoil which such a revolution produces.

There is a class of persons who are never satisfied with anything, but are ready to stir up discontent and create dissatisfaction on the very slightest pretense. The condition of people who live amid constant turmoil is not conducive to peace and happiness, nor the public welfare. A constitution ought to be permitted to remain in force long enough at least, for the people to become acquainted with it before it is overthrown and cast aside as useless. We do not think that the times are very propitious for constitution-making and we think that the very air is filled with vagaries and unpractical theories which, if followed out, will lead us, we know not where.

There are in a republic always on hand a set of men who may be called traders in sedition; who are ready at a moment's notice to jump into the arena and inflame the public mind. There is danger that at this conjuncture, men of more zeal than wisdom may obtain a fatal influence over the masses. "With these men will be joined others, who have neither zeal nor wisdom, common barrators in politics, dregs of society, which, in times of violent agitation are tossed up from the bottom to the top, and which in quiet times sink again from the top to their natural place at the bottom."

A crisis like that which we have mentioned, which makes every honest citizen sad and anxious, fills these men with joy and with a detestable hope. How is it that such men, formed by nature to be objects of mere contempt, can ever inspire terror? How is it that they became dangerous to both Empires and Republics? The secret of their power lies in the indolence or faithlessness of those who ought to take the lead in the redress of public grievances.

"The whole history of low traders in sedition is contained in that fine old Hebrew fable which we have read in the book of Judges. The trees meet to choose a king. The vine and the fig tree and the olive tree decline the office; then it is that the sovereignty of the forest devolves upon the bramble; then it is that from a base and noxious shrub goes forth the fire which devours the cedars of Lebanon."

Let us be instructed.

We do not distrust the future, but we think that there should be inculcated a proper regard for so important a document as the charter of the people, which is known as the organic law, and that it should not be changed without good cause.

One of the wisest and most profound students of history says: "Popular governments make many mistakes and sometimes the people are slow in finding them out, but when once they have discovered them they have a way of correcting them. A popular government is the best kind of government in the world, the most wisely conservative, the most steadily progressive and the most likely to endure."

In many of the States the Legislature is required at stated intervals to submit to the people the question of holding a constitutional convention and if the people vote in favor of the same then one is called by the Legislature. In New Hampshire this question is submitted to a vote of the people every seven years; in Iowa every ten years; in Michigan every sixteen years; in New York, Ohio, Maryland and Virginia every twenty years.

## CHAPTER XXXVII.

### Illinois Ought to Be a Model Republic with a Constitution and Laws to Correspond.

AS civilization advances and mankind reach a higher altitude, a different standard must be adopted than when ruder methods prevailed. The consequences of the past are reaching forward and upward to a loftier ideal than was ever thought of in the infancy of the State.

Illinois ought to be the model republic in our great galaxy of States, and her Constitution and her laws ought to be characterized by the greatest wisdom and the highest enlightenment.

Prior to the year 1800, eight or ten keel boats of about twenty-five tons each, performed all the carrying trade between Cincinnati and Pittsburg. The first government vessel appeared on Lake Erie in 1802; the first steamboat was launched at Pittsburg in 1811, the first on Lake Michigan in 1826, and the first appeared in Chicago in 1832.

Illinois contains 55,405 square miles or 35,459,200 acres of lands. It has 10,000 more square miles than New York and Ohio, and is nearly as large as all New England.

The superintendent of the census in his report in 1860 says: "Illinois presents the most wonderful example of great, continuous and healthful increase. In 1830 Illinois contained 157,445 inhabitants; in 1840, 476,183; in 1850, 851,470; in 1860, 1,711,951.

The gain during the last decade was therefore 860,481, or 101.66 per cent.

So large a population, more than doubling itself in ten years by the regular course of settlement and natural increase, is without parallel. The condition to which Illinois has attained under the progress of the last thirty years is a monument to the blessings of industry, enterprise, peace and free institutions.

\* \* \* \* \* \* \* \*

The remarkable healthfulness of the climate seems to more than compensate for its rigors, and the fertility of the new soil leads men largely to contend with and overcome the harshness of the elements.

The energies thus called into action have in a few years made the States of the Northwest the granary of Europe; and that section of our Union which, within the recollection of living men, was a wilderness, is now the chief source of supply in seasons of scarcity, for the suffering millions of another continent."

Hon. Samuel B. Ruggles, of New York, in his address at the great Canal convention held at Chicago in June, 1863, says: "What human being in his senses, not wholly idiotic or utterly blinded by political bigotry or lust of political power, could assert that this God-given, exuberant, and all but virgin West has now reached its culminating point? For one, I stand awestruck at the immeasurable prospect opening before us. I can see nothing smaller, nothing more diminutive, nothing less stupendous than a yearly product of cereals to be measured, not as now, by hundreds of thousands, but a result so vast, so solemn, so fraught with consequences, so momentous to our nation and to the world, that I can but bow with reverential gratitude before such a wonderful manifestation of the providence of our great Creator. Never before in human history did He lay out a garden so wide-spread and fertile; never before did He provide a granary so magnificent for the use of man.

For what was ancient Sicily, the granary of Rome, or the fertile plains of the Po, or the exuberant valley of the Nile itself, compared with this, our great continental garden, pouring forth yearly volumes of food so enormous, and yet so inevitably, resistlessly increasing? In view of such a power to feed our race who will venture to depict or limit the commercial and the political destiny of this unequaled portion of the earth?"

And he then adds: "The manifest destiny and high office of this splended granary, of which this Chicago of yours and of ours is the brilliant center, stands out as plain as the sun in the heavens.

It is unmistakably marked by the finger of God on these widespread lands and waters, that it is to be our special duty to feed, not ourselves of the new world alone, but that venerable, moss-covered fatherland—that old father world of ours across the ocean —as the pious Grecian daughter nourished her aged sire; to carry abundant food, and that too in the truest Christian spirit, to that over-crowded but under-fed European Christendom, to which we owe our common origin."

Illinois is now the third State in the American Union, and whatever she does will be sure to attract attention. As Mr. Webster once said, "the age is extraordinary, the spirit that actuates it is peculiar and marked, and our own relation to the times we live in and to the questions which interest them, is equally marked and peculiar. We are placed by our good fortune and the wisdom and valor of our ancestors, in a condition in which we can act no obscure part. Be it for honor or dishonor, whatever we do is sure to attract the observation of the world. As one of the free States among the nations, as a great and rising republic, it would be impossible for us, if we were so disposed, to prevent our principles, our sentiments and our example from producing some effect upon the opinions and hopes of society throughout the civilized world. It rests, probably, with ourselves to determine whether the influence of these shall be salutary or pernicious."

If constitution-making is to be further indulged in in this State, then let us have the best that can be framed, and let there be abundance of time in which to frame it. Any defects not of a serious nature can be reached and remedied most speedily by amendments, as the Constitution now provides; and if provision was made for submitting several amendments to the people at one and the same time, there is no reason whatever why every contingency may not be promptly met at once, and that, too, without delay.

## CHAPTER XXXVIII.
### Public Virtue.

BUT there is one thing that no constitutional convention can create, no organic law establish, and no law preserve, and that is public virtue.

To maintain a representative government, men must have the capacity for self-government and no nation can have and possess that capacity without they are fitted for it by habits which involve individual responsibility and perfect honesty and integrity of purpose. The Mexican, Central and South American republics have constitutions similar to ours. But they do not operate with the energy, efficiency, tranquillity and good results that we experience.

The difference is not in the form and plan of their constitutions, but in the people. They have not yet attained the education, poise, elevation, virtue and habits which inspire them to co-operate to make their government as good as possible and to repose with confidence upon its stability and justice. Hence revolts, rebellions or revolutions need scarcely surprise us. These are cruel and wasteful educators, however, and should be avoided.

A government influences the people, and they in turn, the government. No government within the range of civilization can escape the influences of the civilization of the age. Much less so now, when steam and electricity annihilate the barriers of time and distance. Our government exists so near the people that the just complaint of the feeblest citizen can be heard. The people appeal if need be, to the government, without fear of rebuke, and should be able to rely upon it with manly confidence. The government adapts itself to the people and the people to their government.

The stability of our government must ever depend upon the intelligence and common sense of the people, and in order that their confidence may not be impaired they must insist upon the conscientious discharge of every duty incumbent upon their representatives and a fair and impartial administration of the law by every one of their public servants.

Every evasion of law and every perversion of the same is a crime, and every one guilty of such conduct should be arraigned at the bar of public conscience, and punished for it. There are men who are ready to justify every scheme that is formed, every plot that is laid, and every intrigue that is entered into in order to promote and achieve party success.

If men commit crimes against the elective franchise, stuff the ballot box, indulge in wholesale perjury to aid and assist in the wholesale naturalization of men who are not entitled to that privilege, they should be punished, and that, too, severely, and when they have been once fairly tried and convicted, then the governor should be relieved of the constant and increasing importunities of those who undertake to mitigate and excuse such offenses, rendering his life miserable by personal appeals or petitions such as have at times beset his pathway within the memory of men still living.

It should be understood by everybody that "the way of the transgressor is hard," and that punishment stern and unrelenting will be meted out to all those who undertake to thwart the will of the people either by fraudulent voting or by making false returns, or by stealing votes after they have once been deposited in the ballot box.

If there are in the United States or in this State any high crimes and misdemeanors left, these acts constitute them.

We agree with ex-President Cleveland in the views which he expressed in his recent speech before the Young Men's Democratic Club at Philadelphia on General Jackson's day, when he says:

"I believe that among our people the ideas which endure and which inspire warm attachment and devotion are those having some elements which appeal to the moral sense. When men are satisfied that a principle is morally right they become its adherents for all time. There is sometimes a discouraging distance between what our fellow countrymen believe and what they do in such a case, but their action in accordance with their belief may always be confidently expected in good time. A government for the people and by the people is everlastingly right. As surely as this is true, so surely is it true that party principles which advocate the absolute equality of American manhood, and an equal participation by all the people in the management of their government and in the benefit and protection which it affords, are also right. Here is common ground, where the best educated thought and reason may meet the most impulsive and instinctive Americanism. It is right that every man should enjoy the result of his labor to the fullest extent consistent with his membership in civilized community. It is right that our government should be but the instrument of the people's will, and that its cost should be limited within the lines of strict economy. It is right that the influence of the government should be known in every humble home as the guardian of frugal comfort and content, and a defense against unjust exactions, and the unearned tribute persistently coveted by the selfish and designing. It is right that efficiency and honesty in public service should not be sacrificed to partisan greed; and it is right that the suffrage of our people should be pure and free."

For ages there has been a class of writers and speakers, some of them ignorant, others dishonest, who have been constantly representing that governments are able to do, and bound to do, things which no government can, without great injury to the country, do.

Every man of any sense knows that the people support the government, and if it is a good government, ought to support it. But the doctrine that it is the business of the government to support the people is not only unsound but unwise, impracticable and impossible. On the physical condition of the great body of the people, government acts, not as a specific, but as an alterative. Its operation is powerful, indeed, and certain, but gradual and indirect. The business of government is not directly to make the people rich, but to protect them in making themselves rich; and a government which attempts more than this is precisely the government which is likely to perform less. Governments do not and can not support the people. A great statesman of England once said: "We have no miraculous power, we have not the rod of the Hebrew lawgiver, we can not rain down bread on the multitude from Heaven, we can not smite the rock and give them to drink, we can give them only freedom to employ their industry to the best advantage and security in the enjoyment of what their industry has acquired."

Seasons of distress will come to every country, but they are almost always beyond government control. When such a period arrives the effect upon the community and upon the people generally, is not only very marked, but very peculiar. It often makes wise men irritable, unreasonable, credulous, eager for immediate relief, and heedless of remote consequences. There is no quackery in medicine, in religion or politics, which may not impose even on a powerful mind when that mind has been disordered by pain or fear.

At such a time distress inflames the passions and makes those who are sufferers believe all those who flatter them, and to distrust those who serve them.

Men should know the truth even though they denounce and condemn those who tell it to them.

Mankind do not live in alms-houses, and it is only by labor, constant and unceasing, and prudence and forethought, that anybody this side of eternity can keep themselves from want and dependency.

# CHAPTER XXXIX.

## No State will ever be Prosperous under any Constitution unless the People are Educated.

"WHAT is it that makes the great difference between country and country?" says the great essayist Macauley. "Not the exuberance of soil; not the mildness of climate; not mines, nor havens, nor rivers. These things are, indeed, valuable when put to their proper use by human intelligence; but human intelligence can do much without them, and they, without human intelligence, can do nothing. They exist in the highest degree in regions of which the inhabitants are few and squalid and barbarous and naked and starving; while on sterile rocks, amidst unwholesome marshes and under inclement skies, may be found immense populations, well fed, well lodged, well clad, well governed. Nature meant Egypt and Sicily to be the gardens of the world. They once were so. Is it anything on the earth or in the air, that makes Scotland more prosperous than Egypt, that makes Holland more prosperous than Sicily? No; it was the Scotchman that made Scotland; it was the Dutchman that made Holland. Look at North America. Two centuries ago the sites on which now arise mills, and hotels, and banks, and colleges, and churches, and the senate houses of flourishing commonwealths, were deserts abandoned to the panther and the bear. What has made the change? Was it the rich mould or the abundant rivers? No; the praries were as fertile, the Ohio and the Hudson were as broad and as full then as now. Was the improvement the effect of some great transfer of capital from the old world to the new? No: the emigrants generally brought out with them no more than a pittance, but they carried out the English heart and head and arm, and the English heart and head and arm turned the wilderness into cornfield and orchard and the huge trees of the primeval forest into cities and fleets. Man—man is the great instrument that produces wealth. The natural difference between Campagna and Spitzbergen is trifling when compared with the difference between a country inhabited by men full of bodily and *mental vigor* and a country inhabited by men weak in mental and bodily decrepitude."

Again he says, "I believe that it is the right and the duty of the State to provide means of education for the common people. This proposition seems to me to be implied in every definition that has ever yet been given, of the functions of a government. About the extent of those functions, there has been much difference of opinion among ingenious men. There are some who hold that it is the business of a government to meddle with every part of the system of human life; to regulate trade by bounties and prohibitions; to regulate expenditure by sumptuary laws; to regulate literature by a censorship; to regulate religion by an inquisition. Others go to the opposite extreme and assign to government a very narrow sphere of action.

But the very narrowest sphere that ever was assigned to governments by any school of political philosophy is quite wide enough for my purpose. On one point all the disputants are agreed. They unanimously acknowledge that it is the duty of every government to take order for giving security to the persons and property of the community. This being admitted, can it be denied that the education of the common people is a most effectual means of securing our persons and our property? The education of the poor is a matter which deeply concerns every commonwealth. Just as the magistrate ought to interfere for the purpose of preventing the spread of leprosy among the people, he ought to interfere for the purpose of stopping the progress of the moral distempers which are inseparable from ignorance. Nor can this duty be neglected without danger to the public peace."

Mr. Palfrey in his History of New England says, 2d, p. 34, that "The democratic people of New England, in recent times have supposed it to be no invasion of the citizen's liberty to require him to submit his children to instruction in reading, writing and arithmetic, to the end that they may not grow up to be incapable and shiftless, chargeable and troublesome.

And on similar grounds their predecessors in the primitive age considered it to be conducive to the public good and unobjectionable to the individual that he should be saved from the misery to himself and the mischievousness to his neighbors, of ignorance respecting morals and religion."

Edward Everett said: "From the first settlement of New England, and from an early stage of their progress in many of the other States, one of the most prominent traits of the character of our population has been to provide and to diffuse the means of education.

The village school house and the village church are the monuments of our republicanism; to read, to write and to discuss grave matters in their primary assemblies, are the licentious practices of our democracy."

Educate the people, was the first admonition addressed by Penn to the colony which he founded.

Educate the people, was the legacy of Washington to the Nation that he saved. "Educate the people," was the unceasing exhortation of Jefferson, and in this exhortation is joined the unanimous voice of all the wise and good of all ages and of both hemispheres.

## CHAPTER XL.

### The Right of American Citizens to be Protected in Exercising the Elective Franchise.

A GREAT deal has been said, first and last, in regard to the meaning and import of the declaration made by those who lived under the protecting power of the Roman eagle, "I am a Roman citizen."

The majesty and grandeur of such an utterance must have been very great, for it signified legions of soldiers and armies of men who were ready to resent insult, and to conquer and destroy all who sought to resist the power of the State.

> "Then none was for a party,
>   Then all were for the State;
> Then the great man helped the poor,
>   And the poor man loved the great.
> Then lands were fairly portioned,
>   Then spoils were fairly sold.
> The Romans were like brothers
>   In the brave old days of old.
>
> "Now Roman is to Roman
>   More hateful than a foe,
> And the tribunes beard the high
>   And the fathers grind the low.

> As we wax hot in faction,
> In battle we wax cold.
> Wherefore men fight not as they fought
> In the brave old days of old."

These were times when men were chained to chariot wheels to grace a Roman holiday, and mothers smiled to see "their infants quartered with the hands of war," and when it only required "a monarch's voice to cry havoc and let slip the dogs of war."

Contrast this condition of things with that of an American, and let us inquire what it is to be an American citizen.

It is a greater honor and a far more lordly position than that which was ever enjoyed by any of the imperial hosts that divided "all Gaul into three parts," or who set up their mile-stones in the sea-girt isle of the Britons.

The strongest government is that in which there is the assertion of personality. That is the realization of the freedom of the people.

That is not necessarily a strong government which is identified with arbitrary rule or arbitrary power. That government is the strongest which develops in the hearts of the people the dignity and maintenance of law, the institution of rights, the realization of freedom.

For this it is clothed with power and with majesty on earth, such as never existed either in Rome or any land over which her imperial eagles ever flew.

### WHO IS AN AMERICAN?

"He is an American who, leaving behind him all his ancient prejudices and manners, receives new ones from the new mode of life he has embraced, the new government he obeys, and the new rank he holds. He becomes an American by being received in the broad lap of our great Alma Mater. Here individuals of all nations are melted into a new race of men, whose labors and posterity will one day cause great changes in the world. Americans are the Western pilgrims who are carrying along with them that great mass of arts, sciences, vigor and industry, which began long since in the East. They will finish the circle."—*Letters of American Farmer.*

The practical operation of popular institutions of government provides, in innumerable ways, a demand for every species of intellectual effort, not merely within the circle of a capital, but throughout the land. In short, wherever man has been placed by Providence endowed with natural capacities of improvement, there the genius of the republic visits him, with a voice of encouragement and hope. Every day he receives from the working of the social system some new assurance that he is not forgotten in the multitude of the people; he is called to do some act, to assert some right, and to enjoy some privilege; and he is elevated by this consciousness of his social importance from the condition of the serf or the peasant to that of the freeman and the citizen. Why, then, should not the humblest citizen be protected in exercising his right to vote, even if it takes armies and navies to accomplish it?

"All elections shall be free and equal"—is the standing proclamation in our Bill of Rights—and it seems very strange to us, at this day and age of the world, that while all political parties admit the supreme importance of regulating and protecting the elective franchise, and make it a part of their platforms, there are so many who are utterly opposed to any laws by which the power of the government, and especially that of the National Government shall be invoked to make such laws effective. It is only a little over thirty years since the doctrine that we had no National Government at all, but that we were a mere compact of States, and that any acts of the National Legislature might be disregarded, and that any State might secede, and that there was no power to coerce them to submission, was universally entertained by most of the Southern people, and by a large and powerful party at the North who sympathized with them. But these doctrines were declared to be erroneous, after referring them for settlement to the dread arbitrament of war, and we had supposed that we should hear no more of them. But to-day these same ideas are revamped and put forth again, quite as offensively as before, and a great ado is being made over what is called "The Force Bill," a plain and simple bill to regulate the elective franchise at National elections, and of protecting those who are entitled to vote, in voting.

At the outbreak of the war of the rebellion the cry which went up was "coercion" and the horrors of "coercion" were preached throughout the length and breadth of the land; to-day it is "The Force Bill," and men stand aghast at the audacity of those who favor that bill or anything whatever like it. It is the same old cry, and men may apologize for such a course of conduct as much as they please, but it is an attempt to paralyze the arm of the Government in its attempt to protect the freedom of elections and to allow terrorism to rule supreme.

The United States is not only a government but a great National government, and the only government in this country that has the character of nationality. It has jurisdiction over all the general legislation and sovereignty which affect the interests of the whole people equally and alike, and which require uniformity of regulation and laws, and it can call to its support the entire power of the Nation to enforce this jurisdiction, and the "proposition," as Mr. Justice Miller said in the case of *Ex Parte* Yarbrough, 110 U. S. 658, "that the General Government has not the power to protect the elections upon which its existence depends from violence and force, is supported by the old argument, often heard, often repeated, and in this court never assented to, that when a question of power of Congress arises, the advocate of the power must be able to place his finger on words which expressly granted it.

It destroys at one blow, in construing the Constitution of the United States, the doctrine universally applied to all instruments in writing, that what is implied is as much a part of the instrument as what is expressed. This principle, in its application to the Constitution of the United States, more than to almost any other writing, is a necessity by reason of the inherent inability to put into words all derivative powers, a difficulty which the instrument itself recognizes, by conferring upon Congress the authority to pass all laws necessary and proper for carrying into execution the powers expressly granted, and all other powers vested in the government or any branch of it by the Constitution."

"The prejudices and apprehension as to the central government which prevailed when the Constitution was adopted," said Mr. Justice Swayne, in 16 Wallace, 128, "were dispelled by the light of experience. The public mind became satisfied that there was less danger of tyranny in the head than of anarchy and tyranny in the members. Before the war ample protection was given against oppression by the Union, but little was given against wrong and oppression by the States."

We *insist*, in the language of Judge Harlan in 109 U. S. 26-53, "that the National Legislature may, without transcending the limits of the Constitution, do for human liberty and the fundamental rights of American citizenship what it did, with the sanction of the

United States Supreme Court, for the protection of slavery and the rights of the masters of fugitive slaves."

We think that human liberty and the rights of an American citizen in exercising the elective franchise, are entitled to just as much consideration as that of a slave-holder for his slave when he hunted them all over the United States, and that the election bill now pending before the United States Congress is no more a force bill than any other bill which provides a penalty for the commission of a crime.

The idea that it is the business of the State governments, and those alone, to provide laws for the protection of American citizens in casting their votes at National elections and for National representatives is, we submit, simply absurd, and is the last lingering relic of the confederate idea of our government which has come down to us from pro-slavery days "befo the wah."

Is it true that National citizenship of itself has no attribute of any practical value.

Is it true that the higher the source and the more inalienable the rights of man, the less they are within the protection afforded by National citizenship and the National Constitution and the more they are exposed to invasion by the State?

We believe that our Government is a National Government, and that the States should assist that government in upholding it in the exercise of all its just powers, and that in the language of our Bill of Rights, "All elections shall be free and equal." These words should be something else than "sounding brass and tinkling cymbals," and, if it is necessary to call a constitutional convention to give them force and effect, then reckon this as one of the needs of a convention.

The basis of all constitutions and all laws must be eternal justice, and all the rights of all the citizens of this republic must be absolutely equal before the laws.

The days of provincialism are over in this country, and, as John Bright said in one of his great speeches at Birmingham, Dec. 18, 1862, upon America, "I can not believe that civilization in its journey with the sun will sink into endless night in order to gratify the ambition of the leaders of this revolt, who seek to

  'Wade through slaughter to a throne
  And shut the gates of mercy on mankind.'

I have another and a far brighter vision before my gaze. It may be but a vision, but I will cherish it. I see one vast confederation stretching from the frozen North in unbroken line to the glowing South, and from the wild billows of the Atlantic westward to the calmer waters of the Pacific main, and I see one people, and one language, and one law and one faith, and over all the wide continent, the home of freedom and a refuge of the oppressed of every race and of every clime."

## CHAPTER XLI.

### Conclusion.

WHEN the foundations of this republic were laid the world was filled with kings and despotism was supreme. When the first Constitution of this State was formed, steamboats had but just begun to run on the Hudson river, locomotives had been just heard of in England, and it took a month to cross the Atlantic. Now behold the change!

"Power has come to dwell with every people, from the Arctic Sea to the Mediterranean, from Portugal to the borders of Russia. From end to end of the United States the slave has become a free man, and the various forms of bondage have disappeared from European Christendom. Abounding harvests of scientific discovery have been garnered by numberless inquisitive minds, and the wildest forces of nature have been taught to become the docile helpmates of man.

The application of steam to the purpose of travel on land and on water, the employment of a spark of light as the carrier of thought across continents and beneath oceans, have made of all the inhabitants of the earth one society. The morning newspaper gathers up and brings us the noteworthy events of the last four and twenty hours, in every quarter of the globe.

All States are beginning to form parts of one system.

The 'new nations,' which Shakspeare's prophetic eye saw rising on our eastern shore, dwell securely along two oceans, midway between their kin in Great Britain, on the one side, and the oldest surviving empire on the other.

More than two thousand years ago it was truly said that the nature of justice can be more easily discerned in a State than in one man.

It may now be studied in the collective state. The ignorance and prejudices that come from isolation are worn away in the conflict of the forms of culture. We learn to think the thought, to hope the hope of mankind. Former times spoke of the dawn of civilization in some one land; we live in the morning of the world. Day by day the men who guide public affairs, are arraigned before the judgment seat of the race. A government which adopts a merely selfish policy is pronounced to be the foe of the human family. The statesman who founds and builds up the well-being of his country on justice, has all the nations for a cloud of witnesses, and as one of our own poets has said, 'The linked hemispheres attest his deed.'

He thrills the world with joy, and man becomes a nobler spirit as he learns to gauge his opinions and his acts by a scale commensurate with his nature."

The days of war are over, and bright and tranquil years of peace have succeeded. In no country that exists beneath the sun do we mark such progress in all the arts of life, such toleration of domestic peace, such security for liberty and temperate freedom as we behold here. There is no place in all this broad land so well fitted to excite in our minds sad yet grateful feelings as the spot on which we are now assembled.

It was at the fearful price of one whose mortal remains repose in yonder vale, but whose memory is cherished by the inhabitants of the earth with love and affection, that justice and freedom were secured. No one since the days of the inspired lawgiver, who after long communion with the Ruler of the Universe descended from the mountain tops of Sinai with awful aspect and shining face, has ever exerted so great an influence upon the human race, as he who fell beneath the blows of an assassin while overborne by the weight of his country's cares.

A few years ago he lived and moved among us with no pretensions to greatness, but a leader of acknowledged power and of unsurpassed eloquence. He was a member of this bar, and scores who hear me have met him in the court room; have traveled with him on the circuit; have tried cases with and against him and knew him well. He was born nine years before the adoption of our first Constitution, and knew of the efforts put forth at that time to make this a slave State. Soon after he attained his majority, he took part in the legislation of his adopted State; was one who by his vote and influence helped to remove the capital from Vandalia to this city; was well acquainted with Ninian Edwards, Jesse B. Thomas, Elias Kent Kane, Governor Coles, Governor Bond, Daniel P. Cook, Judge Lockwood and all of that class of persons who took part in the great struggle for freedom on our soil in 1822. Every fibre of his being was inwrought with sympathy for the poor, the down-trodden and the oppressed, and his life was as grand as any of the holy prophets of old.

He was a natural born leader of men, and was known in his own region of the world as the "rail splitter," long before his fame had extended to that of neighboring States.

He took ground against slavery at a very early period, and never ceased his opposition to it until his lips were closed in death.

On the soil of Illinois occurred in 1858, before the breaking out of the war, when the slave-holders were seeking to extend slavery into the new States beyond the Mississippi, one of the greatest discussions upon constitutional law and the genius of our institutions that ever occurred in the history of this country. It was on the 17th of June, 1858, that Mr. Lincoln struck the key note of opposition to slavery in this country, when he declared in yonder State House that, "a house divided against itself can not stand. I believe this government can not endure permanently half-slave and half-free. I do not expect the Union to be dissolved. I do not expect the house to fall, but I do expect it will cease to be divided. It will become all one thing or all the other."

No proclamation was ever sent forth by any commander of armies or ruler of nations which was attended with such broad and lasting consequences. If it had been inspired from on high it could not have been attended with more force or carried with it greater weight.

The first sentence was the announcement of an absolute truth embodied in a plain and homely axiom. The other portion of the speech which we have quoted was uttered as his belief and expectation, but it was the truth of prophesy itself. It went like a procession over the land and over the sea. It was like a firebell in the night time and the contest for supremacy between the hosts of slavery and of freedom commenced from that hour, and never ceased until white-winged peace folded her pinions beneath the apple tree at Appomattox.

The generation to which he belonged is fast passing away, but let it be here recorded that no one ever left a sweeter memory or a brighter example to his countrymen than Abraham Lincoln, the great lawgiver of Illinois.

"And, now, we have done. The sceptre may pass away from us. Unforeseen accidents may derange our most profound schemes of policy, victory may be inconstant to our arms. But there are triumphs which are followed by no reverse. There is an empire exempt from all natural causes of decay. Those triumphs are the pacific triumphs of reason over barbarism; that empire is the imperishable empire of our arts, our literature and our laws."

www.ingramcontent.com/pod-product-compliance
Lightning Source LLC
Chambersburg PA
CBHW020911230426
43666CB00008B/1404